CHINA'S INTELLECTUAL DILEMMA

University of British Columbia Press
Asian Studies Monographs

China's Intellectual Dilemma is the first volume in a continuing series of studies in Asian history and society published by the University of British Columbia Press.
Other volumes in the series are:

    2. *Agrarian Class Conflict: The Political Mobilization of Agricultural Labourers in Kuttanad, South India,* by Joseph Tharamangalam

CHINA'S INTELLECTUAL DILEMMA

POLITICS AND UNIVERSITY ENROLMENT, 1949-1978

Robert Taylor

UNIVERSITY OF BRITISH COLUMBIA PRESS
VANCOUVER AND LONDON

CHINA'S INTELLECTUAL DILEMMA

Politics and University Enrolment, 1949-1978

©The University of British Columbia 1981

This book has been published with the help of a grant from the Social Science Federation of Canada, using funds provided by the Social Sciences and Humanities Federation of Canada.

Canadian Cataloguing in Publication Data

Taylor, Robert, 1941-
   China's intellectual dilemma

(Asian studies monographs; 1)
Bibliography: p.
Includes index.
ISBN 0-7748-0131-X

1. Universities and colleges—China—Entrance requirements. 2. Education and state—China. 3. China—Politics and government—1949-1978.
I. Title.
II. Series.
LA1133.T393   378'.105'70951   C80-091227-6

International Standard Book Number 0-7748-131-X
Printed in Canada

To my parents

Contents

Tables

Glossary

ai-hao	interest
ch'a-pan	intermediate class
ch'an-yeh kung-jen	production worker
chu-hsüeh chin	financial aid
chao-sheng k'oa-shih ta-kang	enrolment examination outlines
chao-sheng ling-tao hsiao-tsu	enrolment leadership groups
cheng-chih	politics
ch'eng-fen	social origin
chi-hua ti tiao-p'ei	planned allocation
chi-kung hsüeh-hsiao	technical schools
chi-shu	technique
chiang-hsüeh chin	scholarships
chiao-hsüeh fu-chu jen-yüan	teaching assistants
chiao-wu wei-yüan hui	university council
chiao-hsüeh yen-chiu chih-tao tsu	teaching research guidance groups
chih-shih fen-tzu	intellectuals
chih-shih ssu-yu	knowledge is privately owned
chih-yü	intellectual education
chiu-ti ch'ü-ts'ai	accepting talent according to area
chu-hsüeh chin	financial aid
ch'u-shen	social status
chu-yao	principal (institutions)
ch'ü	area
chuan-chang	special talent
chuan-hsiu k'e	special training courses
chuan-men hsüeh-yüan	technical institute
chuan-men hua	specialization
chuan-yeh hsüeh-hsiao	vocational middle (specialist) schools

chüan-kuo kao-teng hsüeh-hsiao chao-sheng chi-hua	National Enrolment Plan
chüan-kuo kao-teng hsüeh-hsiao chao-sheng wei-yüan hui	National Enrolment Committee
chuan-yeh	specialty
chuan-yeh hua	specialization
chün-chung t'ui-chien	recommendation by the masses
chun-k'ao cheng	examination entry documents
ch'ung-shih	completion
chung-tien	key point
chung-yao	important (institutions)
fen-k'e	divided classes
fu po-shih	candidate doctors
han-shou ta-hsüeh	correspondence universities
hsi	department
hsi chu-jen	department head
hsia fang	secondment
hsiang	village
hsiao-chang	president of a university
hsien	county
hsüeh-hsiao fu-shen	re-examination by institutions of higher education
hsüeh-yüan	technical institutes
i-k'e	medical courses
i-yao	medicine and pharmacy
jen-shih	knowledge
jen-ts'ai	talent
k'ao-ch'ü	examination areas
k'ao-ch'ü pan-shih ch'u	examination area management office
kao-sheng fu-wu t'uan	candidates' service leagues
kung-ku	consolidation
kung-nung ch'eng-fen ti hsüeh-sheng	students of worker and peasant origin
kung-nung pan	worker-peasant classes
kung-nung su-ch'eng chung-hsüeh	worker-peasant rapid middle schools
kung-yeh ta-hsüeh	polytechnical universities
lao-tung ta-hsüeh	labour universities

lien-he chao-sheng	joint enrolment
ling-tao p'i-chun	approval of the leadership
min-pan hsüeh-hsiao	schools run by the masses
ming-t'i wei-yüan hui	Enrolment Examination Topics Committee
neng-li	ability
nung-yeh chung-hsüeh	agricultural middle schools
pan-kung pan-tu	part-time work part-time study (institutions)
pao-chien	to protect health
pao-sung ju-hsüeh	guaranteed entry
pao-t'a	treasure pagodas
pen-k'e	basic courses
piao-hsien	manifestations
p'o-ke	exception rule
p'u-chi	universalization
shen-ch'a he-ke	investigation methods
shih	history
shih-ch'ang	examination halls
shih-chüan p'ing-yüeh wei-yüan hui	Script Assessment Committee
shih-tien	examination centres
shih-tu sheng	provisional students
ssu-nien yen-chiu sheng	four-year researchers
tan-tu chao-sheng	individual enrolment
ti-ch'ü	district
ti-ch'ü kao-teng hsüeh-hsiao chao-sheng kung-tso wei-yüan hui	local enrolment work committees
t'i-kao	elevation
tiao-cheng	regulation
tiao-kan jen-min chu-hsüeh chin	transferred cadre financial aid
t'ien-sheng	innate
ts'ai-neng	ability
tsou-tu sheng	day students
tsung-he ta-hsüeh	comprehensive universities
t'ung-i chao-sheng	unified enrolment
tzu-yüan pao-ming	voluntary registration
wei-sheng	health
wen	humanities

yeh-wu   expertise
yeh-yü chiao-yü   spare-time education
yu-hsien ling-ch'ü   preferential acceptance
yü-k'e   preparatory classes
yüan   dollar

Preface

This study began as a University of London doctoral thesis but has been further developed to take account of the momentous changes in China's higher education since the death of Mao Tse-tung.

I would like to thank Heather Devere, Marjorie Gould, and Beryl Stout for typing various parts of the manuscript, and Janice Mogford for her painstaking care in compiling the index. I am deeply indebted to the Social Science Federation of Canada for its generosity in assisting publication of this book.

With the exception of map spelling, Chinese names have been transliterated according to the Wade-Giles system.

RT

Auckland
1980

1

Historical Perspectives: Chinese Educational Philosophy

Mao Tse-tung, in common with other leaders of Third World countries, dedicated himself to policies designed to strengthen the nation. What made Mao unique was his attempt to prevent the social inequalities inherent in the struggle to modernize. Mao's concern with this problem was in part a reflection of the traditional Chinese relationship between education and society. Thus educational change in China since the Communist accession in 1949 has been encompassed within a dual framework: continual reassessment of China's own philosophical tradition and selective experimentation with foreign institutions.

For many centuries the ethic of Confucius (551-479 B.C.) was the moral basis on which both human relationships and the conduct of government rested in Imperial China: it was also the source of traditional educational philosophy. Confucianism taught that man was by nature good and could be correctly moulded by education; all men had the capacity to reach moral perfection. This belief in the malleability of mankind led to an optimistic appraisal of the miracles which could be wrought in the social and physical environment by the requisite training.[1]

Moreover, the Confucian ethic was essentially humanistic, for its sanction lay in the here and now, not in the world to come. Justification by works rather than by faith meant that the function of education was conceived of as relating directly to the needs of society as a whole. The capacity of the individual had to be developed to the full not for its own sake, but for the contribution it could render to the community.

It was on the basis of Confucian learning that China's administrative elite, the scholar-officials, was recruited, until the abolition of the Civil Service examination system in 1904. The traditional education system was devoted to the study of Confucian classical texts for the examinations; prospective candidates learned definite rules of conduct which they applied, on appointment as officials, to the concrete conditions of everyday life.

The scholar-officials were an aristocracy of merit. The Confucian ethic did not stress innate ability per se, seeing it as of little value if not accompanied by moral training, but taught that all had a capacity to discern the correct ordering of human relationships, the cornerstone of good government. This quality of discrimination has been aptly defined as "the evaluating mind." Men were born equal and the "divine spark" was to be found in all, but they became different from one another through education. Thus the classical tradition had egalitarian implications, and, in theory, the highest positions in officialdom could be reached by every man whatever his social origin, even if, in practice, economic circumstances precluded such social mobility, with poor peasants, for example, unable to afford the long period of study required.

Education, however, was given a very narrow focus. Both clan and state schools were designed to train youth for the Civil Service examinations, but Imperial rulers did not envisage the extension of a general education system to a wider public. There was a low level of literacy among the general population; on this count opportunities for social mobility appear to have been more limited.

Moral quality and personal performance were held in higher esteem than the intellect for its own sake. The scholar-official was recruited on the basis of an amateur ethic, and Confucian rules of conduct equipped him to perform not one but many tasks. Prior to the twentieth century China was basically agrarian; there were no independent centres of economic power competing with government, and all relationships were political. Many Western scholars have attributed the absence of an industrial revolution in China before the impact of the West to the Imperial examination system. Recent research has drawn attention to state-sponsored education in such fields as medicine and hydraulics.[2] Practical studies were thus not neglected, there being no lack of scientific and technical knowledge; but the fact that officialdom was, in theory, the only avenue of social mobility produced a dynamic not conducive to the development of entrepreneurial skills. In this sense, then, the scholar-official's role, like the social milieu in which he operated, was functionally diffuse, however specialized the functions he performed.

China's last Imperial dynasty, the Ch'ing, was, however, powerless to withstand the impact of Western military might and technology during the middle years of the nineteenth century; institutions of government, and by implication the Confucian ethic which inspired them, were gradually discredited, a process which culminated in the demise of the Chinese Empire's political system in 1911.

In 1898 the reformer Chang Chih-tung had called for the introduction of Western technology and the preservation of the Chinese moral tradition. Under the leadership of Chang Chih-tung and other such reformers professional schools for the study of foreign languages, military science, shipbuilding, and navigation were founded during the latter decades of the nineteenth century. But it was not until the early years of this century that a fully-fledged general education system was established; the 1904 regulations, compiled by Chang Chih-tung, decreed that primary schools, middle (in the West, secondary) schools, and colleges were to be set up at various regional levels. Significantly, classics were taught throughout the system.[3] But this attempt to incorporate Western knowledge within the framework of Confucianism caused the ethical basis on which Chinese education rested to decline, as alien institutions came to affect native values.

Moreover, by the turn of the century the Chinese students sent abroad to study in Europe, Japan, and the United States were returning, bringing home knowledge of Western culture and political thought. Cognizant of China's weakness, they sought a new political faith to replace the discredited Confucian ethic and to encompass their twin demands of nationalism and modernization. Meanwhile, Sun Yat-sen, a Western-trained doctor, organized a political movement among Overseas Chinese, designed to overthrow the Ch'ing Dynasty and promote policies of national strength. This later became known as the Kuomintang (KMT) and was reorganized on Soviet lines in 1924. The Revolution of 1911 which created a republic did not, however, herald immediate KMT supremacy but an era of warlords, who failed to prevent further encroachments on China's sovereignty.

It was against this national weakness that Chinese students reacted. The patriotic demonstrations of 4 May 1919 against Japanese territorial demands must nevertheless be seen as part of a wider cultural renaissance, a re-examination of Chinese tradition already underway. The movement was a watershed in both the politics and intellectual life of modern China, because from the study societies of the period came support for the KMT and for the Chinese Communist Party (CCP), founded in 1921.

Within this perspective new educational policies were formulated. Because of her successful modernization policy and in spite of an alleged ''imperialist'' record, Japan became a model for the Chinese, and students returned from that country had a decisive influence on the reform of China's education system between 1906 and 1922. These changes brought a more practical orientation, with separate schools being established for academic, pedagogical, vocational, and technical education.[4] But by 1922, admiration of Japanese scholarship gave way to enthusiasm for the United States. This was reflected in the restructuring of the education system on American lines; individual institutions of higher education were given greater initiative, and specialist colleges could be upgraded to university status. In addition, primary education now lasted six years, and middle school was divided into three-year lower and higher levels.[5]

Educational change was necessarily influenced by the tide of political events. In 1927 the military forces of the KMT, now led by Chiang Kai-shek, undertook the Northern Expedition, which defeated the warlords and enabled them to impose their nominal rule over the whole of China. The Party then sought to tighten its control over education, seeing it as an instrument with which to modernize China. Western knowledge was to be harnessed but simultaneously contained within the Party's own ideological synthesis of Chinese and alien philosophy. During the KMT's golden decade (1927-37) the influence of the Western-educated was at its height.

The inculcation of KMT principles was required at all levels, and curricula in middle schools as well as universities were increasingly standardized. Three cardinal principles governed KMT educational policy: (i) stress on higher education at the expense of other sectors, (ii) official concentration on science and technology rather than the humanities, and (iii) increasing use of foreign materials in the curriculum. These policies had two main results.

The first was a growing neglect of rural education which not only limited social mobility but effectively isolated the urban elite from the masses in the countryside. In theory, at least, the provision of clan schools meant an avenue of social mobility; during the 1930's, in spite of limited scholarship assistance, education was expensive and in practice restricted to a small number of wealthy city-dwellers. Moreover, intellectuals, as part of the urban elite, became more isolated from China's hinterland. The government certainly needed the specialized skills of both the native and the foreign-trained for national reconstruction, but the former political link between intellectuals and public service was severed. They were no longer in contact with the rural masses as they had been in Imperial times,[6] and they became increasingly inclined to sacrifice national for personal interests.

Secondly, but more importantly, the KMT's emphasis on functionally specific technical fields, when coupled with periodic discouragement of political activity among intellectuals, tended to alienate university academics and scientific experts from the process of government. In this way intellectuals became increasingly functional beings: any contribution they made came to be expressed in terms of specialist service to the state. Being dedicated to achievement in their professions, they became even more distant from the masses in the countryside, and the concentration of higher education in a few cities increased urban-rural inequalities.

While the KMT consolidated its control, the Communists were also contenders for political power. By the mid-1930's, however, they were little more than a group of defeated bandits who, after fleeing from Chiang Kai-shek's annihilation campaigns, had found refuge in Northwest China, far from the major centres of population. The Moscow-trained leaders of the CCP now lost power, and the mantle of leadership fell to a guerrilla leader, Mao Tse-tung, who remained Party Chairman until his death in 1976. The large-scale Japanese invasion of 1937 had a decisive effect on the fortunes of the KMT and the CCP. By organizing peasant armies to resist the Japanese, the Communists paved the way for their victory against the KMT in the Civil War (1946-49). In addition, it was in their main base area around Yenan that the CCP leaders were able to experiment with policies later adopted on a national scale after their accession to power in 1949.

Traditional philosophical assumptions remain long after the institutions which they justified have disappeared. Neither the KMT nor the CCP could be unaffected by the traditional relationship between education and society, but in its rise to power the CCP, unlike the KMT, maintained and strengthened its link with the rural masses.

An examination of Mao's thinking concerning education reveals traditional as well as Marxist influences. For example, Mao Tse-tung inherited the Confucian emphasis on personal motivation and practical performance rather than natural endowment, even though he never publicly acknowledged his debt to tradition and indeed in his later years condemned the backwardness of Confucian learning. Mao also stressed that study, especially of Marxist texts, must never be divorced from practical reality. A premium was thus placed not on innate ability in book learning for its own sake but on the application of knowledge through positive commitment to the revolutionary cause. In 1930 Mao Tse-tung called upon Party members to "oppose book worship":

> Many who have read Marxist books have become renegades from the revolution, whereas illiterate workers often grasp Marxism very well. Of course, we should study Marxist books, but this study must be integrated with our country's actual conditions. We need books, but we must overcome book worship, which is divorced from the actual situation.[7]

But the CCP's educational philosophy, as Mao formulated it, differed from the Confucian view in one fundamental respect: while Chinese philosophers traditionally saw government as an extension of the laws of the universe, thus stressing harmony and continuity, the CCP has sought to remould the physical environment, thereby promoting social change and economic development.

There is little in Mao Tse-tung's theoretical writing which does not deal at least implicitly with education. Against the turbulent background of revolutionary war in the 1920's and 1930's Mao began to outline the function higher education would perform after nation-wide Communist victory had been achieved. He also defined the role of the intellectual, which would in turn determine enrolment policies and subjects taught. In his 1939 essay "Recruit Large Numbers of Intellectuals" Mao Tse-tung adopted the then current definition of the term "intellectual" *(chih-shih fen-tzu)*, which referred to all those who had received middle school or higher education, with the addition of others with equivalent attainment.

But the CCP's adherence to Marxist doctrine led Mao to formulate policies of socio-economic change; here intellectuals would play a key role. Mao's definition of this new-style intellectual reflected a fusion of the Confucian and Marxist influences to which he had been exposed. Mao consistently stressed the Marxist view that education was part of the superstructure, the realm of ideas, and served the economic base; but the Confucian heritage caused him to emphasize personal performance and moral commitment. The new intellectual would therefore owe his status not merely to class position but much more to proven ability to act in the manner demanded by the CCP: anyone who possesses this quality, as well as the required level of education, is a "proletarian intellectual," that is, an individual who is dedicated to the CCP's political and economic goals regardless of his social origin. In summary, proletarian intellectual status would thus be earned by behaviour rather than inherited by class origin; although the masses may be seen as possessing it, this quality is not innate but moulded in revolutionary struggle. Moral, read political, commitment is the crucial factor.

Moreover, as proletarian intellectual status was acquired rather than ascribed, it could not be monopolized by a privileged class of mental workers. Significantly, however, the old-style intellectuals, hitherto uncommitted to CCP objectives, would not be rejected but remoulded, as the new proletarian intellectuals could not be created without their help.[8] Thus Mao Tse-tung exhorted workers and peasants to raise their cultural level and become intellectuals and simultaneously called upon intellectuals to become workers and peasants.

Now the traditional link between education and society was being carried a stage further; Mao Tse-tung wanted the government to re-establish its link with the masses, especially in the countryside and implied the ultimate integration of mental and manual labour. Role interchangeability and the theme of moral commitment were both echoed in Mao's statement commemorating the twentieth anniversary of the May the Fourth Movement:

> But the intellectuals will accomplish nothing if they fail to integrate themselves with the workers and peasants. In the final analysis, the dividing line between revolutionary intellectuals and non-revolutionary or counter-revolutionary intellectuals is whether or not they are willing to integrate themselves with the workers and peasants and actually do so.[9]

If the Confucian moral imperative and the dictates of Marxist doctrine were both present in Mao's formulation of the proletarian intellectual concept, the exigencies of war against the Japanese between 1936 and 1945 were also to have a profound effect on his educational thinking.

Intellectuals, attracted by the CCP's nationalist stand against the Japanese but not completely committed to Communist ideology, had come to Yenan from all over the country. It was because of the need to win over such intellectuals to the revolutionary cause that Mao Tse-tung outlined the CCP's theory of knowledge in 1942 in his speech "Rectify the Party's Style of Work":

> What is knowledge? Ever since class society came into being the world has had only two kinds of knowledge, knowledge of the struggle for production and knowledge of the class struggle. Natural science and social science are the crystallizations of these two kinds of knowledge, and philosophy is the generalization and summation of the knowledge of nature and the knowledge of society. Is there any other kind of knowledge? No. . . . All relatively complete knowledge is formed in two stages: the first stage is perceptual knowledge, the second is rational knowledge, the latter being the development of the former to a higher stage.

But even though knowledge originates in the struggle of practice, practical experience must not be divorced from theoretical knowledge:

> True, these people [those engaged in practical work] are often rich in experience, which is very valuable, but it is very dangerous if they rest content with their own experience. They must realize that their knowledge is most perceptual and partial and that they lack rational and comprehensive knowledge; in other words, they lack theory and their knowledge, too, is relatively incomplete. Without comparatively complete knowledge it is impossible to do revolutionary work well.[10]

The war situation allowed the CCP to experiment with education in laboratory conditions and demanded that this be given a practical orientation, thus reinforcing Mao's earlier principles. Flexibility was now the keynote; during the war against the Japanese many kinds of institution at various levels were run according to local conditions in the various Communist areas. The example of Yenan University, for which Temporary Regulations were issued in May 1944, will illustrate the Party's theory of knowledge in action. The main enrolment targets were Party and local leaders in political, economic, and cultural fields, but the university also sought to remould intellectuals from other parts of China. Flexible timetables and periods of study facilitated the integration of education and productive labour, which was in turn geared to the economic needs of the Yenan base area.

Instruction was based on two methods derived from the Party's educational philosophy: theory and practice, and collective study. Combining education and productive labour was designed not only to impart technical knowledge but to mould the viewpoint of students so that they became dedicated to the Party's revolutionary goals, and a political message was always implicit in instruction. Theory and practice meant open-door study; students helped to solve practical problems which arose in the base area's economic enterprises and on graduation returned to production for three months, after which they carried out further theoretical work at the university. Participation in labour during study both inside and outside the university promoted role interchangeability of student and worker.

It was against this background of education-labour integration that collective study was adopted. A main feature of guerrilla warfare was flexibility; each individual commander had to be given considerable tactical initiative. Similarly, the chain of command between officers and men was more informal than in conventional warfare, and this pattern was also reflected in the relationship between teacher and student at Yenan University. Private study was at the heart of collective study, on the basis of which students and teachers combined book learning and practical experience in production. Teachers were first among equals; they emphasized the main points in study, but the purpose of their lectures was to prompt students' questions and encourage independent research. At the end of a course teachers provided summaries, collating and answering the questions which had arisen in the students' research. Any hierarchical ranking which divided teacher and student was denied, as the CCP's theory of knowledge claimed that both could contribute to learning. This was a two-way process, and the teacher had no monopoly of knowledge.[11]

But the CCP leaders aspired to be the government of a united China and in their ambitious programme of socio-economic change education would play a new role. During the Sino-Japanese War educational institutions had been designed to forge a national consciousness and fulfil the everyday practical needs of the base areas; once nation-wide victory had been achieved, education would be directed to helping rebuild a devastated national economy. It was to matters such as these that Mao Tse-tung addressed himself in his political report "On Coalition Government" (1945) and his article "On New Democracy" (1940). Ideologically, the CCP was part of the international Communist movement and saw the Soviet Union as China's mentor in education as in other fields. But Mao's emphasis was always on selectivity in the adoption of foreign experience. He consequently stressed the value of Soviet experience but declared that China's own heritage was not to be disregarded. In discussing the wider context of cultural work, Mao affirmed:

The new culture created in the Soviet Union should be a model for us in building our people's culture. Similarly, ancient Chinese culture should neither be totally rejected nor blindly copied but should be accepted discriminatingly so as to help the progress of China's new culture.[12]

Again, in discussing a national, scientific, and mass culture, Mao urged that "we should not gulp any of this foreign material down uncritically, but must treat it as we do our food."[13] In the event, Mao Tse-tung had left many questions unanswered, especially in relation to exactly how foreign institutional models were to be integrated with Chinese values and which elements were to be accepted, which rejected. The CCP's rapid victory over the KMT in the Civil War and its accession to power in 1949 made such questions even more urgent.

2

Chinese Education and Society since 1949

On their accession to power in 1949 the Chinese Communists were faced with enormous tasks of national construction. During the Yenan period the Party had built a national consciousness among the peasantry in the areas they controlled; now its leaders turned their attention to the rehabilitation of a war-ravaged economy and their ultimate goal of transforming China into an advanced industrial society. Certainly the CCP possessed certain advantages its predecessors did not have; it was the first ruler of a united China in over a century. But policies of national construction now involved the State promotion of economic and political development. The proletarian intellectual would play a key role in this process.

The proletarian intellectual concept contained within itself the seeds of conflict, however; its traditional component was rooted in a functionally diffuse society and extolled an amateur ethic, but its Marxist element stressed socioeconomic change, which demanded professionally qualified manpower. Accordingly, a premium would be placed on functional specificity, that is, the acquisition of different branches of specialized knowledge by scientific and technical personnel in order to promote economic development and material abundance. But the proletarian intellectual would ultimately be judged not by his acquisition of expertise per se but the extent to which he used it to express commitment to the Party's revolutionary social goals. But there was always the danger that the means would replace the end, with economic development pursued for its own sake. Similarly, the proletarian intellectual might see specialized knowledge as an objective in itself, losing sight of the final goal of a Communist society. In that case moral commitment would be subsumed under vocational function, the proletarian intellectuals' specialist role; this, in turn, could result in China moving away from Mao Tse-tung's vision of a classless Chinese society, which stressed role interchangeability of mental and manual labour.

This latent conflict within the proletarian intellectual concept eventually became actual and was necessarily reflected in the implementation of university enrolment. By the same token enrolment can also be considered a barometer of change in China's education system since 1949. Thus the purpose of this study is to examine policies governing admission to institutions of higher education against the moral imperative of revolutionary commitment and the functionally specific needs of national construction.

During the early years of the regime the demands of national construction dictated certain priorities in education. In the short term, at least, egalitarian social goals were to be sacrificed for the needs of a developing economy. Major priorities included engineering manpower, medical personnel, and middle school teachers. The training of these high calibre personnel required emphasis on higher education at the expense of the lower sectors; the necessary creation of regional centres of excellence meant that the uneven geographical distribution of universities, a legacy of the KMT's urban orientation, would be perpetuated for the immediate future,[1] even if the Party was pledged ultimately to correct it. There is every reason to assume, however, a fair degree of initial unanimity within the CCP leadership concerning education, and if Mao had any reservations about the priorities of his lieutenants who had the task of implementing policy, no open conflict was yet apparent.

The evolution of educational policy has necessarily been influenced by the prevailing economic and political climate in China, and for purposes of introductory analysis, the period since the Communist accession may be divided into four major phases: (i) 1949-57, a period of economic rehabilitation, the institution of Soviet-type central planning, and the reorganization of higher education on Russian lines; (ii) 1958-65, characterized by stress on national economic self-sufficiency and the revival of the Yenan tradition in education, although retrenchment policies followed in the latter part of this period; (iii) 1966-76, when Mao launched the Cultural Revolution, after which "moderates" conflicted with "radicals" over China's development strategy. These years also saw the reform and subsequent consolidation of the education system; and (iv) the period since Mao Tse-tung's death in 1976 during which the new leadership has set in motion an ambitious modernization programme, necessitating re-emphasis on the study of science and technology.

In this chapter changes in the enrolment process will be introduced within the above framework.

The 1950 Sino-Soviet Treaty of Friendship and Alliance was a landmark in the politics of post-1949 China, and by its provisions, China received economic and technological assistance from the Soviet Union. Russian experts were sent to give advice concerning the development of heavy industry, the major priority in China's First Five-Year Plan (1953-57). Educational policy would thus be strongly influenced, if not determined, by centrally planned manpower requirements. There seems to have been general agreement within the CCP leadership about learning from the Soviet Union, yet this structure implied far-reaching value change, in potential conflict with the CCP's own tradition of education. Meanwhile, however, a series of educational conferences was held to discuss the reorganization of the Chinese system. In June 1950, at the First National Conference on Higher Education, the Vice-Minister of Education, Ch'ien Chün-jui, called for "regularization," suggesting that the Soviet system rather than the short-term training classes of the Yenan period should be the model for reform.[2]

The Soviet system was adopted because it made possible the allocation of the required quantity and quality of personnel to a specialized field. This necessarily involved a tight hierarchical relationship between individual institutions of higher education and the Chinese Central Government. Thus each institution trained a centrally determined number of specialists required by national construction. But this system also possessed certain disadvantages; changes in policy, for example, could only come from the centre and this severely restricted the independent initiative of individual institutions and educators.[3]

This situation was a significant departure from the KMT system, where university presidents enjoyed considerable power, and the Yenan tradition, which promoted local initiative, though always within a framework of unified leadership from the centre.

Here the relationship between Party and State organs in China since 1949 comes into focus. In Western parliamentary systems political parties usually alternate in government and opposition; in Communist countries, however, any organized dissent, except within very narrowly permitted confines, is, by definition, treason. In China, the CCP permeates every area of national life, ensuring obedience to its directives. Party control over decision-making at the national level is assured; high ranking officials in government bodies, like Ministries, are usually prominent Party figures. In addition, Party committees are established at regional levels, for example, at those of the province and the *hsien* (county), and in institutions like factories, schools, and universities.

Institutions of higher education were initially controlled by the Ministry of Education and then from 1952 to 1958 by the Ministry of Higher Education. Some specialist institutes were partially directed by Ministries concerned with functional branches of the national economy, but a Ministry of Education always remained the general co-ordinator of central control. In addition, most universities and institutes were financed either by the Ministry of Education or other Ministries.

But the pre-eminent position of the Party in education, as in other walks of life, meant that the universities were subject to dual control. The president of a university *(hsiao-chang)* was appointed by the state and subject to the orders of the Education Ministry. He represented the institution at national conferences, directed all teaching, research and administration, and appointed personnel. He was, however, also responsible to his institution's Party committee, which played the crucial role of ensuring that central directives were carried out in accordance with CCP ideology and policy.

In practice, however, the adoption of the Soviet system of vertical control in China tended to promote the leadership of specialists at the expense of the Party committees. Even if direction from the centre left only limited local initiative, the specialist "responsible principalship" system meant that the university president assumed complete overall responsibility for both administrative and teaching affairs.[4]

Party membership, however, determined the authority which a president actually possessed. If a Party member, he directed the institute; if not, his position was prestigious but nominal, real power being exercised by one of the vice-presidents who were very often Party members. Party control was thus assured. The most important administrative body in the institution was the university council *(chiao-wu wei-yüan-hui)*, membership of which included such figures as the university president, the vice-presidents, and the department heads *(hsi chu-jen)*.[5] In any case, decision-making always remained effectively in the hands of the CCP. In addition, many professors appointed before 1949 were forced to undergo periodic thought reform to inculcate loyalty to the new regime, and even in purely academic matters, they were subordinate to Party members. Any influence such non-Party professors had was strictly limited and final decisions always rested with the CCP.[6]

The Soviet model not only demanded central planning and vertical control but a division of labour within higher education. Between 1950 and 1952 the education system was reorganized on Soviet lines. Private and foreign institutions were taken over and their faculties distributed among newly created units. There were now three categories of institution: (i) the comprehensive university *(tsung-he ta-hsüeh)*, which was interdisciplinary and embraced the arts and the sciences. In 1955 there were fourteen institutions of this kind;[7] (ii) the technical institute *(chuan-men hsüeh-yüan)*, which taught subjects such as petroleum, coal-mining, geology, chemical engineering, construction engineering, agriculture, forestry, medicine, and teacher training; and (iii) polytechnical universities *(kung-yeh ta-hsüeh)*, which had a broader curriculum than the technical institutes and were formed by rearranging the technical colleges of the old universities inherited from the KMT period. A prominent example was the newly founded Ch'inghua Polytechnical University.[8]

The comprehensive universities were to train scientific research personnel and teaching staff for all branches of higher education and middle schools. Their teaching was designed to provide students with a high level of theoretical knowledge in the natural or social sciences. Because of greater funding and superior facilities, the comprehensive universities became elite institutions, despite frequent assertions to the contrary. The comprehensive universities' theoretical study guaranteed the existence of the other two categories, and one source called them the signpost of national, cultural, and scientific development.[9] The other two categories also had crucial roles to play, however; the technical institutes trained experts of all kinds, and the polytechnical universities produced high calibre scientific and technological personnel.

The reform of academic and administrative structure within institutions was also undertaken. Prior to such reorganization a pilot project was initiated to test the relevance of Soviet experience to Chinese conditions. This was the Chinese People's University, founded in 1950 and designed to train old cadres, that is, leadership personnel in Party and State organs, in economics and finance.[10] These old cadres, many of peasant origin, were now being seconded to higher education to learn new branches of knowledge. This training would enable them to play a key role in the consolidation of Party control over city industry, hitherto managed and owned by private enterprise. Social science teachers were also sent to acquire further depth in their respective subjects.

At a conference to discuss initial teaching experiences at the Chinese People's University, shortly after its foundation, the Vice-Minister of Education, Yang Hsiu-feng, called not only for emulation of the Soviet Union's scientific achievement but its university administration as well. The rearrangement of administrative structures and teaching units was undertaken in accordance with Soviet-type functionally specific manpower needs. In contrast with the American-style KMT higher education system, where universities consisted of separate colleges and schools, each university or institute was now to be divided into departments *(hsi)*, which had under their jurisdiction a number of specialties *(chuan-yeh)*. Under this new system of academic organization, the department which, in the pre-1949 period, had been a teaching unit, now became the body responsible for basic level administration. In the department's former place came the specialty, the Soviet *spetsialnost*, as the new academic unit. In this way several closely allied specialties were grouped together in a department. These specialties were in turn divided into numbers of specializations *(chuan-men hua)*, the Soviet *spetsializatsiya*. A detailed study plan was compiled for each specialty or specialization, embodying a list of courses offered. For example, the specialty ''internal combustion engines'' in the Department of Mechanical Engineering at an engineering institute was designed to produce experts with concrete knowledge and practical experience in the construction of such machines. Methods and content of instruction were uniform in all specialties of that type throughout China. The minute divisions in academic disciplines which characterized the specialty system were seen as the most suitable means of training cadres for national construction, and by their nature would enable graduates to be fitted for specific positions in the country's programme of economic development.[11]

Teaching research guidance groups *(chiao-hsüeh yen-chiu chih-tao tsu)*, the

Soviet *kafedras,* were composed of all teachers of allied courses in a specialty and became the basic unit of instruction. They compiled study plans and taught accordingly, exchanged teaching experiences, directed research programmes, and trained postgraduates for academic posts.[12] Significantly, teaching research guidance groups were also introduced in middle schools, where they performed similar functions.

Curricula reform followed changes in academic structure. In 1953 and 1954 the Ministry of Higher Education held a series of conferences to discuss Soviet teaching materials. Large numbers of Russian textbooks, incorporating the fruits of Soviet scientific and technological research, were then translated. Some of these may well have been unsuited to China, but they were uniformly adopted throughout the country, thus abandoning the Yenan tradition of local experimentation.

While higher education was reorganized on Soviet lines, other parts of the education system remained structurally the same as they had been in the pre-1949 period. The middle schools were still divided into higher and lower sectors, the primary level took six years of study as in the American-style KMT system, and vocational schools were retained. There have since been minor adjustments, but this pattern has remained basically unchanged. A new feature, however, was spare-time education which included, for instance, literacy classes. This, in part, reflected the CCP's Yenan experience and was designed to raise the cultural and technical levels of workers and peasants. ''Rapid schools'' were also established to facilitate the latter's promotion to higher rungs of the ladder, especially to universities and institutes.

It was not necessary to make education compulsory, as it continued to be held in high esteem; advancement was not automatic, however, since there were always more aspirants than places. But the age at which pupils began school was raised from six to seven, as in the Soviet system.

If, in general, the structure of lower sectors remained unchanged, Russian influence was felt to some extent in the adoption of new curricula, especially science textbooks in middle schools.[13] The content of political education was also changed from KMT doctrine to Marxist-Leninist ideology.

The education system, as it stood after the reform of universities and institutes in the years 1950-52, is shown on the next page.

It is against this background of institutional reform that the evolution of the enrolment process must be understood. Higher education had been redesigned to produce specialized manpower, and during the period 1949-57 the CCP formulated central enrolment plans. Before reorganization there were considerable local variations in higher education, and in 1950 and 1951 each institution was responsible for its own enrolment, albeit within the framework of centrally devised general regulations. But the years from 1952 to 1957 brought the gradual introduction of a centralized system. The first phase of this process took place in

1952 and 1953. In those years enrolment was conducted through the Six Large Administrative Areas, into which China was divided by the CCP during its consolidation (1949-54). In the last year this phase gave way to a second stage, the admission of students on a countrywide basis.

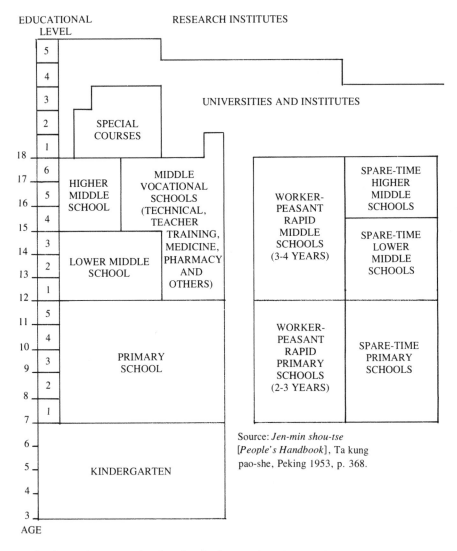

Source: *Jen-min shou-tse* [*People's Handbook*], Ta kung pao-she, Peking 1953, p. 368.

Soviet style economic planning had necessitated central control through a hierarchical chain of command between 1953 and 1957. The bulk of national investment had been placed in heavy industry, which had expanded rapidly, but agriculture's performance was less impressive. An increase in agricultural productivity was crucial, however, to feed a growing population, provide raw materials for light industry, and produce exports for the purchase of capital goods. A high price had been exacted in social terms as well, for differences in living standards between city and countryside increased.

The First Five-Year Plan had had a limited economic success, but new policies initiated in 1958 called for a more balanced development of industry and agriculture. The Great Leap Forward (1958-61) was intended to make good the severe shortage of capital in the countryside by intensive utilization of China's abundant resources of labour; there was also greater stress on production relations than on production forces, that is, emphasis on the organized direction and mobilization of the peasantry as opposed to an increase in technological input. Numbers of co-operatives were now amalgamated into ''communes,'' which were not only agricultural units but took over such functions of local government as education and health. Industries were also established in the commune setting. Devolution of power from the Central Government to the regions gave greater initiative to local Party cadres. Mao Tse-tung believed that these policies would serve social as well as economic goals. In general, however, the Great Leap proved a disaster; targets were too ambitious, crop figures were later shown to be exaggerated, the products of local industries in the countryside were unusable, over-zealous cadres drove the peasantry too hard, and the overall result was severe economic dislocation.

Mao Tse-tung lost prestige and yielded the Headship of State to CCP Vice-Chairman, Liu Shao-ch'i, although he remained Party Chairman. By 1962 Liu and his associates were instituting policies of economic retrenchment, more rational planning returned, and the communes were readjusted, the peasantry being once again given material incentives. By 1965 national economic health was being restored. The economic developments of the Great Leap and its aftermath were necessarily reflected in educational policy.

By 1958 Mao was having very serious misgivings about the direction of China's education system. In the early years of the regime he had accepted that in the short term social goals would have to be sacrificed for the demands of a developing economy. The Soviet higher education system had originally developed in a very different society, and its adoption by the CCP was a very radical departure from China's own tradition. But while institutional structure, academic organization, and curricula content came to bear the imprint of Soviet experience, teaching methods continued to be influenced by the traditional Chinese relationship between education and society, via the experimentation of Yenan. Gradually, however, the hierarchical and technological nature of Soviet institutions also left its mark on teaching methods: the unity of theory and practice and collective study came to be seen as instruments designed solely for furthering the theoretical study of experts rather than as having social values in themselves.

Moreover, national construction placed a premium on certain types of specialized knowledge, like various branches of engineering, which soon attracted higher material rewards, a situation where experts were increasingly able to bargain with society for the price of their services. As a result, disparities were appearing in facilities and standards within higher education; in a vicious circle of inequality more prestigious institutions maintained standards and attracted the best entrants. This process of stratification will be called the elite-mass structure: the elite being the institutions which imparted crucial expertise to excellent students, the mass being the less favoured bodies teaching less important subjects to the least able entrants. These patterns of elitism, together with the concomitant emergence of new centres of privilege being created by economic development, were gradually producing a meritocracy, a class of persons who owed their prominent positions to their ability, real or apparent.

Mao Tse-tung saw these tendencies as undesirable and sought to correct them. One consistent theme in the Party's educational philosophy, as he had formulated it, had been the integration of education and productive labour; this reflected, too, the Marxist millenial vision of all-round development and role interchangeability of worker and intellectual. Mao Tse-tung's dissatisfaction with the emerging elite-mass structure was forcefully expressed in a new educational policy, initially outlined in the Joint Directive of the Central Committee, the ruling body of the CCP, and the State Council, the equivalent of the Cabinet in Western parliamentary systems. This was issued on 19 September 1958. Education was to serve the interests of proletarian politics and was to be integrated with productive labour. This practical element had long been present in the education system, but was now given greater emphasis, and part-time institutions were established at the middle school level and in higher education. (Part-time schools are, however, to be distinguished from spare-time education, which operated much less formally, providing literacy classes and technical training on an ad hoc basis).

The part-time institutions were justified in both economic and social terms. There was a serious shortage of schools, and large numbers of graduates were consequently unable to be promoted. Rural aspirants were particularly disadvantaged; nearly all middle schools were in the cities. Part-time schools and universities were to be run by factories and communes under Party leadership; these would pay their own way without need of State expenditure, providing new sources of local technical manpower. But, to Mao, their social function was preeminent because they eliminated the three separations between city and countryside, mental and manual labour, and worker and peasant.

Part-time institutions certainly offered educational opportunity for those previously denied it, but their standards were considerably lower than their full-time counterparts. Moreover, contrary to Mao Tse-tung's intention that full-time institutions ultimately take on the part-time form, disparities between the two types increased. Patterns of inequality were being reinforced, for there were now two education systems.

There is evidence to suggest that some national figures such as Liu Shao-ch'i, certain officials in the Education Ministries, and various academic authorities in the universities, unlike Mao, viewed these developments not with apprehension but qualified approval. Their task was to implement policy, but in so doing, they reinterpreted the educational philosophy which Mao had formulated, and the elite-mass structure was intensified as a result. Furthermore, by 1962, they were also giving part-time education an economic rather than a social role; to them it was essentially supplementary, not, as Mao believed, a model for the full-time system.

Later, Liu Shao-ch'i was accused of pursuing policies opposed to those of Mao and formulating his own theory of knowledge. An article in the *Kuang-ming jih-pao*, a Chinese Communist newspaper specializing in intellectual policy, charged Liu with stating that ability *(tsai-neng)* is innate.[14] But an analysis of Liu's writings does not support this contention. In his book *How To Be a Good Communist*, for many years required reading for Party cadres, Liu Shao-ch'i quoted Confucius' concentration on study as evidence that the ancient philosopher did not consider himself to have been born a sage. In short, Liu was claiming that capacity to become a sage was within reach of all, but only possible through personal effort, or in Marxist terms, via the struggle of practice.[15]

Thus Liu agreed with Mao as to the origin of man's ability and, by extension, knowledge *(jen-shih)*. But although he saw knowledge as an instrument for promoting the collective good, the individual remained Liu's frame of reference, even if the individual's contribution was in the Party's interests: "Members of our Party should not have personal aims which are independent of the Party's interests; their personal interests must harmonize with the Party's interests."[16] Likewise, in his "Directive to the Democratic Construction Association and Federation of Industry and Commerce" in 1959, Liu Shao-ch'i stated: "Personal interests must be looked after, for without personal interests there will be no group interests. . . . Therefore, instead of caring for the public and not one's self, one should care for both."[17] There seems little doubt that Liu was more prepared than Mao to come to terms with individual interests.

Similarly, Liu made concessions to personal aptitude, suggesting that individuals might be suited to different categories of work:

> Technical work occupies a very important place in our Party work, and comrades engaged in it are doing their share in the Communist cause no less than comrades engaged in other jobs. . . . Naturally, in assigning work to members, the Party organization and the responsible comrades

should, as far as possible, take their individual inclinations and aptitudes into consideration, develop their strong points and stimulate their zeal to go forward. However, no Communist must refuse a Party assignment on the grounds of personal preferences.[18]

But Liu's emphasis here on the development of the individual according to his aptitude for various specialized skills and, by implication, certain branches of scientific knowledge is not strictly meritocratic. Although he does not refer to innate ability as such, he later conceded that in practice achievement will vary markedly even among those with similar experiences in revolutionary struggle. For instance, in speaking of the varying quality of Party members in revolutionary struggle, Liu asserted:

For example, several Communists take part in a revolutionary struggle together and engage in revolutionary practice under roughly the same circumstances and conditions. It is possible that the effect of the struggle on these Party members will not be at all uniform. Some will make very rapid progress and some who used to lag behind will even forge ahead of this. Other Party members will advance very slowly.[19]

Liu, by giving considerable weight to differing personal performance, would surely, in Mao's view, have come perilously close to acknowledging innate ability.

In conclusion, Liu's preparedness to accept differences in individual aptitude, interest, and performance may well have predisposed him to accept the social changes being increasingly dictated by the adoption of the Soviet model in higher education. During the years from 1953 to 1957 he saw the training of specialized manpower as more immediately crucial than the eradication of social inequality; by 1962 he was according part-time education a utilitarian not a social role. Liu Shao-ch'i did not postulate his own theory of knowledge in opposition to Mao Tse-tung, but he emphasized the practical economic aspects of the proletarian intellectual concept.

Changes in the educational process closely followed the general lines of domestic policy in China during the late 1950's and early 1960's. The beginning of the Great Leap, 1958 and 1959, brought decentralization of university admissions work, with greater initiative being given to provincial authorities and a limited freedom of action granted to individual institutions of higher education. By the early 1960's policies of retrenchment were reflected in moves to partially recentralize the enrolment process, involving a system of unified leadership combined with regional management. Thus during the years from 1960 to 1965 there was greater central control; the independent initiative of individual institutions of higher education was now reduced, although provincial authorities still retained certain powers over the enrolment process in their areas.

By 1965 Mao Tse-tung was having very serious reservations about the state of Chinese society. The retrenchment policies of Liu Shao-ch'i and his colleagues had only intensified the social inequalities emerging in the previous period; as the economy further developed, it began to create new centres of power and privilege. Meanwhile, when Mao gave up the position of Head of State in 1959, possibly under pressure but ostensibly to concentrate on Party affairs, he withdrew from day-to-day administration, and other Party leaders gradually succeeded in isolating him from the masses. Liu consolidated his control over the Party apparatus, which, in turn, dominated State organs. To Mao, a drastic situation called for sweeping measures, and he started to plan a mass campaign which would, at one stroke, eradicate social cleavage and destroy his opponents at the centre of political power.

The Cultural Revolution (1966-69) may thus be seen on two levels: it was a power struggle and a conflict over political ideals. The power struggle component demonstrated Mao's ability as a manipulator of men and organization. When, at a top Party meeting in 1959 a prominent military figure, P'eng Teh-huai, criticized Mao's brainchild, the Great Leap Forward, he was dismissed from office and replaced by a famous guerrilla leader, Lin Piao, Mao's firm supporter; thus, even though he lost influence in the Party, Mao retained it in the army, which he now saw as the repository of revolutionary wisdom, to be copied by other sectors of Chinese society. It was from the army that Mao would stage his comeback in 1966. Meanwhile, Mao sought the co-operation of top Party bureaucrats in mass campaigns to check arrogant cadres; this was to test the loyalty of the Liu faction, which increasingly failed to live up to Mao's ideals.

The shock-troops of the Cultural Revolution were the Red Guards, composed of middle school and university students. Under the direction of a specially appointed Cultural Revolution Group, headed by his wife Chiang Ch'ing, Mao assigned them the task of "bombarding the headquarters," that is, attacking certain Party leaders at both central and local levels. Initially, Liu Shao-ch'i and his supporters sent work teams into the universities in an attempt to contain the Red Guard movement, but without success. Mao still held the army in reserve, but it nevertheless provided crucial logistic support which increased the mobility and authority of the Red Guards. The latter, however, proved difficult to control and caused disruption of essential services. They also became deeply factionalized, with some of them taking the side of Liu Shao-ch'i as well as local power-holders. Consequently, in 1967 the army was instructed to bring the Red Guards under control and to play a prominent role in running local administration in the midst of increasing chaos. The Red Guards had, in any case, by now served their main purpose of discrediting and helping to dismiss Liu Shao-ch'i and his closest supporters. The Party organization had been essentially destroyed, and the apogee of army predominance came at a high Party meeting in early 1969 which heralded the end of the Cultural Revolution; this fuelled Lin Piao's own ambitions, and he and certain other military figures were reluctant to relinquish the power which had accrued to them. The Party organization, however, was now being reconstructed and Mao increasingly relied on Chou En-lai, Premier and leader of the "moderate" faction, who now became, through his own diplomatic finesse, a counterweight to Lin. Lin's coup against Mao failed, and he attempted to flee the country, later dying in an air crash.

Soon, however, the moderates and factions in the army which had helped Mao to destroy Lin incurred the disfavour of the "radicals" headed by Chiang Ch'ing. By the early 1970's this conflict took on the nature of a succession struggle; the radicals exploited Mao's apprehension concerning the pragmatic economic policies being pursued by Chou En-lai and the State Council. To Mao, these policies looked like a return to 1965, and when he sanctioned the Anti-Lin Anti-Confucius Campaign (1973-74), the radicals sought to channel it against Chou En-lai. Mao had never acknowledged his unconscious debt to Confucius, and he now asserted that all reactionaries were, by definition, followers of backward Confucian teaching. The campaign, however, lost impetus and gradually died away; the moderates gained in strength in the Central Government and in 1975 Chou's protégé, Teng Hsiao-p'ing, recently returned from the disgrace and oblivion to which he had been assigned in the Cultural Revolution, wrote his *Outline Report of the Academy of Sciences*, a blueprint for a new education, on the lines of the pre-Cultural Revolution system.

Though the radicals possessed regional enclaves of strength, their control of the media made them appear more powerful than they actually were. As Mao's grasp of affairs grew steadily weaker, the radicals still claimed to speak in his name; Mao, however, appointed a hitherto little-known agricultural expert, Hua Kuo-feng, a second rank Party figure, as a compromise successor. Meanwhile, Chou En-lai predeceased Mao, and on the latter's death in September 1976, the new leadership, headed by Hua Kuo-feng, moved swiftly to discredit Chiang Ch'ing's radical group, a process in which military support was of great importance. During the period since late 1976 Hua Kuo-feng and Teng Hsiao-p'ing, returned to power after a second but temporary defeat at the hands of the radicals, have continued Chou En-lai's modernization policies, which have necessitated a re-emphasis on academic study.

The Cultural Revolution may therefore be seen as a power struggle, but it must also be understood in a wider sense. It is tempting to see this momentous campaign as beginning in 1966, but certain features of it had been implicit in mass movements and inner-Party struggles ever since the days of Yenan. Mao had inherited the Confucian assumption that man's nature was essentially good and could be correctly moulded. There was another side to this optimistic appraisal of the malleability of man, however; even paragons of virtue could fall from grace through negative behaviour. Liu Shao-ch'i was such an example, and not even he could be immune from criticism.

There was always a populist strain in Mao's adaptation of Marxism-Leninism to Chinese conditions; he constantly sought to bridge the gap between the Party and the masses. One instance of this had been the Hundred Flowers Campaign of 1957, the results of which reverberated throughout China's intellectual world. Mao believed that the old intellectuals had been sufficiently remoulded, and the younger generation adequately schooled, to be allowed to undertake criticism of the current relationship between Party cadres and the masses. But the flood of criticism which eventually ensued from academics and students alike questioned not only administrative abuses and cadre corruption but the very role of the Party in national life. So-called "rightists," including some student leaders, were sent to the countryside to be re-educated through manual labour; this presaged the rusticated youth programmes of the post-Cultural Revolution period, when millions of former Red Guards were sent down to the rural areas.

In spite of the damning indictment of the Hundred Flowers, Mao, at the beginning of the Cultural Revolution, still placed his faith in youth. If older Party cadres had succumbed to the temptations of city life, power, and wealth, the younger generation could still be remoulded and trained as revolutionary successors. They were too young to have experienced the revolutionary struggles of the pre-1949 period, however, but in attacking power-holders throughout China, they would now, in theory, be so tempered.

At the beginning of the Cultural Revolution universities were closed, and when they began to reopen in the late 1960's and early 1970's, there was a re-emphasis on practical studies and "open-door" instruction. Students in science and technology worked in factories inside and outside their own institutions; those in the arts and humanities "took society as their workshop" so that their creative writing could reflect the everyday lives of workers and peasants. It was intended that this integration of education and productive labour would enable full-time education to take on a part-time form. The younger generation would not lose the contact they had earlier made with the masses; through open-door education the momentum of revolution would be maintained.

Proletarian control of higher education was to be assured by the leadership of the "Workers and Peasants Mao Tse-tung Thought Propaganda Teams," the first of which entered Ch'inghua Polytechnical University in July 1968. These have recently been abolished, however, and the Party control apparatus in institutions of higher education at last revived.

The early 1970's brought new enrolment processes, consonant with the institutional changes which were taking place and reflecting Mao Tse-tung's attempt to reintegrate education and society. Mao's aim was to prevent the re-emergence of a privileged elite divorced from the masses. Academic competition for university entry had been intense during the two earlier periods; the elite-mass structure in higher education had come to be reflected in Chinese society itself. The June 1966 Joint Directive of the Central Committee of the CCP and the State Council outlined a new process of recommendation and selection, by which middle graduates were to spend two years of manual labour in the countryside before applying for entry to higher education, instead of being examined for university immediately after higher middle graduation. In theory, political qualifications were now crucial; candidates would be recommended at local levels by poor and lower middle peasants. "Steadfast revolutionaries" among the latter were themselves also eligible to apply for selection. Selection, however, passed through several local government levels, at each of which a certain number of applicants was eliminated. Moreover, as this system was consolidated, it became more competitive; there were many more aspirants than places in higher education.

Certainly, the enrolment process had been decentralized and there was less control from the Central Government. But the Party's function was even more predominant; each stage was supervised by local cadres, and the masses' role, in theory crucial, was in practice less important than it first appeared.

Other subtle changes were already in evidence. The last stage of the process was re-examination by the institutions to which candidates had applied. By 1973 a coherent pattern was emerging, and there was strong evidence to suggest that some prestigious universities, like Ch'inghua, were exercising to the full their right to reject, presumably on academic grounds, candidates previously recommended at the local level. In addition, this growing stress on specialized knowledge was accompanied by the revival of a hierarchical structure of enrolment organs on the pre-1966 pattern.

Moreover, although the principle adopted in the immediate post-Cultural Revolution period had been that institutions of higher education should recruit locally, addressing themselves to area manpower needs, a 1971 directive stated that major national universities, recently reopened, would accept students from all over the country, with each province given a fixed quota. This suggested a significant modification of the new enrolment process, which now began to differ according to type of institution. The radicals opposed these changes but, in the long term, to no avail.

Since the death of Mao Tse-tung China's new leaders have embarked on an ambitious modernization programme designed to turn China into an advanced industrial power, thus furthering the policies set in motion by Chou En-lai during the mid-1970's. This programme is China's latest response to the West and requires massive injections of foreign technology. The apparent willingness of China's leaders to play a greater role in international trade suggests a very considerable departure from Mao Tse-tung's insistence on national self-reliance; earlier reluctance to finance imports through long-term credits has given way to the acceptance of foreign investment in China's industry. These changes have been legitimized by selective quotation from, and reinterpretation of, Mao Tse-tung's writings; he had, after all, advocated that foreign countries be studied, albeit critically. Hua Kuo-feng and his colleagues are convinced that China's sovereignty and integrity can only be guaranteed by a strategy of rapid economic development.

The main task of the education system is to train technological manpower. Egalitarian social goals will be sacrificed for the foreseeable future. Development is in any case rarely even; specialized and regional centres of strength must be created as pacesetters for the rest of the country.

In early 1978 an Education Ministry report outlined these priorities in greater detail. The major emphasis was to be placed on higher education, with science and technology given funds and facilities at the expense of the arts and humanities. Full-time education has now become the model; the part-time system is essentially a supplementary alternative to train lower level technical personnel and provide a limited channel of mobility for workers and peasants. Productive labour is now seen as a practical means of illustrating theory; successful aspects of Maoist experiments have thus been incorporated in China's new education.

The system is in many respects much as it was in the late 1950's and early 1960's; its ethos is competitive and meritocratic. Liu Shao-ch'i has now been rehabilitated; greater rein than ever is being given to aptitude and individual excellence. University students are already becoming a privileged elite.

Since 1977 the enrolment process has resembled the unified control characteristic of much of the pre-1966 period. National priorities have again required a hierarchy of enrolment organs. In spite of centralization, however, provincial authorities and individual institutions have had considerable initiative in the implementation of enrolment. Finally, procedures once again vary according to type of institution; the wheel of privilege has come full circle.

3

Eligibility and Preparation of Candidates

The CCP's educational philosophy was reflected in the formulation of university enrolment regulations. The main feature of that philosophy was stress on moral commitment and personal performance, the implication being that all, whatever their social origin, could become proletarian intellectuals through ideological re-moulding and correct conduct. In the early years of the Communist regime there was a desperate shortage of specialized personnel and every effort was made to utilize "bourgeois" academics and recruit students inherited from the previous government.

Enrolment was thus closely related to the urgent need for qualified manpower. Regulations issued during the period from 1950, the first year that students were admitted to higher education under the new regime, and 1957, the end of the First Five-Year Plan, show that the categories of eligible applicant underwent minor changes, but in conception remained generally consistent. Any changes reflected the progress of national construction and its need for various kinds of scientific and technological personnel.

In 1957, for example, the initial requirement for examination registration was a cultural level (sometimes referred to as a level of scholarship) equivalent to that of higher middle graduation. This broad stipulation was designed to accommodate diverse kinds of applicant, both within and outside the education system. For instance, in addition to graduating higher middle students, it encompassed those who had formerly studied in technical institutes, failed to complete the course, but subsequently carried out private study. This rubric also appeared to apply to those who had graduated a long time before from higher middle schools, but only provided that they had not previously been examined for institutions of higher education and were under a certain age, usually twenty-seven.

Seven basic categories were outlined, the first two groups coming from within the educational system, the others part of the work force: (i) graduates of higher middle schools and worker-peasant rapid middle schools of the year in question, who had graduation certificates (rapid middle schools consisted of revision classes and were established to enable worker and peasant candidates to reach the standard required for entry to higher education); (ii) the year's graduates of outstanding academic calibre from vocational middle schools could apply for registration. These vocational schools were an integral part of the education system, but their students were very often seconded from work units and for this reason required the approval of their employers. They were also required to produce relevant verification documents; (iii) serving personnel from Party and government organs, commercial and industrial units, and mass organizations, like trade unions, who held letters of verification from their original employers and who were under thirty years of age; (iv) retired and seconded soldiers, who held verification letters from their local *hsien* governments or from the Party committees in their military units, and who were also under thirty; (v) various kinds of intellectual youth. This was a wide grouping and its confines were not always made clear; it seems to have included, however, youth who had long since left school but were as yet unemployed. Some of these, presumably of bourgeois origin, appear to have undergone special programmes of thought reform. The upper age limit for these youth was twenty-seven and they had to present evidence of their qualifications in the form of verification letters from their local governments; (vi) Overseas Chinese students who had returned to China and held the necessary documents from the country's Overseas Chinese Affairs Organs; and (vii) Hong Kong and Macao students, who could produce verification letters from the Promotion Guidance Committee, set up in Canton for higher middle graduates returning to China from those two areas. The age stipulation for the two latter categories of eligible applicants was below thirty.[1]

Three major conclusions may be drawn from the enrolment regulations quoted above. Firstly, there is a noticeable absence of any restriction based on social origin, even if in practice counter-revolutionary elements would have been excluded, especially in the early years of the regime, by virtue of the verification documents required from relevant authorities. In this context a comparison with Soviet university enrolment regulations is instructive. Despite minor changes, a policy of discrimination on the basis of social origin continued in effect until 1935 in the USSR.[2] The Chinese regulations thus left open the possibility of applicants of bourgeois origin proving their acceptability by performing in the manner demanded by the Party. Secondly, the categories outlined reflected not only that proletarian intellectual status would be based upon achievement rather than ascription, but also the Party's attempt to tap talent wherever it might be found. In reality, the Party could not fail to recognize that bourgeois students at various levels, inherited from the Kuomintang regime, possessed various skills which were capable of direction in the interests of national construction. In 1956 a correspondence column explicitly stated that there was no definite ratio laid down for acceptance between different categories of candidate.[3]

The categories of eligible applicant outlined in the enrolment regulations would in any case necessarily reflect the criteria on which the concept of proletarian intellectual was based. Red Guard statements published during the Cultural Revolution accused Party revisionists of manipulating the enrolment process to ensure the entry of children of high cadres, while denying the admission of children of workers and peasants as well as the sons and daughters of bourgeois elements who had been reformed. The main objective, however, was to discredit Liu Shao-ch'i, and evidence to hand does not support the Red Guard charges.

What is significant about Red Guard sources in this context, however, is not any adherence to factual evidence but their return to the fundamentals of the Party's educational philosophy. The concept of proletarian intellectual had stressed achievement rather than ascription; it followed that applicants from all social backgrounds were eligible for entry if they were prepared to reform themselves in accordance with the Party's political criteria. Knowledge came from the struggle of practice in the material world and generational change would eventually eliminate ascribed social background. The Red Guards at least partially refuted their own charges against Liu Shao-ch'i when they quoted Mao Tse-tung's essay "On the Correct Handling of Contradictions among the People" (1957): "Although very many of our university students are not children from the homes of workers, yet, with a few exceptions, they are patriotic and uphold socialism." Without doubt reformed youth of bourgeois parentage were being admitted to higher education.

Social background has never been adequately defined in Chinese Communist educational writing, but articles in Red Guard tabloids, when considered together with the enrolment regulations issued in the early years of the Chinese Communist regime, provide glimpses of class divisions as they specifically affected entry to higher education. For instance, in 1967 the Red Guard newspaper, *Chung-hsüeh wen-ming pao*, in claiming that few students came from worker and peasant families, gave the following outline on which categories of eligible applicant had apparently been based during the pre-Cultural Revolution period.

Five categories of youth were defined as "non-red," as not coming from the ranks of workers and peasants: children of (i) landlords, (ii) rich peasants, (iii) counter-revolutionary bad right-wing elements, (iv) those capitalists who had not been reformed, and (v) high intellectual elements from the old regime. There were also five types of "red" youth: the offspring of (i) workers, (ii) peasants, (iii) revolutionary cadres, (iv) revolutionary soldiers, and (v) revolutionary martyrs. Youth included under neither of the two designations above consisted of the children of government functionaries, well-to-do middle peasants, and the middle peasant strata in general.

Nevertheless, these categories were not rigid, but a general guide. In Chinese Communist terms the key to designation of social background has lain in personal performance. Here two main concepts come into focus: (i) social origin *(ch'eng-fen)* and (ii) social status *(ch'u-shen)*. While the former refers to the social category of the family into which a child is born, the latter becomes the status that derives from family influence. But the Party's educational philosophy, in implicitly accepting social as far exceeding family influence, suggests that all youth who have been nurtured in the requisite environment are equally eligible to enter higher education. *Ch'u-shen* declines in importance as socialist society is reached. The instruments that ensure this equality are thought reform and the conscious will of the individual to achieve it: "Youth with a good *ch'u-shen* do not have any special quality which sets them apart from those with a bad *ch'u-shen*." Social influence and personal achievement override family background and ascribed position.

The same Red Guard source described this quality of performance as *piao-hsien* or manifestations. *Ch'u-shen*, as drawn from *ch'eng-fen*, is a result of home environment; firstly, *piao-hsien* is created by and in turn creates social influence, and secondly, provides home influence for future generations. *Ch'u-shen* and *piao-hsien* are therefore of a different nature. The influences a person has received can only be assessed from *piao-hsien*, the criterion which determines whether a youth is revolutionary or not. *Ch'u-shen* is but a general guide to political character; the key lies in thought reform. These principles were inherent in the Party's educational philosophy which reflected the moral perfectibility of man, as expounded in Confucian writing. In theory, at least, moral commitment would always outweigh social origin.[4]

In any case, between 1950 and 1956, higher middle graduates, predominantly from urban schools and the main target of university enrolment, were in short supply and had to be supplemented. For example, between 1952 and 1956, the country's higher education enrolled 530,000 students, while the same years only produced 410,000 higher middle graduates. From 1952 onwards the Central Committee of the CCP ordered local Party committees to direct departments of the State apparatus to mobilize, in a planned fashion, serving cadres,[5] retired soldiers, primary schoolteachers, vocational middle school graduates, and intellectual youth to register for enrolment examinations. For these categories a quota system was in operation. The Central Government decided upon the total number to be registered throughout the country and then allotted a quota to each of the Large Administrative Areas. The area government in turn allocated a certain figure, on the basis of which Party and government organs at the level of *hsien* or above would select candidates for registration. Those selected then presented relevant documents and certificates to enrolment committees.[6]

In 1956 a joint decision of the Party Central Committee and the State Council directed that serving cadres in Party and government organs should be allowed on their own initiative to register for examination. In this way it was claimed that 480,000 intellectual youth had been mobilized for examination registration and as a result the enrolment plans had been fulfilled and student quality raised.[7] In July 1956 a press report underlined the problem of candidate sources by giving a detailed breakdown of statistics for each category of eligible applicant:

> Higher middle graduates registered for examination this year number 144,000; this is 40,000 more than last year. Serving cadres from State organs, factories, mines, and enterprises are leaping forward to register, and their total has increased from last year's 21,000 to the present 79,000. Primary schoolteachers registered for examination in teacher training institutions number 65,800. Candidates also include serving workers in public and private joint-stock enterprises [institutions used to incorporate free enterprise into the state sector] who number 3,500; intellectual youth from the industrial and commercial world number 770.[8]

Finally, the categories of eligible applicant, by placing the restriction of "outstanding academic calibre" on graduates from vocational middle schools, indicated the need to maintain a precarious balance between specialized manpower already trained to various levels and the demand to produce experts to a still higher level of competence. Because of pressing production work needs, not all middle level technical personnel could be spared for further training. Moreover, despite the equivalent level rubric, the whole tenor of the enrolment regulations in encompassing potential candidates with vastly different educational standards was to implicitly deny the maintenance of any uniform quality among institutions of higher education. Because of the varying standards between institutions at the middle and the higher levels, the principle of vertical ranking within the education system was also modified in practice.

Nevertheless, although the regulations laid down very broad and flexible categories of potential candidate, the eligibility of those registering from outside the education system was limited because they did not necessarily have equal opportunity to study in the academic field of their choice. Certain categories, for example, were restricted in the subjects for which they could register. One rationale for the recruitment of serving personnel had been the shortage of specialized manpower and the paucity of candidate sources, but evidence would also suggest that the Party leadership saw entry to higher education as only one means of improving the technical expertise of young cadres and intellectual youth. In 1956 articles in the press called for the further development of spare-time *(yeh-yü)* study programmes for serving personnel.[9]

For example, the spare-time schools in industrial enterprises which had the task of raising production workers' cultural and technical levels performed two functions: retraining personnel without removing them from production and providing candidates for higher education. Spare-time education in industrial enterprises represented a limited channel of mobility for workers of exceptional calibre.

Another case in point was that of teachers in middle schools and teacher training institutions at the same level who were urged to make themselves more professionally competent without leaving their employment to enter higher education. Local education bureaux were directed to organize retraining programmes so that teachers' demands for further study might be satisfied.[10] There were nevertheless instances of brief courses being given to enable teachers to qualify for similar posts in institutions at a higher level.

In general, however, it was clear that, if operated satisfactorily, the system of spare-time study could obviate the necessity of the temporary withdrawal of needed manpower to higher education. Thus it was a question of how many elements from outside the education system could be spared for full-time study, and it became imperative that they usually study in academic fields closely associated with their former employment or experience. The destination of such candidates will be examined through three subject areas: teacher training, health and medicine, and fine arts.

Those people from outside the education system who could register for higher teacher training institutions can be divided into two main types: graduates of equivalent institutions at the middle level and primary schoolteachers.[11] According to the "Decision Concerning the Reform of the Educational System," passed on 11 August 1951, graduates of teacher training institutions at the middle level were to serve in primary schools for a specific period of time before they became eligible for promotion to higher education. Clearly, many primary schoolteachers, dissatisfied with low salary and poor working conditions, saw considerable material advantage accruing from university study. Thus, in spite of the fact that the enrolment regulations conferred eligibility to register on such categories, in practice they were limited by service requirements. These were made more specific in a 1957 article calling for the ideological education of middle level teacher training graduates, who from that time onwards would only be able to register for higher education after three years service. However, small numbers of this group could be promoted to higher education immediately after graduation, providing that their total did not exceed 5 per cent of that year's graduates.[12] It seems likely that there were many exceptions to this rule, which reflected the need to adjust supply and demand in staffing the education system.

Similar arguments prevailed in the examination registration of primary schoolteachers and reflected frequent changes of emphasis. In 1956 primary schoolteachers still remained eligible to be examined for higher teacher training institutions, but with the qualification that the best of them already selected to be teachers in middle and teacher training schools could not register for higher education.[13] In fact, an educational newspaper indicated in 1957 that serious staffing problems were occurring in primary education as a direct result of higher education admission policies: ''We must especially note that great numbers of primary schoolteachers have been examined for and entered higher education and this has done considerable damage to primary education. In these circumstances we hope that teacher comrades will be able to work peacefully and to tackle primary education well.''[14] In summary, teaching personnel accepted for further study were directed to academic disciplines associated with their former employment or experience. On graduation, they would return to teaching, perhaps at a higher level. The norms governing their promotion varied with staffing needs in the teaching profession and to that extent modified the enrolment regulations.[15]

The mobilization of serving personnel for enrolment registration was well illustrated by the planned transfer of specialist cadres serving in the health field. Units of this system under the Health Ministry itself as well as those belonging to other sectors like industry, agriculture, and communications and transport were to arrange for middle level specialist cadres with a limited amount of medical knowledge to register for examination. It was made clear that such cadres were to apply for entry to medical institutes and were only able to do so if their departure did not prejudice current work needs in their units.[16] Similarly, the enrolment targets for the four institutes of Chinese medicine, established in 1956, included the best graduates from medical middle schools. These were to be admitted after passing the examination subjects laid down for medical institutes, and after graduation were to be distributed to associated teaching, research, and health units. These medical middle graduates were classified under the vocational health rubric.[17] Again, the eligibility of these candidates to enter the institution of their choice was limited, even though those from the various kinds of vocational schools would, in professional terms, have been ranked above higher middle graduates.

The need to retrain specialized personnel at a higher level and for flexibility in the implementation of the enrolment regulations was shown in the recruitment of students for fine arts institutes. In 1957 a Shanghai source, while stressing the eligibility of various elements outside the education system for examination registration in fine arts, nevertheless emphasized key enrolment targets. These included professional performers and those who had shown excellence in fine arts activities outside their work or during specialized fine arts meetings. Additionally, the academic requirement was lowered in some cases to a cultural level equivalent to lower middle graduation, ostensibly to include those workers and peasants serving in industrial and agricultural enterprises whose outstanding talent seemed to offer a future in fine arts.[18] This stipulation suggests that there was a good deal of local variation. Since 1957 fine arts institutes throughout the country, because of their exceptional nature, were adopting the method of individual not unified enrolment, which meant that each institute had considerable initiative in the implementation of enrolment regulations. Finally, in addition to the retraining of personnel and those who had shown excellence in fine arts activities, the current year's graduates of fine arts middle schools also formed one of the major enrolment targets.[19] In short, fine arts personnel and middle graduates were generally recruited for academic fields closely associated with their former employment or experience. In comparison, then, with the general run of higher middle graduates, fine arts middle graduates were less than equal in terms of opportunity to study in fields of their choice, and in spite of the egalitarian tone of the enrolment regulations, eligibility was severely circumscribed.

Most of these candidates in the three subject areas of teacher training, health and medicine, and fine arts came from outside the education system, and this was one of the means used to facilitate the entry of workers and peasants. But at the same time these policies were related to the demand for trained manpower in various fields. They were, however, also essentially designed to pave the way for the creation of proletarian intellectuals, as conceived of by Mao Tse-tung in his earlier writings. But, in the long term, these enrolment policies were to perpetuate rather than eradicate the inequalities within the education system in such a way that the concept of proletarian intellectual became synonymous with vocational function. This idea came to be expressed in terms of advancing national construction: the Liuist interpretation was becoming predominant.

In addition to the conditions laid down in the enrolment regulations and the provisions for entry to specific kinds of institution, other more wide-ranging methods were employed to increase the worker and peasant contingent in higher education and create proletarian intellectuals. The first method to be examined is that of preferential acceptance *(yu-hsien ling-ch'ü)*. In *The Guidance on Enrolment in Institutions of Higher Education, Summer 1955*, issued in the name of the Education Ministries, certain categories of candidate were to be preferentially accepted when their performance in the examinations reached the acceptance standard of the specialty for which they had registered, or when it was equivalent to the majority of applicants. The following were all subject to the preferential acceptance rubric: (i) production workers from factories, mines, and farms, (ii) children of workers and peasants, and cadres of worker and peasant origin, (iii) retired soldiers and seconded soldiers, (iv) students from the minority peoples, and (v) Overseas Chinese students.[20]

As suggested above, those outside the education system were mainly admitted to disciplines with which they already had some connection through employment experience. However, the categories for preferential acceptance are broader than those mentioned above in connection with specific disciplines. This rubric applied to the humanities, the sciences, engineering, medicine, and agriculture, but one source referred to preferential acceptance in relation also to music, fine arts, and theatrical institutes.[21]

The preparation of each of these preferential acceptance candidate categories is dealt with in detail later, but it is significant that this rubric of admission underwent certain changes in 1956 and 1957. In contrast to the 1955 rubric, the first category in the 1956 regulations adds "this year's graduates of worker-peasant rapid middle schools." Moreover, while the 1955 Regulations spoke of "children of workers and peasants," the 1956 provisions refer to the sons and daughters of revolutionary martyrs, clearly a smaller group. This seems a limitation, although the qualification must be added that worker-peasant rapid middle school graduates would have included worker-peasant children other than those of martyrs. Significantly, the 1956 rubric mentions serving personnel who had taken part in revolutionary work for fully three years.[22] Thus the trend in 1956 seemed to be toward greater selectivity of workers and peasants. That this was an attempt to maintain and raise academic standards is demonstrated by an article in an educational journal in 1956:

> If their [preferential acceptance categories] examination success does not fulfil the lowest acceptance level, we cannot lower the standard to accept them, for this would give us no way of guaranteeing the quality of new students, and would in turn adversely affect the standard of trained cadres . . . such a policy would also not be in the interest of these preferential acceptance categories, for they would not be able to keep up with course work, they might have to remain in a grade, drop out, or generally damage their own health.[23]

While this was undoubtedly a warning for the future, it clearly represented regret at the low standards of the past and was an attempt to tighten entry requirements even in the face of the essential aim of increasing the number of workers and peasants in higher education. The 1957 provisions for preferential acceptance mention both the three-year limitation for serving personnel and the specific reference to children of martyrs.[24] Moreover, the inequalities inherent in the preferential acceptance system were again shown by the fact that these elements were being admitted to certain academic fields related to practical branches of national construction. Detailed examples given indicate that these entrants were being concentrated in particular vocational areas.

In summary, although preferential acceptance had as its justification the recruitment of workers and peasants in order to make them intellectuals, they seem to have been concentrated in various production-related technical subject areas, and to that extent their eligibility was limited. Furthermore, by 1957 there was a trend towards greater social and academic selectivity in the preferential acceptance system.

In 1958 a Chinese youth periodical assessed the operation of the preferential enrolment system in the wider context of conditions for entry to higher education. Overall it was claimed that the selection of the best candidates from all enrolment categories on the basis of the three conditions of politics, scholarship, and health had not taken place but rather candidates had been placed according to their success in the academic enrolment examinations. This gave priority to expertise *(yeh-wu)*, not politics *(cheng-chih)*. Therefore, those candidates whose academic success was high but who were politically inadequate had many opportunities of entry, yet those whose political conditions were good but who lacked scholarly achievement had much less chance of acceptance. Significantly, the latter were said to be predominantly of worker and peasant origin, although no further details were given.

According to the preferential acceptance rubric, the principle had been established that when workers and peasants were equivalent in standard to other candidates, they would be given priority of entry. It was clear, however, that the rubric had not solved the problem, since this source claimed that workers and peasants were comparatively lacking in academic knowledge, and in general they did not perform as well as other candidates in the enrolment examinations. It was thus difficult to accept them for entry.[25] These facts could not but be a reflection on the special academic preparation which such worker and peasant candidates were being given.

The second method employed to facilitate the entry of worker and peasant candidates was the worker-peasant rapid middle school *(kung-nung su-ch'eng chung-hsüeh)*. These institutions were explicitly designed to create proletarian intellectuals: to satisfy the need for technical experts and cadres loyal to socialism. In practice, they were preparatory schools for higher education, since they were attached to certain university institutions.[26] Courses in rapid middle schools were three or four years in length, and those eligible for entry were stated to include worker and peasant cadres and industrial workers who had taken part in revolutionary struggles or production work for a number of years and whose standard of education was deemed equivalent to that of a primary school graduate. Significantly, this stipulation suggested that students in rapid middle schools would be given training comparable to those in any ordinary middle school; on that basis they would need to acquire the knowledge of a six-year regular education system in three or four years. In 1957 a source discussing their composition indicated that from their inception in 1950 until 1955 when they ceased enrolling, these schools numbered 87 and 63,000 students had entered them during that period. The origin of their students was said to be as follows: worker and peasant cadres represented 44.7 per cent, workers 23.7 per cent, and soldiers together with others 21.6 per cent. The remainder was not specified. At the same time, however, it was stated that by 1957 graduates of worker-peasant rapid middle schools numbered 21,000. This figure would tend to suggest that many students failed to reach the standard required and consequently could not enter higher education; this is supported by a reference to model workers who were said to have "just studied" in worker-peasant rapid middle schools.[27]

The fact that many students in the rapid schools were not promoted is also borne out by figures provided in the 1959 issue of *Jen-min shou-ts'e*. These may be tabulated as follows:[28]

TABLE 1: WORKER-PEASANT RAPID MIDDLE SCHOOLS

Year	1950	1951	1952	1953	1954	1955	1956	1957
Number of Schools	24	41	51	58	87	65	56	58
Number of Students	5,000	13,000	19,000	28,000	51,000	36,000	32,000	22,000

Two major conclusions may be drawn from the above figures: (i) even if the number of schools and their total enrolment reached a peak of 87 and 51,000 in the year 1954-55, they were still in operation as late as 1957, and (ii) enrolled students greatly exceeded graduates. The rate of graduation suggests that considerable selectivity was employed in promoting such students to the universities to which they were attached. Moreover, although in general graduates of these schools took part in enrolment examinations, there was also a system of direct entry whereby the very best graduates could be admitted without examination.[29] It seems unlikely that many of the worker-peasant rapid middle students would have been able to reach the requisite standard for entry in so short a time, and there was in that case a very real need for selectivity. On these terms, the rapid schools became a channel of mobility for the exceptionally able among workers and worker-peasant cadres. Certainly the cause of creating proletarian intellectuals was being furthered, but since promotion of rapid students to universities was to some extent at least based on academic criteria, this concept was nevertheless being expressed in terms of vocational function. The worker-peasant rapid middle schools contained within them the seeds of academic and social inequality.

But even though the schools were serving as a limited channel of mobility for the very able, that is not to suggest that the general academic standards of the schools were high. Cultural Revolution sources claim that on a visit to Ch'inghua University in 1955, Liu Shao-ch'i disagreed with the principle of opening school doors for workers, peasants, and soldiers, and, by implication, the concept of proletarian intellectual. Liu appears to have said that the rapid middle schools should discontinue recruitment of students, since a three-year programme was not realistic for the academic ground to be covered. But in calling for their closure, it could be argued that Liu Shao-ch'i was not necessarily attempting to exclude workers and peasants from higher education; he was rather suggesting that it was unrealistic to take short cuts in study merely to admit them to higher education at all costs. That it was necessary to add an extra fifty points for workers and peasants who took enrolment examinations indicated that in the main rapid school graduates were lower in standard than the majority of candidates.[30] To Liu Shao-ch'i, this lowering of standards was not justified.

In summary, the worker-peasant rapid middle schools theoretically reflected one of the key assumptions of the CCP's educational philosophy: that workers and peasants could become intellectuals through the requisite training. A privileged stratum of mental workers would not be allowed to come into being; the monopoly of bourgeois specialists inherited from the old regime would be broken as the best worker and peasant cadres would be turned into technical experts. Moreover, since these came from outside the education system, a link would be forged between education and society. To that degree the worker-peasant rapid middle schools corresponded to Mao Tse-tung's interpretation of the Party's educational philosophy. But, in practice, the emphasis on the exceptional ability of the rapid school graduates for promotion to higher education suggested the interpretation of Liu Shao-ch'i, where proletarian politics came to be subsumed under vocational function. It was indeed likely that worker and peasant cadres might forget their class origins when further training had raised their professional status. The same could be said of production workers. These new cadre experts might become more and more isolated from the rural and urban proletariat whom they led, leaving the way open for the emergence of a privileged stratum, which would subordinate politics to expertise. Ironically, the cessation of enrolment in worker-peasant rapid middle schools, like its operation, represented the Liuist interpretation, for on their closure they were to be turned into ordinary middle schools, thus becoming an integral part of the established education system.

But the functioning of the rapid schools and their significance in the later struggle between the two educational lines can best be illustrated by reference to the attitudes of academics in individual institutions to their establishment and operation. On 24 March 1952 the Hong Kong newspaper *Ta-kung jih-pao* stressed that the rapid schools had opened their doors to workers and peasants and by so doing had turned higher education into people's education. The newspaper then continued by making what later were proved to be exaggerated claims for the establishment of worker-peasant schools: "The majority of the institutions of higher education have set up worker and peasant rapid middle schools to serve as preparatory classes for entry to higher learning." This statement soon proved to be very wide of the mark. But as late as 1 March 1954 the *Kuang-ming jih-pao* echoed earlier optimism by asserting: "For the last three years each of the country's institutions of higher education has thoroughly addressed itself to the aim of opening its doors to workers and peasants." Later in the year, on 27

September, the same paper announced the admission of both worker-peasant cadres and production workers to rapid middle schools established at Peking University.

However, in spite of such optimism, the task of establishing such schools was meeting with less than enthusiasm on the part of individual institutions. During the early months of 1953 complaints were voiced in the press that in some institutions the significance of schools of this type had not been realized and that in others they had not been adequately conducted. In some cases it would appear that the schools had not been properly established:

> The organs of leadership in very many institutions of higher education have still not been able to give the necessary attention to the subject of worker-peasant rapid middle schools. . . . In some institutions such work has been seen as a nuisance, and leading organs have been unwilling to set up worker and peasant rapid middle schools.[31]

The Education Minister Ma Hsü-lun emphasized:

> We must gradually put into effect the decisions concerning the establishment of worker and peasant rapid schools, which have not been conducted well. There are naturally a number of reasons for this, but the fact that institutions have not given sufficient attention to the matter is the main one. We trust that all will now take notice.[32]

Nor did the results achieved by the 87 operative worker-peasant rapid middle schools give cause for inspiration. Their success would obviously be judged by the ability of their students to adapt to the rigours of higher education. As it happened, many workers and peasants who had graduated from these schools found it difficult to adjust to the study routine demanded by the universities. Graduates of the rapid middle schools not only lacked the self-discipline required for sustained study, but also their knowledge of such basic subjects as mathematics, physics, and chemistry was abysmally low. Even allowing for their originally low cultural level, students of the rapid schools were not provided with an academic basis sufficient to equip them for higher education.

Various measures were recommended to remedy this situation. The study load of worker and peasant students in universities was to be lightened so that they might concentrate on the main curricula, and their participation in the activities of the Party and the Youth League (an elitist body from which Party members were recruited), such as meetings to study Marxism-Leninism and government policy documents, was to be curtailed during their first year.

Yet while the Ministry of Higher Education criticized the leadership in universities for neglecting rapid schools, these authorities were not entirely to blame for the schools' inadequacies. A co-operative attitude among individual faculty members would be crucial if the purpose of rapid schools and the entry of their graduates to universities were to be fulfilled. In the event, teachers were accused of being unsympathetic to the special needs of worker and peasant students, and in some cases appear to have been openly hostile. For example, on 1 March 1954 the *Kuang-ming jih-pao* noted that some teachers lacked sympathy with worker and peasant students, and in certain cases seemed to have had neither understanding of, nor respect for, the studies of workers and peasants. A considerable proportion of these faculty members would have been bourgeois academics inherited from the Kuomintang period, who had not been remoulded sufficiently to understand the moral imperative of creating worker and peasant intellectuals. From the professional angle, they no doubt regarded the special effort needed to educate workers and peasants as academically unsound and probably believed that other priorities should be given precedence. Moreover, the social and political background of many such faculty members predisposed them to adopt the Liuist interpretation of the Party's educational philosophy.

Nevertheless, the worker-peasant rapid middle school programme was not entirely without success. In the autumn of 1954 the Communist Party organ *Jenmin jih-pao* praised the example of the worker and peasant rapid middle school attached to Ch'inghua University: "This summer's graduates were thirty in number and not only did all of them succeed in gaining entrance to a university through the enrolment examination system, but one of them came first among those from the North China Area taking the examination for Ch'inghua University." The paper went on to proclaim the high calibre of worker and peasant students in the University. For example, of the twenty-eight worker-peasant students in one specialty, 80 per cent had reached the exceptional grades of excellent or good in the previous year.[33]

It is difficult to account for the outstanding success of a few worker-peasant rapid middle schools and the abject failure of others. Certainly, however, Ch'inghua, like Peking University, was an institution of some prestige, and it may well have attracted, or in some way been able to recruit, the best from among the workers and peasants.

If the charges of Cultural Revolution vintage that bourgeois academics in the universities collaborated with Liu Shao-ch'i and his supporters in the Education Ministries cannot always be substantiated, evidence would nevertheless indicate that university teachers often favoured the Liuist interpretation of the function of the rapid schools and worker-peasant entry to higher education. The evidence quoted concerning the attitudes of faculty members to worker-peasant students also suggests that teachers were concerned primarily with academic performance. While they were prepared to encourage the promising among the proletarian contingent, they saw no reason to waste time on hopeless cases, into which category the majority of workers and peasants seemed to fall. Both in the Party and academic circles in general there seems to have been a fair degree of unanimity as to the desirability of fostering talent among workers and peasants, but faced with numbers of workers and peasants of indifferent academic quality, faculty members increasingly came to justify training the best of them in terms of national construction needs. University teachers were prepared to train them as technical experts only if they were exceptionally able, not by mere virtue of their social origin.

The Maoist and Liuist interpretations of the Party's educational philosophy shared emphasis on personal performance: the difference between them in this context centred on the function of the rapid schools. Firstly, while the Liuist saw their importance in the utilization of scarce academic ability, the Maoist considered them an important vehicle for creating intellectuals from the ranks of workers and peasants. Secondly, the August 1951 "Decision Concerning the Reform of the Educational System" also referred to the need for institutions of higher education to run preparatory and supplementary classes for worker and peasant cadres, students from the national minorities, and the children of Overseas Chinese. These were different from the rapid schools in that they were established as the need arose within institutions of higher education rather than attached as separate schools. The necessity for them appears to underline the academic deficiencies of workers and peasants and others outside the education system admitted to institutions of higher education through various special methods. To some extent at least the existence of these preparatory or supplementary classes showed that measures to admit students from outside the education system had resulted in the entry of candidates who were not equal to the academic standards demanded in higher education.[34]

Thirdly, the policy of increasing the number of workers and peasants in higher education and creating proletarian intellectuals was reflected in the introduction of the intermediate class (ch'a pan) system in 1956. These classes were not separately constituted but an integral part of higher education. Announcing that institutions were to enrol intermediate students, the Ministry of Higher Education stated their objective as raising the quantity and quality of cadres trained in the education system. Nevertheless, although it was announced that initially enrolment of intermediate students would be confined to engineering and agricultural institutes together with humanities and natural science specialties in comprehensive universities, initiative was given to individual institutions to decide whether to conduct classes, based on their own conditions.[35]

Like those of the rapid middle schools, the enrolment targets laid down for the intermediate classes came from outside the education system. These were outlined as follows: (i) past graduates of special training classes *(chuan-hsiu k'e)*; (ii) those who had earlier acquired a specialized skill in institutions of higher education (for both these categories the age stipulation was below thirty-five[36]); (iii) Overseas Chinese students who had learned a specialized skill in institutions of higher education outside China; (iv) students from Hong Kong and Macao; (v) those who had acquired a specialized skill in spare-time and correspondence universities *(han-shou ta-hsüeh)*;[37] and (vi) intellectual youth who had left school but were as yet unemployed, and other youth. The first, second, and fifth target groups were composed of serving personnel who were required to have the approval of their original work unit in registering for enrolment examination. The third, fourth, and sixth categories would have been required to submit verification documents from relevant authorities.[38]

The *ch'a pan* mirrored two concerns: to increase the number of worker and peasant students and to create proletarian intellectuals. To the extent that these regulations assumed that those from outside the education system could be turned into intellectuals, intermediate classes echoed the link between education and society. But their purpose was also to train and retrain manpower at various levels of competence. Needless to say, political criteria would not have been left out of account, but the emphasis in the intermediate regulations left no doubt about the functionally specific criteria used to express the purpose of the classes. Candidates would have been through a selection process, based on professional competence, before registration for examination. The first and second categories would have been especially selected to raise their level of professional competence and in some cases intellectual depth; the fifth would have included those who had shown themselves of high academic calibre suitable for further training. All these were exceptional cases.

The comprehensive universities had the twofold aim of producing research personnel in the natural and social sciences on the one hand, and training teaching staff for middle and higher education on the other. The fact that intermediate class entrants were to be admitted to comprehensive universities indicated that the former's purpose was not merely retraining, but also represented an attempt to recruit the outstanding elements outside the education system as high level academic personnel. The intermediate students in comprehensive universities would have taken courses in the natural sciences and the humanities; those in institutes and polytechnical universities, subjects in the applied sciences. Thus while those intermediate class students in technical and polytechnical institutes would be retrained to a higher level of expertise, those in comprehensive universities would have been chosen as suitable to acquire intellectual depth.

The recruitment of the third and fourth groups, Overseas Chinese students and those from Hong Kong and Macao, was intended as a measure to tap all available talent. These Overseas Chinese students, often sympathetic, even if not totally committed, to the Communist regime, have been returning to China to further their academic or professional studies.

But it was in the case of intellectual youth, the final category, that the order of priorities for the intermediate classes was shown most clearly. References to intellectual youth in other sources indicate that at least a proportion of that category consisted of those who had been subject to reactionary thought but were in the process of re-education. Such youth, whatever their bourgeois origin, were also being seen as potential talent to be utilized wherever possible. The *Kuang-ming jih-pao* explained in March 1956 that because socialist construction was proceeding apace and the country's international position was being established, very many youth were turning away from their reactionary past towards a desire to study and progress in service to the people.[39] These sentiments, if applied to the intellectual youth category, tend to express political commitment through the acquisition of technical skills useful to national construction, the implication being that proletarian politics is synonymous with vocational function. Therefore, in spite of the fact that the intermediate classes were fulfilling their function of increasing the number of worker and peasant entrants, the primarily academic criteria used for the acceptance of the enrolment targets were anathema to Maoist thinking. The intermediate classes represented an attempt to accommodate specialized personnel who had already been trained to certain levels of competence in various fields. For these reasons intermediate class candidates did not participate in unified enrolment examination as did the majority of university applicants but were examined by individual institutions. Therefore, dates within which application and examination were to take place were laid down centrally, with specific times designated by individual institutions, providing these did not prejudice the timetable for the reopening of the academic year.

Similarly, the Ministry of Higher Education formulated general guidelines of examination subjects for intermediate candidates, on the basis of which concrete outlines were compiled by individual institutions according to relevant specialty standards. The Ministry's regulations stipulated that examination subjects would include politics, national language, and foreign languages, together with relevant specialist skill subjects. Compulsory examination subjects were not to exceed seven.[40] Specific information concerning academic entrance examinations for intermediate candidates is unfortunately sparse, but institutions would certainly have demanded standards considerably above those of unified enrolment applicants.

Every attempt was made to place intermediate entrants at academic levels to which they were suited through previous training. The term *ch'a pan* means to classify a pupil from another school according to his grade (in this case academic level) and entrants were enrolled normally at the middle year stages of specialty courses, not at the first and graduation year levels.[41] Intermediate classes were designed to effect a balance between the demand for manpower already trained and the need to raise its technical level.

In conclusion, the three methods of preferential acceptance, rapid middle schools, and intermediate classes were derived from the CCP's educational philosophy and sought to create proletarian intellectuals through facilitating the entry of worker and peasant students. But both preferential acceptance and rapid middle schools, to the extent that they concentrated on certain categories of candidates, denied the assumption that proletarian intellectual status was achieved by performance rather than ascribed by social origin. The criteria used to assess these categories of candidate also became increasingly elitist on purely academic grounds when the regulations were translated into practice. Finally, the intermediate classes shared both this partial rejection of that achievement articulated in the proletarian intellectual concept and the increasingly selective enrolment conditions based on academic criteria, but in one respect carried the process of selectivity a stage further. As suggested above, in the case of intellectual youth, proletarian politics was equated with vocational function in the implementation of the intermediate class regulations. In their implementation these three methods came to be interpreted as means of satisfying functionally specific manpower needs. The latent conflict between the so-called two educational lines gradually came into the open through differing interpretations of the function which the institutional methods should perform. It was not until 1958, however, that the conflict was clearly in evidence.

The development of special methods to effect their entry to higher education did not, of course, preclude the admission of those of worker and peasant origin to ordinary middle schools in preparation for promotion to universities. But while the rapid schools had as their target specific elements from outside the education system, the ordinary middle schools would admit the children of workers and peasants in general. The "red" and "non-red" categories of youth have already been briefly outlined and served as the frame of reference for judging social origin, but it must also be emphasized that the special entry devices, particularly that of preferential acceptance, had as their targets both those with and those without leadership positions or Party membership. Attacks levelled during the Cultural Revolution against Liu's supporters in the Party accused them of excluding not only youth from the five non-red categories but the children of ordinary workers and peasants from higher education. The accusation that very few students from the non-red groups were admitted to universities has already been refuted, and the second of these charges cannot be sustained in the light of statistical evidence relating to social origin of students in institutions of higher education.

The proportion of worker and peasant children in institutions of higher education would to some extent necessarily depend on how many of them were receiving middle level education. For this reason, the CCP sought to increase the number of worker and peasant children in middle schools through institutional adjustment and financial aid, which, if successful, would in the long term obviate the necessity of such special devices as preferential acceptance at the higher education level. Special measures were necessary because of a shortage of middle schools, particularly in the rural areas. In 1957 an educational periodical listed four special concessions being given to worker and peasant children in middle schools: (i) preferential enrolment, (ii) financial aid, (iii) encouraging factories, mines and villages to run middle schools, and (iv) attaching lower-middle classes to primary schools.

As only the second and fourth of these categories were given in-depth coverage by Chinese Communist sources, attention in this study will be focused on financial aid and institutional adjustment. The presence of worker and peasant children would, in any case, have been closely related to the cost of education and the accessibility of schools.

A survey of two institutions in each of the three provinces of Hopei, Shantung, and Shansi showed the practical application of financial aid to students. An examination of the distribution of this aid indicated minute divisions in the system of monetary awards granted to particular students rather than exclusive concentration on dire need. On this basis most students would have received some financial aid, but there was little variation between the highest and lowest amounts distributed. In one school there were as many as eleven different levels of grants given to students. Schools were given a certain initiative in the distribution of grants, as it was claimed in the report that some institutions lowered the rates set down in the guidelines from the local education bureaux. Heads of classes (teachers) appear to have been responsible for deciding the amount to be awarded in individual cases, and as they could not always accurately ascertain the nature of the financial difficulties in the students' homes, distribution tended to be based on general impression. The majority of the students came from villages and these especially were in need. In general, however, grants appear to have been generous enough to cover most expenses. Here a distinction must be made between financial aid *(chu-hsüeh chin)* and scholarships *(chiang-hsüeh chin)*. Arguments for change to a scholarship system were resisted on the grounds that this would inevitably favour academically able students who in general were not to be found among those worker and peasant children with financial difficulties, but among those with means. Students of bourgeois origin would have been increasingly favoured under a scholarship system.

But in spite of the provision of financial aid, payment of tuition fees and the general cost of keeping a child at middle school would have placed a heavy burden on poor rural families and those of factory workers. Children from poorer homes, particularly in the countryside, could not be spared from productive labour. Moreover, peasant children were disadvantaged by the concentration of middle education in major centres of population; this level generally required boarding, and attempts were made to solve this problem by attaching lower middle classes to primary schools and establishing new middle schools in the villages. Similar efforts were directed at running middle schools financed by factories and mines to cater for children who would otherwise, because of financial need, have been deprived of middle education.[42] Such structural changes, if widely adopted, would have been more effective than any financial aid scheme.

When taken together with the competitive nature of the regular school system, financial aid would only have conferred a limited advantage on small numbers of worker and peasant children. Competition for entry to both lower and higher middle schools as well as higher education was intense and based essentially on academic criteria; worker and peasant children were undoubtedly at a disadvantage because of home environment. In January 1955 the educational periodical *Jen-min chiao-yü* stated that in some localities those lower middle applicants failing to qualify in the entrance examinations for higher middle school had reached 76 per cent of the total number of candidates. At the same time higher middle graduates were in short supply, and the failure rate for candidates at the university level was much lower, although academic authorities were expressing reservations about the quality of entrants to higher education.

That there was much discussion within the Party concerning the reform of middle education on these grounds is shown by proposals debated in 1957. It was claimed that the middle schools were academically specialized and the study load was too heavy. Two alternative reforms were suggested for solving these problems. The first entailed the simplification of teaching materials in middle schools so that basic knowledge would be taught, leaving specialized study to higher education. Higher education would provide preparatory classes to make good any deficiencies. The second alternative would be to leave the university system unchanged, while increasing the number of years spent in middle schools. Under this system lower middle school would have been extended to four years, while higher middle education would have required instruction for two years on the basis of divided classes *(fen-k'e)*. Divided classes would have narrowed the students' focus to fewer subjects, thus strengthening them in those fields. They would then have been better able through earlier specialization to meet the needs of the universities.[43]

These reforms were not implemented, but they underline the issues involved in the Party's thinking on the role of middle schools. The proposal to establish preparatory schools for higher education under the first reform alternative was foreshadowed by the institutional adjustment operated through the lower middle classes attached to primary schools. While both these types of class reflected the CCP's educational philosophy that children of workers and peasants could benefit from special instruction through devices additional to the regular education system, the regular middle school establishment and the second reform alternative tended to favour the Liuist interpretation. However, because of the stress on intellectual criteria in middle schools as the sine qua non of entry to higher levels of the education system, academic performance remained a crucial factor in the promotion of worker and peasant children; the four special concessions provided only a very limited channel of mobility for the exceptionally able.

In conclusion, these measures were said to have raised the percentage of children of worker and peasant origin in middle schools. The following statistics were given for the period from 1951 to 1956:

1951	51.27%
1952	56.06%
1953	57.12%
1954	60.73%
1955	62.32%
1956	66.02%

Such percentages are virtually identical with those given in *Ten Great Years,* which also provides equivalent data of 69.1 per cent and 75.2 per cent for the years 1957 and 1958 respectively.

These figures were averages for the whole country, but it was claimed that the percentages were even higher in provinces where the entry of worker and peasant children had received particular attention through, for instance, the lower middle classes, especially run by primary schools. For example, in the province of Hopei in 1956, 92.56 per cent of new entrants in lower middle education and 89.8 per cent in middle education as a whole were said to be children of workers and peasants.[44] The reservation must be made, however, that Hopei Province was unlikely to have been typical of the country as a whole, as it included the Peking Metropolitan area. It is not easy to verify scattered statistics of this kind, but they do indicate the Party's concern with the need to train proletarian intellectuals from the ranks of workers and peasants.

The preparation candidates received for the enrolment examinations reflected the concept of proletarian intellectual and depended on whether they came from inside or outside the education system. In order to increase the worker and peasant contingent in higher education, thereby furthering the goal of creating proletarian intellectuals, cadres were made eligible for examination registration. For this, two systems were in operation: (i) the planned transfer through a quota system of, for example, specialist cadres and workers in factory or mining enterprises, and (ii) the voluntary registration of other cadres if they could be spared from their work.[45] Furthermore, any discussion of examination preparation brings into focus those other categories of candidate outside the education system given eligibility by the enrolment regulations.[46] These were also to apply voluntarily for registration. As most of these categories were concerned with industrial production and candidates would, as a general rule, return to it after completion of their studies, the two systems of planned transfer and voluntary registration had to take into account the necessary balance between trained manpower and the need for expertise at a higher level.

Against this background of candidate eligibility, industrial and commercial enterprises were directed not only to transfer and encourage candidates to register for examination, but also to provide the conditions within which they could best carry out revision to that end. In these tasks, enterprise management was to be assisted by the trade unions. In May 1956 the *Kung-jen jih-pao* urged trade union organizations to arrange times and places for candidates to study, to encourage the latter to remedy their academic deficiencies, and to appoint teachers to instruct them in revision. Moreover, trade union organizations were in a position to know the personal situation of candidates, especially financial burdens and family problems. The role of the trade unions was thus political and practical: on the one hand, they exhorted the leadership of enterprises to fulfil their responsibilities regarding candidates' revision, and on the other, they were able to furnish the conditions under which the applicants could best study. Playing the part of mediator, the trade unions acted as a transmission belt between leadership and workers and were intended to overcome such ideological evils as conservatism, vested interests, and short-sighted viewpoints, which tended to inhibit certain units from permitting cadres and workers to register for examination.[47]

Indeed, the co-operation of enterprise leadership was essential if candidates were to qualify for admission to higher education. Although applicants in enterprises were of a cultural level equivalent to higher middle graduation, reports published in 1956 indicate that extensive revision was necessary if applicants were to reach the required standard in specific examination subjects. In March 1956 the *Jen-min jih-pao* called upon all relevant units to ensure that serving cadres and production workers in public-private joint enterprises had an adequate revision period. A three-month period was considered essential for candidates to gain knowledge in fields with which they were not familiar and to relearn subjects which they had studied in the past but forgotten.[48] That such cadres had lost the habit of regular study and were thus considerably lower in standard than higher middle school graduates was shown by the difficulties they encountered in revision. Therefore, in addition to basing their revision on the examination outlines published by the Education Ministries, cadre applicants were given special summaries of such courses as history and chemistry by the teachers of the special revision classes. These teachers included those temporarily seconded from local middle schools and universities, together with leadership personnel in particular enterprises. There were, however, instances of cadres who could not follow the teachers' lectures and found difficulty in taking notes.[49] Much praise was given to the new techniques developed by the revision teachers, who provided succinct summaries of national language, history, and political general knowledge curricula, discarding peripheral materials. Exaggerated claims were made that these methods enabled the teachers to shorten the lecturing period, thereby allowing the candidates more time for private study. However, there is little doubt that these measures amounted to little more than "cramming" and did not provide much understanding of the subjects as a whole.

Needless to say, attendance at revision classes required a flexible work routine for cadres. It seems unlikely that the three-month revision stipulation was adhered to, in view of pressing production work needs, even though those registering would have been only a very small percentage of the total work force in a particular enterprise. Reports on the progress of cadres' revision suggest that they were not granted full leave, but rather were given a regular timetable of revision classes, initially within the enterprise concerned. But there appear to have been major differences in approach to revision, owing to the disparity of the type of organizations to which cadres belonged. For example, while industrial and commercial enterprises appear to have permitted cadres to have regular periods for revision, certain Central Government organs appear to have been far more generous. For instance, one source stated that those cadres in the Education and other Ministries who were registering for examination were given either half or all of their work-time to attend the revision classes set up in the organs concerned.[50] Similar rules apparently existed for administrative cadres in schools and universities where work routines were presumably more flexible. At the University of Wuhan cadres approved for examination registration were formed into small groups to carry out revision. Educational institutions in Hupei province reduced the duties of teachers registered for examination, and rearranged their teaching periods, thus enabling them to revise.[51]

Revision, however, was not only confined to enterprises and units in which cadres worked. While they initially undertook study there, those from outside the education system were later organized to attend special revision schools and classes established by local authorities. In July 1956 it was reported that cadres, retired soldiers, seconded soldiers, and unemployed intellectual youth had taken part in revision schools and classes set up in local areas. These schools and classes can, however, be divided into two kinds, depending on their enrolment targets: (i) intellectual youth who had left school but were as yet unemployed, and (ii) other categories from outside the education system.[52]

The guidelines for the first type were set out in a joint communiqué of the Central Committee of the Youth League and the Education Ministry, published in February 1956. These directives will be discussed under three main headings: (i) organization and leadership, (ii) aims and entry conditions, and (iii) study contents, methods, and timetable.

Firstly, revision schools were to be established in large and medium-sized cities for unemployed intellectual youth over twenty-five. But in cases where there were less than twenty-five people in this category in small and *hsien* cities, revision classes or small groups were to be organized. Unlike the revision schools, these would not be separate entities but would be attached to the regular higher middle schools. Administrative control of the revision schools and classes was vested in the city education bureau which addressed itself to such questions as teaching staff, the direction of teaching, study facilities, and convening work conferences. An office, manned by cadres sent from both the education bureau and the city Party organization, was set up to co-ordinate daily activities, while the education bureau was itself responsible for academic organization. Party and Youth League organizations were to ensure that the objectives of the revision school were being realized. For example, the Party and League both played a major part in the mobilization, ideological education, and cultural activities of students.

The aim of revision schools was to prepare intellectual youth, usually of a cultural level equivalent to that of the second year of a higher middle school, for enrolment examinations, and intellectual youth who held evidence of those qualifications were eligible for entry. Enrolment was voluntary.

Study content was both academic and ideological. Academic study concentrated on the higher middle third year curricula, as reflected in the enrolment examination, but teaching methods were very flexible, involving lectures together with private study and discussion groups. In addition to instruction by regular school teachers, usually seconded from middle schools and universities, outside personnel were often brought in to deliver explanatory reports on the purpose of schools. There was a great deal of variation in teaching methods, according to local conditions: for example, whereas the general regulations for the revision schools stated that the study period would begin after the spring holidays and last for six months, with four hours of teaching six days a week, an added provision allowed each locality to vary this routine.

Finally, tuition fees were charged, although they appear to have been only nominal, as it was stated that those without means could delay or be exempt from payment. Any insufficiencies in the revision school's funds were to be rectified by local governments on request from the education bureaux.[53]

By March 1956 the *Kuang-ming jih-pao* was reporting favourably on the implementation of these directives throughout the country. In the vanguard was the Peking City Education Bureau which had dispatched a part of the best middle school teachers in the area to conduct revision classes for intellectual youth. Among the 1,093 intellectual youth attending these schools and classes in Peking were 588 higher middle graduates and 505 with an equivalent level of scholarship.[54] Meanwhile, Shanghai revision schools were said to have begun registration, and it was estimated that about 5,000 candidates would be entering them. The Peking and Shanghai institutions can be seen as models for education bureaux elsewhere, as preparation for the establishment of similar schools followed in the provinces of Shensi, Kiangsi, Szechwan, Hunan, Kwangtung, and Hopei.

The second category of revision schools was designed to draw in cadres, workers serving in public-private joint stock enterprises, retired and seconded soldiers, and young intellectuals in the industrial and commercial world. Another joint communiqué issued by the two Education Ministries and the Central Committee of the Youth League on 10 March 1956 called for the establishment of cadre revision schools on the basis of those already being set up for intellectual youth.[55] Once again, these schools were run on an area basis by local education bureaux, and teachers from middle schools and universities were similarly dispatched to conduct them. Regular institutions were specifically asked to co-operate in this task. Initially there seems to have been a certain reluctance on the part of education bureaux to carry out this work, since Party committees were urged to ensure their compliance.[56] The same ideological errors characteristic of some leadership in enterprises were appearing in education bureaux: vested interests and bureaucratic attitudes which neglected candidates' revision. Nevertheless, it was reported in June 1956 that cadres in industrial enterprises and Central Government Ministries in Peking had participated in classes for serving personnel after having initially carried out revision in their respective organs. These revision classes were divided into two categories based on subjects preferred by candidates: (i) the natural sciences, engineering, agriculture and forestry, and medicine, and (ii) the humanities, law, finance and economics, physical education, and fine arts. Candidates would be examined accordingly.[57]

Yet there is no doubt that in spite of the elaborate measures laid down for conducting the revision of the two categories of candidate considered above, neither enterprise units nor education organs were unanimous in their support. In fact, this failure to co-operate, especially on the part of enterprises, appears to have been a continuing theme. In March 1956 the *Jen-min jih-pao* claimed that the reason for emphasizing revision schools was to remedy the high failure rate of serving cadres: in 1955 three-quarters of these had been unsuccessful in the entrance examinations.[58] In general, the leadership of production units was accused of obstructing cadre enrolment in higher education in two ways: (i) by refusing to approve their registration for examination, and (ii) by not allowing them leave to revise. Diverse reasons were given for not allowing cadres to register. Some leadership personnel claimed that the desire of serving cadres to register for examination indicated "individualist" tendencies and dissatisfaction with their work. But, in general, the excuses given were related to work needs in a particular enterprise, and for these, loopholes were to be found in the regulations governing cadres' registration. A State Council directive on this issue explicitly stated: "All serving cadres who satisfy the conditions for examination registration may register." However, this is flanked by specific conditions which modify the original right: "providing that there is no loss of production, that his work is good, he serves the leadership and his political thought is advanced.''[59] These conditions appear to have been used to the full by leadership personnel when they found it necessary.

Three examples will be used to demonstrate the tactics employed by leadership personnel to deny cadres permission to register. The first case involved a cadre in the retail department of the Post Office who was eligible to register freely for examination. A leading cadre, after having consulted the deputy-head of the relevant area Post Office Bureau who was also the Party branch secretary, was refused permission on the following grounds: ''Cadres in this office offering themselves for examination do so only on the basis of the transfer principle, not on the basis of voluntary registration. We desperately need manpower, and therefore you had better not register.'' Later higher authorities in the Post Office stated: ''If you have to go for examination, then you will have to revise courses in your own time.''[60]

In the second case a worker in an enterprise in the city of Anyang accused leadership personnel of shelving a communication from the Anyang City Education Bureau encouraging serving cadres to offer themselves for examination and guaranteeing them revision time. When this worker inquired at the bureau, he was told that personnel there had no authority to approve registration, presumably without the permission of the enterprise leadership. Then, a few days later, three leading people at the enterprise gave three reasons for not allowing him to register: (i) there was no certainty of his being accepted by an institution of higher education, (ii) since in the past he had suffered from a lung ailment, he was not physically fit, and (iii) as work needs were pressing he could not be spared.

In the third case a twenty-six-year-old cadre in the Second Ministry of Machine Building was refused permission to register. He was a higher middle graduate who had continued to study in his spare time. Again, the needs of the work force were given as the reason for refusal.[61]

It is to be noted that in all three cases candidates were eligible according to the enrolment regulations for examination registration. But in each case leadership personnel were able to use the rubric of work needs, apparently quite legitimately, to refuse approval for registration. To this extent the eligibility of cadres was limited in practice, if not in theory. But even if such elements were permitted to register, they had only cleared one hurdle. Many leadership personnel did not honour the provision whereby cadres already approved for registration were to be given leave of absence to revise. This situation was said to be true of the Peking Broadcasting Correspondence School. In other cases enterprise leadership awarded half-day revision time, but in reality did not reduce the work load of the candidates accordingly.[62] The reservation must be added, however, that the provisions which allowed cadres to revise for the examinations were also amenable to abuse by candidates. In June 1956 the *Kuang-ming jih-pao* complained that serving cadres had unduly emphasized the importance of revision and neglected the work of their units. The paper added that while each industrial enterprise or government office should guarantee necessary time for revision, this "half leave of absence" would be given subject to conditions in particular units.[63]

In spite of earlier optimism, an indication of the limited success with which the revision schools and classes had been attended in 1956 was the decision to abolish officially directed revision in 1957. The first reason given was that the enrolment task and the sources of candidates had both undergone change; but this seemed to be outweighed in importance by a second which stated that in the past the operation of revision schools had been considerably impeded by staffing, facilities, and revenue difficulties. Serving personnel and intellectual youth candidates were exhorted to carry out revision themselves, according to their own circumstances and on the basis of the enrolment examination outlines, published by the Education Ministries. For example, one group of serving personnel, primary schoolteachers, was urged to carry out revision but only on condition that this did not adversely affect their duties, suggesting that the latter may well have been the case in 1956.[64]

In summary, while some cadres may have abused their privileges, the majority of serving personnel appear to have been denied the opportunities for revision to which they were entitled. To this extent the opportunities given in the enrolment regulations were restricted in practice.

The entry of serving personnel to higher education was related to questions of manpower. To that extent their eligibility in practice came to reflect the Liuist interpretation of vocational function: a fine calculation of manpower needs in enterprise units and the demand that cadres be trained to a higher level of professional competence.

Revision schools were also established for the remaining categories outside the education system: Overseas Chinese and students from Hong Kong and Macao. These applicants were not statistically significant, but facilities for their revision are noted here to show how the CCP's concept of proletarian intellectual was demonstrated in practice through eligibility for university enrolment.[65] From the beginning of their regime the CCP leaders sought to win the favour of Overseas Chinese and students from Hong Kong and Macao for practical as well as political reasons. The latter's approval would enhance the legitimacy of Chinese Communist rule, while the recruitment of foreign-educated Overseas Chinese youth of high scholastic calibre would help to provide needed specialized manpower.

Because of their background, Overseas Chinese candidates were generally of a high academic standard, and official sources implied that their defects were ideological rather than intellectual. Newspaper reports suggested considerable failure rates for this category in 1955 and 1956: special revision schools in Peking, Amoy, and Canton were established in 1956 and 1957 for those Overseas Chinese students who had failed the enrolment examinations.[66] The rejection of Overseas Chinese is surprising because they were subject to the rubric of preferential acceptance which should have facilitated their entry.

The ideological emphasis of the schools is indicated by an article in the *Jen-min chiao-yü* which mentioned the deliberate policy of distributing successful Overseas Chinese candidates among as many institutions of higher education as possible, in order to better eradicate previous foreign influences.[67] The nature of this revision is further borne out by the fact that many Overseas Chinese graduates of comprehensive universities and technical institutes were allocated to teaching and scientific research posts in higher education and academic organs.[68] The few examples given and the lack of detailed statistics make a definite conclusion difficult, yet the facts that Overseas Chinese were recruited with a view to manpower needs and that some of them were apparently good enough to undertake research tend to belie a purely academic function of revision schools. In addition, such candidates would have needed help in adjusting to an unfamiliar education system. Revision schools with similar emphasis were run in Canton in 1956 for the benefit of Hong Kong and Macao students who had failed in their first attempt to enter higher education. Experienced instructors and students from teacher training institutes were dispatched to supervise their revision.[69]

Therefore, although one reason for accepting Overseas Chinese and Hong Kong and Macao students as candidates for higher education was the desperate need for qualified manpower, arrangements made for their entry reflected the fundamental tenet of the CCP's educational philosophy that proletarian intellectual status was based on ideological as well as on academic performance.

Like Overseas Chinese and Hong Kong and Macao students, candidates from the national minorities, both within and outside the education system, also formed only a very small percentage of applicants. They were culturally distinct, and special facilities would have been provided for them.[70] But, with the exceptions noted, the preparation of the candidates outside the education system mainly centred upon academic criteria, the area in which they were most deficient.

The major source of candidates from within the education system was the regular middle school; academically their graduates had been amply prepared for promotion, but ideologically they were considered deficient. During the first two years of the regime very few middle school students would have come from worker and peasant families, even if their proportion was increasing by the middle and late 1950's. In any case, although all such graduates, whatever their social origin, would have received education since the Communist accession, they had nevertheless been subject to other pre-Liberation influences. Bourgeois individualist ideas might still be strong.

Ideological education was therefore supremely important in persuading youth to choose their study preferences in accordance with the needs of the State. Directives issued early each year, for example, stressed priority subjects like engineering and teacher training. This was the first step in the ideological preparation of higher middle graduate candidates. For example, in March 1957 a joint communiqué issued by the Ministry of Higher Education, the Ministry of Education, and the Youth League addressed itself to this question. Candidates' selection of preferences was therefore not merely a matter of academic knowledge, but of socialist awareness.[71] Positive direction was needed to achieve this. In the first instance, enrolment handbooks outlining the scope of examination subjects were published each year by the Education Ministries, and detailed materials on individual institutions' specialties were made available. These were academically informational, and candidates were urged to consult them. At the same time the middle school Youth League organizations played the crucial leadership role of exhorting applicants to subordinate individual to collective interests.

Consequently, not only were middle schoolteachers, students, and parents involved in preparation for enrolment, but other elements in society as well. But the organizational framework within which this work was to be carried out was formed by enrolment organs, local education bureaux, other government departments, and the middle schools themselves.

Candidates were permitted to choose a specific number of specialties and institutions. This determined the subjects in which they would be examined, since examinations were divided into categories according to the academic disciplines selected. This rubric regarding the selection by candidates of specialties and institutions varied over the years, but it is noteworthy that revisions made to this system in 1957 gave a wider choice to candidates.[72]

Specialties and institutions, however, did not in all cases offer the attractive rewards and career prospects which candidates personally sought. This is evident from press comment on candidates' selection of preferences. For instance, in 1956 the *Kuang-ming jih-pao* bemoaned the fact that in past years candidates had only considered their own wishes for material gain regardless of their aptitudes. As a result, the paper claimed, such subjects as mining and meteorology, which offered inhospitable conditions of employment, and physical education and teacher training, where future salaries were low, attracted comparatively few applicants.[73] These tendencies seem to have gone unchecked in 1956, in spite of ideological preparation, because in 1957 other sources spoke of the need to propagate information concerning subjects students had not greatly favoured. By 1957 cadres were increasingly being trained in certain institutions of higher education for local needs and the importance of urging students to register for examination in fields such as teacher training and agriculture and forestry was strongly stressed. In this sense, enrolment would become much more the method of manpower distribution in response to national needs than it had been in the previous period.[74]

But, however much candidates might be encouraged to apply for subjects critically in need, personal aptitudes could never entirely be ignored. In fact, alternating emphases between candidates' wishes and the public interest were also characteristic of ideological education. In 1957 one source, while hailing the interests of national construction, at the same time emphasized the need for balanced propaganda; exaggerating the importance of certain subjects and disregarding candidates' own preferences were equally to be deprecated. Education, not coercion, was to be the order of the day: personal aptitudes and national needs were not mutually exclusive but must interact. Those university authorities who had lauded their own specialties to attract students while denying the significance of other fields came under attack. Published introductions to specialties must reflect difficulties as well as advantages for only then could candidates be expected to choose wisely.[75] Thus, when an accurate picture was given of a specialty in question, a candidate would be in a better position to make an appropriate choice. General guidelines were consequently laid down in periodicals for the benefit of prospective candidates. It was stated, for example, that those who had scored well in natural science would be well advised to opt for scientific and engineering specialties; likewise, those whose success lay in the humanities should select appropriate specialties. More specific articles, however, referred to mental and physical limitations; colour blindness, for example, was seen as a distinct disadvantage in aeronautics specialties. For reasons not adequately explained, women were reckoned to have aptitude in the humanities, education, and health fields, although praise of Soviet women engineers in the media encouraged girls to apply for, and be accepted by, related specialties. In general, however, the above assumptions are not very dissimilar from Western attitudes. Selection of a specialty connected with their scholastic attainment hitherto and suited to their health would not only increase the possibility of candidates' being accepted, but would also mean that they would study better after entry.[76]

These concessions to aptitude were, of course, intimately related to the CCP's theory of knowledge. Aptitude is not synonymous with ability, for it implies skill in a particular area of activity. But if aptitude was created, for example, through previous training, it followed that it could also be subjected to change. The point at which aptitude was proven was also debatable. In fact, in supporting the contention that a person's preference, based on aptitude, is a result of training, an article in a youth periodical, clearly reflecting Party views, justified a shift away from emphasis on aptitude by claiming that youths' knowledge of, for instance, production technology, was extraordinarily limited. This being the case, it could not be said that candidates' interest had been produced by work experience. In any event, it was not so decisive that it could not be changed. Therefore, if candidates were allocated by planned distribution or persuaded to select a different preference, they would only need to concentrate on building up interest in this new subject to obtain good study results.[77] Moreover, there were said to be cases of people who had changed their study preference after entry to university with great success. Although this latter argument was by no means watertight enough to justify preference policies, it emphasized that interest and aptitude were not innate *(t'ien-sheng)* but were created by practice; it was also clearly designed to encourage those not successful in gaining admission to their preferred specialty to acquire new interest by determined application.[78] The interest *(ai-hao)* of youth was said in any case to be many-faceted, and it would not be difficult for them to adjust to new disciplines. At the same time it was being argued that interest must not exceed the conditions of social reality, but must follow the country's construction needs and change with them.

This policy was also applied to the allocation of graduates. If a university graduate had been allocated to unsuitable employment, he could ask to be reallocated to a position where his aptitude and training could be more fully utilized. If he were reallocated to a post close to the subject he had studied, and yet was not very enthusiastic about it, ideally he would be able to develop his interest and individuality through concentrated study. Although this argument referred to graduates, it was similarly based on the principle that interest is developed through experience.[79] In fact, individuality could only come to full flower through concentrated effort in contribution to national construction.[80]

When discussions of aptitude and interest led to questions of individual development, the two interpretations of the Party's educational philosophy were shown in sharp relief, the Liuist one being reflected in the implementation of policy. Questions of individual aptitude always hinged on the exact point at which interest could be said to have developed. In one of the periodic shifts towards the importance of individual aptitude, a youth periodical stated that if a candidate lacked necessary understanding of a specialty when selecting it, he might not study well if accepted for entry.[81] Any concession to aptitude would always bring into focus the individual as the main frame of reference. In his writings Liu Shao-ch'i had made the individual the centre of attention to a degree not credited in Mao Tse-tung's expression of the proletarian intellectual concept. Individual aptitude and national construction were never mutually exclusive. Nor did the CCP's educational philosophy or the Liuist interpretation ever entirely reject one at the expense of the other. It was a matter of emphasis. But in making greater concessions to individual aptitude, the Liuist interpretation paid more attention to the demands of functional specificity than to the full meaning of the concept of proletarian intellectual. In this context the Liuist thesis was expressed especially cogently in an article on the relationship between individual development and social needs, published in the *Jen-min chiao-yü* in January 1957:

At the present time the nation especially needs to develop industry, and there are very many engineering subjects in enrolment. The remuneration of technical cadres in industry is comparatively high, and so the majority of candidates all want to study engineering. Such decisions on the part of candidates can be considered discernment, and form the basis on which individual development and social needs may unite.

Allusion to the full meaning of the proletarian intellectual concept, the creation of the man who was intellectual as well as worker or peasant, is absent. Moreover, the Maoist interpretation would not have lavished praise on candidates' motivation to study engineering through the expectation of high financial reward.

Here the individual in a functionally specific capacity had become the frame of reference. This remained the case even when contradictions existed between social needs and government allocation on the one hand and the development of individuality on the other:

At present there are only 249 specialties in our country's higher education, but the work sectors in industry, agriculture, culture, and education are very numerous, and however many and however good the personnel produced by higher education, they still cannot completely satisfy work needs. It is possible that the situation in future may change; that it may develop so that some people may not be allocated to work connected with their study. Individuality may undergo further refinement through being sent to different work. Individuality can be developed through struggle at unfamiliar work as through work in one's own field.[82]

Certainly, this passage suggested that personal preferences must be subordinated to the national interest, but it justified such adaptability through Liuist practical necessity, not the Maoist moral imperative. Thus while this argument provided justification for the distribution of candidates to fields of study other than those they had chosen, it nevertheless took individual interest as its starting point. If the relationship between the individual candidate and functional specificity implied in the article quoted above began to promote service to national construction in terms of personal preferences, the operation of the enrolment system itself confirmed the same tendency, and Red Guard sources strongly indicate that those responsible for policy implementation inclined to the Liuist view. The way was clear for candidates to judge the potential rewards of different fields of study and to place institutions in order of supposed merit. This may have resulted from a poor indoctrination process, but it undoubtedly also reflected Party ambivalence as to personal and public interest. In July 1956 a press source examined the relationship between candidates' preferences and the enrolment plan:

All the candidates' preferences taken together do not tally with the nation's enrolment plan ratios: while the registration numbers for some institutions and specialties are large, in the case of others they are very few. For example, in the Nanning examination area there are 3,967 candidates but only 9 have registered for examination in forestry. In this way there is a definite contradiction between candidates' preferences and the State's enrolment plan.

While it was claimed that the majority of candidates were prepared, if necessary, to follow planned distribution, some applicants lacked complete understanding of the nation's construction work and only considered engineering subjects as important. If they could not be accepted for the latter, they preferred not to be admitted at all.[83] Further evidence for this is shown by the fact that some students failed to fill up the required number of preferences, thereby reducing their chances of acceptance.[84] Similarly, some candidates only considered famous institutions like the universities of Peking and Ch'inghua and would rather be examined for them the next year than be accepted for lesser schools.[85]

The selection of preferences was followed by the enrolment preparation given to candidates from the higher middle schools. This involved ideological as well as academic training for the examination, and reflected the traditional relationship between education and society. For example, agencies of socialization such as candidates' families and the Youth League were urged to correct heterodox attitudes among candidates regarding enrolment. The latter organization would also have acted as a check upon incorrect views among middle schoolteachers. Some candidates, for instance, were said to be over-confident, believing that because the enrolment plan numbers were heavy and the sources of candidates few, there was no problem about their being accepted.[86] This kind of complacency could only be eradicated by the determined co-operation of the organizations involved in enrolment preparation. Similarly, teachers' attitudes towards preparation came under fire and were normally related to consideration of a particular middle school's interest at the expense of the national one. Thus some teachers were accused of not seeing the whole picture; they felt that they were failing in their duty if the majority of their students were not admitted to higher education. Low status employment, for example in industry or agriculture, seemed a very inadequate reward for higher middle graduates. In this way some teachers were charged with failure to see the purpose of enrolment within the overall context of national needs.[87] At the other extreme, some middle schoolteachers were apparently neglecting to help the students' revision by waiting for candidates to seek their aid rather than positively directing the latter's study.[88]

Also critical in candidates' preparation was family influence; it is not surprising that here traditional attitudes regarding the prominent position of the intellectual with his monopoly of knowledge persisted, even among workers and peasants. Thus some families saw their children's promotion to higher education as an investment. There were cases of higher middle students who had failed to be promoted being afraid to go home lest they lose face.[89] It was to eliminate tendencies like these that the Youth Leagues encouraged those accepted for higher education to further their academic study and mollified the feelings of those rejected by persuading them to make an equivalent worthwhile contribution in another area of national life.[90]

The Youth Leagues would also have played a part in forums on the aims of higher education, run for new students on their entry to universities and institutes. In the ideological aspect of enrolment preparation, the Youth Leagues were supported by the work of mass organizations and the media. Trade unions, for example, discussed employment opportunities in relation to the State's needs; provincial newspapers and radio stations publicized eligibility regulations and information concerning specialties in local institutions. Ideological preparation for enrolment showed the influence of the traditional relationship between education and society. But accepted candidates would be more advantaged than rejected applicants in terms of future job opportunities and this underlined the differences between the functions each group was to perform in society. Ideological preparation was justified in terms of the CCP's educational philosophy, but its implementation only differentiated the specific roles which candidates were later to play. Ideological education was sufficient neither to bridge the gap between those accepted and those rejected, nor to ensure that all academic disciplines in higher education were seen as equal in their contributions to national needs.

Ideology also permeated academic revision methods and contents. In directing the students' revision, middle schools gave general lectures and then concentrated on specific topics. For example, any subject which had not been adequately covered earlier now received priority. During revision teachers also clarified any points which the students had not understood,[91] and before the beginning of the preparation period, middle schoolteachers responsible for students who were in their graduating year participated in forums to discuss revision methods. It was here that concrete plans were made.

One problem raised by certain teachers, however, was whether they should conduct revision on the basis of the middle school teaching outline or that of the university entrance examination published annually by the Education Ministries. This was especially pertinent, as proposed reforms of the middle system mentioned earlier had indicated a very real hiatus between middle and higher education, and in 1957 an article in the *Jen-min chiao-yü* took a critical view of the current link between the two. For example, the physics and chemistry examinations had the advantage of focusing middle curricula on student understanding of natural science laws, but at the same time the scope of the examination topics was too wide-ranging and difficult for higher middle graduates. The problem that this presented led teachers to take the enrolment examination outlines as their guide for revision. The teachers then brought together the questions raised by students and wrote direction outlines. These were afterwards corrected or added to by teachers in small groups, and the final drafts of these outlines would form the basis on which students would revise.[92]

But this approach did not produce entirely propitious results. There were cases cited where students' revision involved concentration on subjects outside the middle school courses and teachers' lecturing exceeded the subject matter of the course textbooks. In short, the examinations required more comprehensive study. This led to the rote memorization of probable examination answers which in turn hindered the all-round development of students' understanding of basic subjects. Rote learning, it was claimed, impaired students' ability to think in depth.[93] It would appear, then, that the revision direction outlines were only partially successful in overcoming tendencies inherent in the very scope of the enrolment examinations.

The significance of these outlines was not confined to the practical aspects of revision, however, because they also underlined the value of collective study. In the formulation of revision materials, a teacher's individual competence was not considered a substitute for collective effort, and the adoption of this method by teachers was designed to better prepare students ideologically and academically, thereby dispelling the tense atmosphere during revision.

Collective study was not restricted to teachers. Under the leadership of the Youth Leagues, student mutual aid through discussion in small groups was applied to the selection of preferences and afterwards to the revision of curricula. Private study was at the basis of mutual aid, but the advantage of the latter was that it provided discipline in group situations and joint research. The effectiveness of revision was said to be raised as a result.[94] This co-operative effort by teachers and students reflected traditional assumptions concerning the nature of man and knowledge: its function was not only practical but moral.

But against the moral assumptions implicit in these revision methods stood individualist tendencies. Collective understanding might be seen merely as a means of ensuring individual academic excellence rather than as a social value in itself. The individual would then again become the frame of reference. High academic performance was at a premium in the competitive enrolment examinations.

Collective study, however, failed to solve the overall problem of the considerable discrepancy in standards between middle school curricula and higher education enrolment examinations. Some middle schools were more successful than others in overcoming this problem, but significantly, complaints were voiced by university students concerning preparation for enrolment examinations. Alumni of the First Middle School in Loyang sent letters to the head of the school, their former teachers, and fellow students urging that the scope of the physics and chemistry teaching be increased. If this were not done, they claimed, the students would not be able to gain entry to good universities, and if they did succeed in gaining admittance, they would not be able to keep abreast of the courses.[95]

Certainly, excessive rote memorization of special subjects in the outlines for both the humanities and natural science examinations was having an adverse effect on standards within institutions of higher education. This was indicated in a report written by the Head of the Peking Steel Institute. It appeared that the fundamental principles of the natural sciences were being neglected in the race for entry to higher education; Chinese language studies had apparently been similarly affected. Teaching in middle schools had manifestly failed to train students to write succinctly and clearly and to read with rapid comprehension of fundamental arguments. It had encouraged rote learning without understanding. Students at the Institute found difficulty in taking notes and grasping the central points in study. The report argued that the teaching of language in middle schools enabled students to study the scholarship of the past and eventually make their own contribution to knowledge.[96]

The academically competitive nature of the higher education enrolment examinations led also to the emergence of elite middle schools which became noticeably more successful than others in promoting their candidates. One was the August the First School in Peking, so-named to commemorate the founding of the People's Liberation Army in 1927, and one of several middle schools established in the early years of the regime for orphans of revolutionary martyrs and children of high-ranking cadres, especially those serving abroad. Despite a directive issued by the State Council in 1955 ordering that such schools cease enrolment, they appear to have continued in operation because of influential parents and through the connivance of provincial and municipal education authorities as well as supporters of Liu Shao-ch'i in the Education Ministries. Like the principles governing preferential acceptance and worker-peasant rapid middle schools, the decision to operate the cadre children's schools represented at least a partial contradiction of the CCP's educational philosophy. All were capable of being educated, yet the pupils of these schools were, by definition, set aside from others. Certainly, orphans of revolutionary martyrs and children of cadres abroad were to be educated in these schools because of special circumstances, but the elitist implications of such institutions were nevertheless far-reaching.[97]

In fact, these schools illustrate how organizational structure can subvert educational philosophy. The fact that they only admitted entrants from high ranking cadre families meant that their students were exceptional, socially if not academically. Because of the leverage which parents and connections of the students could exert on the school authorities, special measures came to be taken to ensure their promotion to prestigious universities. Highly qualified teachers were dispatched from outside by the municipal education bureau to instruct students in small groups. These schools also exhibited tendencies found in the ordinary middle schools, but in an extreme form; academic study focused on the main courses related to enrolment examination topics, and in the case of the weaker students, the more secondary subjects not contained in the direction outlines were neglected for one whole term. Moreover, in the case of the cadre children's schools, such expedients as ignoring secondary subjects were supported by teachers. Furthermore, in order that students might concentrate as much as possible on academic subjects for the enrolment examinations, the nationally stipulated two hours per week of manual labour they would normally have been required to undertake during term-time became perfunctory, and in some cases appear to have been abolished altogether. Finally, under pressure from powerful cadre parents, the school authorities allowed students to repeat an academic year's work so that they could take the examinations again and thus enter more prestigious institutions of higher education.

The August the First School was a classic example of the inequalities emerging in the preparation of different categories of candidate for the enrolment examinations.

4

The Administration of University Enrolment

Varying emphasis on the quantity and quality of specialized manpower during the period from 1949 to 1957 influenced admission procedures and reflected the Chinese leaders' conception of the demands of a developing economy.

The aims of enrolment were succinctly summarized by the *Kuang-ming jih-pao* in 1955. After four or five years' study the students would have been trained to become cadres loyal to socialism and with modern scientific knowledge. On graduation they would be sent to participate in the economic development programme outlined in the Second Five-Year Plan.[1] At the same time a similar source called for greater attention to be paid to quality: an implied criticism of earlier years.[2] Two years later this call was reiterated when the CCP leadership resolved that the number of students must be increased, but only if quality could be guaranteed.[3] Enrolment administration involved central planning and the numbers of students to be allotted to individual subjects were laid down by the Central Government. For example, in discussing the question of the allocation of successful candidates, a Kwangsi source stated that each institution's student numbers were determined according to the national enrolment plan *(ch'üan-kuo kao-teng hsüeh-hsiao chao-sheng chi-hua)*. National construction depended on definite numbers of qualified personnel.[4]

The development plan for higher education demanded unified arrangement from the centre, which would best be carried out through positive and creative co-operation of individual institutions. By 1957 it was being claimed that central control had been inflexible, often stifling local initiative.[5] The CCP's educational philosophy did not deny the need for functionally specific types of expertise, but in one sense the results of central planning and control of enrolment can be said to have opposed the traditional relationship between education and society. The concept of proletarian intellectual implied not a privileged stratum based on academic criteria, but the integration of mental and manual labour. In designating the categories of eligible applicant, the Party theoretically gave equal weight to elements both inside and outside the education system, even though the singling out of workers and peasants for special attention was a partial contradiction of the Party's educational philosophy. But the central planning of enrolment administration by the Education Ministries and other concerned departments of the Central Government caused the Party's role, pre-eminent in mobilizing eligible cadres to register, to be subordinated to the State apparatus in admission procedures. The Party's function was thus relegated to that of supervision rather than leadership of enrolment administration. By extension, the admission procedures, instead of fostering the moral imperative by which all were capable of being educated, concentrated increasingly on the importance of those within rather than those outside the education system.

Given the minute divisions inherent in the Soviet academic system, enrolment administration only intensified the exclusive nature and potential inequality characteristic of functional specificity. Moreover, the direction of successful candidates to particular academic fields in the name of the enrolment plan led the students to involve themselves in narrow academic concerns and neglect the broader political criteria contained in the proletarian intellectual concept.

In the enrolment plan certain types of expertise were said to be at a premium. In 1951 the order of priorities was stated as follows:

> Naturally we need industrial construction personnel first of all. Next come medical personnel. Teacher training to produce middle schoolteachers comes third. Fourthly, mathematics, physics, chemistry, finance, political science, law, agriculture, literature, and history personnel are all urgently required.[6]

Although the enrolment numbers for these priorities did not necessarily appear in the order above, figures issued for the years 1955, 1956, and 1957 assert the pre-eminent importance of engineering, teacher training, and medicine.

The statistics quoted below are figures projected for the enrolment plan and issued at a comparatively early stage of the admission process. They are not to be regarded as definitive but nevertheless reflect the major priorities in higher education. Thus, while in the main these early projections correlated with later figures for entrants, they are to be considered statements of intention rather than exact statistics.

In 1954, for example, approximately 90,000 students were to be admitted, among whom those in engineering would represent 37.42 per cent and those in medicine 10.17 per cent.[7] Leo Orleans, basing his analysis on *New China News Agency* sources, confirms that there were 33,800 entrants in engineering subjects and 9,300 in medical fields in 1954.[8] These two fields, with the addition of teacher training, were also the main priorities for 1955, 1956, and 1957. In June 1955 the *Kuang-ming jih-pao* stated that altogether 90,000 new entrants would be enrolled, and of these engineering would receive 35,000, teacher training, 21,000, and medicine (apparently including pharmacy and health), 9,000. Similarly, in 1956, out of a projected enrolment of 165,500, engineering would take 62,400, teacher training, 45,000 and medicine, 14,300. Finally, in 1957 out of a total of 107,000, engineering, teacher training, and medicine were to enrol 37,210, 36,000, and 8,500 respectively.[9]

A brief observation must be made concerning figures for medicine. In the 17 March 1956 issue of the *Jen-min jih-pao* the term "protect health" *(pao-chien)* is mentioned in the projected enrolment figures, while the 1955 reference uses the term "medicine and pharmacy" *(i-yao)* and that for 1957 the expression "medical courses" *(i-ke)*. Variation of Chinese Communist terminology does not necessarily imply changes of category, but it would seem from other evidence that since the overall enrolment figures for 1956 were about 80,000 higher than the previous year, the term *pao-chien* must include other health workers at a lower level of expertise.

In any case, the statistics found in Chinese sources encompass major categories of academic disciplines, even if the total figures for these subjects do not reach the overall figure given in the enrolment plan. The table below provides a graphic comparison of the consistent priorities for 1955, 1956, and 1957:[10]

TABLE 2: ENROLMENT PRIORITIES (1955-57)

Year	1955	1956	1957
Engineering	35,000	62,400	37,210
Teacher training	21,000	45,000	36,000
Medicine	9,000	14,300	8,500
Agriculture and Forestry	8,000	15,000	6,000
Natural Science	5,000	9,700	7,790
Humanities	5,000	7,500	4,970
Finance and Economics	3,000	4,500	2,300
Politics and Law	1,900	2,500	1,300
Physical Education	1,300	1,500	1,000
Fine Arts	600	900	730
TOTAL	90,000	170,000	107,000

However, although the targets set forth in the chart give specific numbers for various disciplines, other sources make it abundantly clear that these were always flexible. Projected numbers were based on directives laid down in the First Five-Year Plan, but the figure for 1956 exceeded that in the Plan by 40,000.[11] In addition, at the end of the First Five-Year Plan period in 1957, the total of 441,000 students enrolled in higher education was slightly above the target of 434,600.[12]

Table 3 shows the planned number of students to be enrolled in institutions of higher education during the period of the First Five-Year Plan. This is followed by the planned number of graduates in this five-year period, the total number of students in 1957, and relevant percentages.[13]

Candidate sources from within the education system were inadequate to meet enrolment needs,[14] and for this reason the importance of revision for candidates outside the education system became paramount. Where quality and quantity of applicants were forthcoming, the original projected numbers could be exceeded. It was explicitly stated, however, that quality should not be sacrificed. Shortage of applicants for specific fields was, of course, primarily related to selection of preferences, and perhaps, secondarily, to the lack of qualified candidates in general. While it appears to have been easy to attract candidates to register for examination in engineering and medicine, fields like teacher training and forestry were not especially favoured. In 1956 the authorities were prepared to allow 20,000 more to enter teacher training; this policy was supported by public relations which explained a vicious circle of supply and demand of teachers:

> At present, middle school graduates are not sufficient [for enrolment needs]. Why are middle school graduates not sufficient? . . . Why not run more middle schools? One main reason is that middle schoolteachers are insufficient. Therefore this year's teacher training enrolment numbers are even higher than those for engineering; this is because the country desperately needs teachers.[15]

Significantly, this statement implicitly calls for the solution to the problem of acute candidate shortage through the further development of middle school education rather than by extending the eligibility of outside applicants.

The importance of other fields where candidates were in short supply was propagated in information given about forestry. Graduates in that field were frequently allocated work with spartan conditions in distant areas of the country and this discouraged prospective applicants. Projected numbers for forestry in 1956 were said to be double that of 1955; the Greening of China Conference in 1956 had pointed to the necessity of training more personnel, publicizing forestry's vital role in land reclamation and raw material production.[16]

TABLE 3: PLANNED ENROLMENT NUMBERS (1953-57)

Course	Planned Enrolment 1953-57	Percentage of Students Enrolled	Number of Graduates 1953-57	Percentage of Graduates	Number of Students in 1957	Percentage of Students	Ratio of 1957 to 1952 (per cent)
Engineering	214,600	39.5	94,900	33.6	177,600	40.9	266.8
Agriculture & Forestry	41,800	7.7	18,800	6.6	37,200	8.6	240.7
Economics & Finance	16,400	3.0	25,500	9.0	12,700	2.9	57.9
Political Science & Law	10,600	2.0	4,800	1.7	9,300	2.1	242.3
Public Health	57,600	10.6	26,600	9.4	54,800	12.6	221.4
Physical Culture	6,000	1.1	2,800	1.0	3,600	0.8	1,107.7
Natural Sciences	32,600	6.0	13,800	4.9	27,100	6.2	283.4
Arts	29,300	5.4	21,600	7.6	20,400	4.7	150.9
Pedagogy	130,700	24.0	70,400	24.9	89,000	20.5	282.0
Fine Arts	3,700	0.7	3,800	1.3	2,900	0.7	79.3
TOTAL	543,300	100.0	283,000	100.0	434,600	100.0	227.4

The reform of higher education on Soviet lines was designed to train cadres for national construction. Nowhere is this better exemplified than in the case of engineering. According to the figures given in the First Five-Year Plan, the number of students in engineering institutes was to be distributed among thirteen specialized fields as shown in Table 4.[17]

It was further stated that as the number of engineering students given in the table was not expected to fully meet the country's needs, annual plans were to provide suitable adjustments in the proportion of students to be enrolled in the relevant specialized fields, in order to guarantee major national priorities. Projected figures for enrolment within small divisions of the major categories were therefore outlined in detail accordingly for relevant years. For example, in 1957 the engineering category was divided into figures for the specialties included within it. Although slightly different terminology was used for the annual plans, it is noteworthy that in that year machine-building (or machine and tool making), as in the overall First Five-Year Plan target, was to receive the highest number of students, 9,990. This was followed by electrical engineering with 3,360; geology, 3,100; dynamics, 2,700; mining, 2,460; chemical engineering, 1,860; metallurgy, 1,200; light industry 570; food products, 300; and paper-making and wood-processing, 120.[18] Similarly, in 1955 medicine had included 6,600 to be accepted for general practice, 700 for hygiene, and 700 for child health.[19]

But by 1957 it was being admitted that earlier annual enrolment plans, especially that of 1956, were over-ambitious and had also produced inflexibility in the allocation of candidates. The *Wen-hui pao* stated that while candidates would continue to be accepted for entry on the basis of politics, health, and scholarship, at the same time even greater attention would be given to candidates' preferences. The acting Minister of Higher Education, Ting Hua, emphasized that the task of that sector in training personnel under the First Five-Year Plan was already being over-accomplished. The target was 543,300 but in the previous four years 456,000 had been enrolled. Thus although the number of entrants for 1957 was smaller than that for 1956, it was nevertheless close to the figure prescribed by the Five-Year Plan. The 1956 plan was said to have been too high; its 1957 counterpart had therefore been formulated on the basis of need and what was possible.[20] The greater numbers in 1956 might well have reassured many candidates concerning their entry, but the inflexible nature of minute specialization and an excess of applicants for popular subjects suggest that a considerable proportion would have been sent to academic fields not of their choice, with resulting adverse effects on study.

This tight schedule of numbers for academic disciplines throughout the country necessarily meant that a quota of candidates to be admitted to institutions and departments would be allocated by the Central Government. An official handbook published in 1951 gave specific figures for academic units in the Chiaotung Technological University. One entry stated: "The numbers of new

Specialized Field	Planned Enrolment 1953-57	Percentage of Students Enrolled	Number of Graduates 1953-57	Percentage of Graduates	Number of Students in 1957	Percentage of Students	Ratio of 1957 to 1952 (per cent)
Geology & Prospecting	17,500	8.1	10,000	10.5	12,500	7.1	219.2
Mining & Mine Management	16,000	7.4	7,600	8.0	12,400	7.0	258.8
Power	15,500	7.2	7,500	7.9	13,300	7.5	232.8
Metallurgy	10,000	4.7	3,200	3.4	8,900	5.0	398.4
Machine & Tool Making	54,100	25.2	19,300	20.4	46,100	26.0	395.2
Manufacture of Electric Motors & Electrical Supplies	9,400	4.4	1,700	1.8	8,800	5.0	870.2
Chemical Technology	10,600	5.0	5,100	5.4	9,100	5.1	219.3
Paper Making & Lumbering	700	0.3	600	0.6	600	0.3	127.1
Light Industry	4,400	2.0	3,300	3.4	3,600	2.0	138.0
Surveying, Drafting, Meteorology & Hydrology	4,600	2.2	2,100	2.3	3,500	1.9	273.0
Building Construction & City Planning	37,400	17.4	25,100	26.4	28,200	15.9	163.5
Transport, Post & Telecommunications	9,600	4.5	4,700	5.0	8,500	4.8	200.5
Others	24,800	11.6	4,700	4.9	22,100	12.4	406.2
TOTAL	214,600	100.0	94,900	100.0	177,600	100.0	266.8

students to be enrolled this year in this institution are already being decided. The two departments of physics and mathematics will each enrol 40; chemistry will admit 60.''[21] The Chinese Peoples' University is a further example. In 1956 it was stated that its original departments of industrial economics, trade economics, planning statistics, finance and credit, law, journalism, and archives would altogether enrol 1,240, while newly established departments of philosophy, history, and economics would enrol a total of 1,000.[22] Theoretically, in the allocation of numbers of entrants to academic disciplines, individual institutions of higher education enjoyed virtually no freedom of initiative. Numbers were fixed by the Education Ministry (from 1952 to 1958 in co-operation with the newly formed Ministry of Higher Education) on the basis of overall decisions made by the State Council.

To ensure that enrolment work was implemented according to the national allocation plan, the CCP moved rapidly towards a unified system in the administration of university admissions. During the period from 1949 to 1957 the administration of admissions work passed through two distinct stages.[23] Initially, the Central Government only set down the spirit and guidelines within which the new system of enrolment work was to be implemented. Before any reform of enrolment administration was possible, rehabilitation of personnel and facilities was necessary. The universities had to enrol students, even though ideal procedures had not yet been put into effect.

The considerable variation in institutions of higher education throughout the country was mirrored in the cautious enrolment regulations for the summer of 1950. While these statutes established in great detail the categories of person who might be admitted, the content and timing of enrolment examinations, and the date for registration, great flexibility was shown in the actual implementation of enrolment.[24] For example, in 1950 and 1951, selection standards were relaxed as each institution undertook its own enrolment.

This is not to say that universities and institutes were completely free to exercise their own initiative, even in the sphere of enrolment administration. Within the framework established by the 1950 Enrolment Regulations, overall control of the administration process was in the hands of the Education Ministries of the Large Administrative Areas.[25]

In effect, control by the Area Ministries represented the first step in the direction of unified enrolment *(t'ung-i chao-sheng)*.[26] The 1950 Enrolment Regulations stated:

> The Education Ministry of each Large Administrative Area will be able to exercise its own control within this schedule and will conduct joint or unified enrolment . . . according to the concrete circumstances of that particular area. If unified enrolment presents difficulties, the Education Ministry

of each Large Administrative Area may allow . . . each institution to undertake its own enrolment. Nevertheless, each institution must connect its enrolment processes with the examination subjects officially laid down. Methods of enrolment must be reported . . . to the Education Ministry of the Central Government via the equivalent Ministry of the Large Administrative Area.[27]

But any independence that institutions enjoyed was limited to one aspect of enrolment, implementation. Certainly, they had a considerable voice in the selection of students and admission standards, but even in this early period such matters as enrolment numbers were dealt with by the Administrative Area Education Ministries, in accordance with decisions reached by the Central Government. This pattern was repeated in 1951.

The second stage, 1952-57, saw the transition to a fully fledged system of unified enrolment. In 1952 and 1953 the Party put into effect unified enrolment by area, the major change being an attempt to achieve better co-ordination of enrolment to fit in with the country's overall needs. To this end, the enrolment numbers for every institution of higher education had to be reported to the Education Ministry by each Large Administrative Area, and these were to be then examined and approved on the basis of the country's national enrolment plan. From 1954 onwards came a second phase of unified enrolment, this time countrywide.

In 1955-56 unified enrolment, with certain exceptions, was being carried out through the organizational leadership of the province (city), with individual institutions responsible for implementation. The original Large Administrative Area was nevertheless to remain the scope within which enrolment took place.[28] The exceptions permitted, however, made the term "unified enrolment" to some extent a misnomer. Nevertheless, the basic characteristic which distinguished the final stage of unified enrolment in the period 1954-57 was vertical control from the centre. All the measures taken from 1952 onwards were directed to that end. Beginning in 1952, an annual unified enrolment plan was formulated and its concomitant, the "First Five-Year Plan for the Development of Higher Education," was initiated.[29]

In addition to central planning, a second justification for unified enrolment was the uneven distribution of prospective students throughout the country. Moreover, North China had many universities but few higher middle schools; in the South the situation was reversed. Measures were thus taken to remedy the uneven distribution of candidates. For example, because sources of candidates in the North China, North-East and North-West Large Administrative Areas were few and insufficient for their enrolment needs, those registering were as a general rule examined for institutions in the same regions. In very exceptional cases, however, they could be registered for examination for designated institutions in outside areas. On the other hand, as for those areas where candidate sources were many, like East China, the Central South, and the South-West, and exceeded enrolment needs, their prospective students could register for examination in the North China, North-East and North-West Areas, as well as their own. However, although candidates in the latter three areas could register for their own and the other three, mutual transfer for prospective students between East China, the Central South, and the South-West Areas was not permitted.

An exceptional rubric gave concessions to individual aptitude, however. If an equivalent specialty was not available in their area, those with a special aptitude could apply for an institution in any other area if they obtained official approval.[30] But the institutions for which such candidates opted had all to be in the same area.

A source published after the acceptance of students in 1955 confirmed that these distribution policies had been carried out: the three areas of North China, the North-East, and the North-West had received new students from surfeit areas. In addition, Inner Mongolia was now mentioned as a candidate-deficit area. Institutions were encouraged to pay great attention to the ideological education of new entrants,[31] to convince them of the justice of the allocation system.

Similar regulations were in force in 1956 with slight differences. Now candidates in only two of the surfeit areas, East China and the Central-South, in addition to registering for institutions in their own regions, could also apply for admission to those in the deficit areas of North China, the North-East, and the North-West. Candidates from the South-West, apart from applying for entry to institutions in their own area, could register for examination only in North China and the North-West.[32] In 1957 the same system was in operation with slight modifications.[33] Unified enrolment meant planned allocation *(chi-hua ti tiao-p'ei)*.

Three major conclusions are to be drawn concerning unified enrolment: (i) although unified enrolment meant vertical control from the centre, it allowed for exceptional cases within an overall framework; (ii) concessions were made to individual aptitude, a system which could in time perpetuate the inequalities which already existed in the higher education system, and (iii) candidates experienced problems of adjustment to institutions in unfamiliar areas. Post-entry ideological education included orientation to local conditions to ensure contentment in study.

But, most importantly, unified enrolment was a theoretical ideal, and the many questions it posed could only be answered in practice. By 1957, three major exceptions had come to be permitted within the framework of unified enrolment and national allocation: (i) fine arts institutions, (ii) universities of national importance, and (iii) institutions related to specific area needs. But the freedom of initiative granted to institutions and areas in these exceptional cases applied in the main to implementation; such crucial aspects as numbers to be enrolled were subject to national allocation.

The first category of institutional exceptions was composed of the fine arts, music, and theatre institutes which were to carry out individual enrolment *(tan-tu chao-sheng)*. This meant that such matters as examination methods were determined by the institution in question. Alternatively, such institutions of a similar nature in the same area could organize joint enrolment *(lien-he chao-sheng)*, where conditions were appropriate. In 1955 the *Kuang-ming jih-pao* reported that enrolment for fine arts institutes would take place in seventeen major centres including Peking, Sian, Shanghai, Wuhan, and Chengtu.[34] There were similar arrangements in 1957.

Secondly, institutions considered of pre-eminent national importance were to enrol candidates throughout the country. In 1956 and 1957 these included Peking University, Ch'inghua University, Harbin Technological Institute, Chiaotung Technological University, Peking Agricultural Institute, Peking Teacher Training Institute, and Peking Medical Institute. In addition to accepting candidates from the areas in which they were located, such institutions could also accept students from elsewhere according to numbers set down by the Central Government. Furthermore, special regulations were to be formulated for institutions concerned with such sectors as defence, industry, and foreign relations, which also could enrol candidates throughout the country. Apart from the above universities and institutes, certain specialties in some institutions were able to enrol candidates, not from the whole country, but from designated areas outside their own. In this connection can be mentioned the railway management and construction specialties in the Peking Petroleum Institute, which could enlist a number of students from the North-West and the North-East. All specialties in the Wuhan Water Transport Institute could accept a small number of their students from the North China and East China Areas.[35]

Other institutions of national importance, such as the Chinese People's University and the Peking Foreign Language Institute, were also not restricted by area enrolment. Unlike the other institutions of national importance already discussed, however, they carried out individual enrolment,[36] with initiative similar to that enjoyed by fine arts institutions. This meant that such matters as examination methods, as in the case of fine arts, were determined by individual institutions.

The third exception concerned the requirements of localities. By 1957 greater attention was being paid to the satisfaction of local needs, which could conceivably be better dealt with by partial decentralization of enrolment. These changes did not necessarily come about through deliberate policy but in response to a specific local situation. In 1957 these adjustments were reflected in enrolment directives, but earlier regulations had foreshadowed these changes. In 1956, for example, a Szechwan newspaper stated that candidates for teacher training were only allowed to register for institutes in their own province.[37] This indicated a trend towards enrolment of local candidates on the basis of local needs.

The enrolment processes of 1957 brought a reassessment of earlier practices. Unified enrolment had possessed certain advantages: it had effected a balance of numbers between candidate-deficit and surfeit areas, guaranteeing a definite quantity and quality of students for those institutions in need, while providing promotion opportunities for candidates who might otherwise have been denied them. But ultimately the defects of the system had outweighed its advantages: not enough attention had been paid to the principle of accepting able candidates according to area. Because of the redistribution system, areas which had been able to enrol the required quantity of candidates had emphasized quality rather than the entry of local students when given a wider selection from which to choose. Institutions were also clearly giving full consideration to preferences, especially those of the most able applicants who were being accepted for entry to the more prestigious specialties.

This policy had produced undesirable side effects. Not only did students from distant areas have difficulty in adjusting to new conditions, but more importantly, the disparity in standards between areas and institutions, far from being reduced, was intensified. Some parts of the country were consequently well served, others not.

Closely related to these problems was the unnecessary transfer of candidates from one area to another under the unified enrolment system. This is not to say that all redistribution of candidates between areas was unsuitable, but certainly some features of it resulted in unnecessary administration and wastage. There seemed little point, for example, in the practice whereby the Honan Teacher Training Institute in 1956 accepted candidates from Tientsin, while the Tientsin Teacher Training Institute received students from Honan.[38] It is difficult to avoid the conclusion that, in some cases, institutions had exercised their own initiative only too well, and the satisfaction of candidates' preferences had meant that very often the better candidates had been accepted for entry in the field of their choice.

The major justification for modification of the unified enrolment system was to pay greater attention to area needs. The 1957 regulations were posited on the assumption that higher middle graduates within a given area would be able to fulfil the manpower requirements of its provinces and cities. This policy, however, was only to be applied to certain categories of institutions of higher education. For example, teacher training, medical, and agriculture and forestry institutes which were training cadres for a particular province or city would, in principle, adopt the method of enrolment according to area. Training would be directed towards local needs and graduates would subsequently be employed in their own area. But those institutions of pre-eminent importance which were training cadres for the whole country, namely various technological institutes and all the comprehensive universities, would continue to enrol as in the past and would, if necessary, do so in outside areas. These measures were designed to decrease the flow of candidates between areas, enabling students to be familiar with area conditions and economizing on manpower and resources both in the enrolment process itself and in national construction. This new system naturally involved readjustments in entrance requirements and candidates' preferences. The major determining factor, however, was still the ratio between each area's enrolment plan and its sources of candidates.

By 1957 higher middle graduates were becoming more plentiful. Orleans, basing his argument on Soviet sources, claimed that there were 202,600 graduates from higher middle schools at the end of the 1956-57 academic year. The higher education intake in 1957 was 107,000.[39] But it was clear from the prescriptions laid down that some areas would find it difficult to obtain students of suitable calibre. Therefore, it was stipulated that, as the economic and educational circumstances of the areas differed, the acceptance standard in academic examinations would vary accordingly, and the phenomenon of allocating too many students too distantly was to be avoided. Finally, attention was to be paid to the historical traditions of areas and institutions of higher education.[40]

In April 1957 the *Jen-min jih-pao* called for even more concessions to be given to candidates' preferences, and by implication their aptitudes, in order to arouse students' enthusiasm in study, and help their adjustment to the specialties to which they were allocated.[41] But these two measures would tend to perpetuate, not eliminate, inequalities between standards in various areas. Therefore, by 1957, the system of unified enrolment was being considerably modified. Some institutions were being addressed to national, others to local needs, and institutes such as those of fine arts could conduct individual, or where appropriate, joint enrolment.

Because of this modification of unified enrolment, elaborate regulations had to be formulated to take account of those candidates who were registering for two types of institution simultaneously, that is, those conducting individual, and those implementing unified, enrolment. Candidates were instructed to take verification letters from their individual enrolment institutions so that they might also be registered for unified enrolment.[42]

All these exceptions suggested that only one important element of the unified enrolment system remained intact, that of vertical control from the centre which determined allocation plans and general guidelines for examinations. But enrolment based on the needs of provinces and cities, as well as the special dispensations for institutions of national importance and institutes admitting students on their own account, hierarchically ranked higher education according to functionally specific criteria and national priorities. Though the decentralization entailed in catering for local needs would tend to lessen the concentration of high calibre students in certain areas and institutions, dividing higher education into categories for the enrolment process would maintain other inequalities. The better candidates would still be likely to apply, and have the greater opportunity of being accepted, for the comprehensive universities and the more prestigious technological institutes.

Moreover, 1957 appears to have brought a greater emphasis on candidates within the education system. A *Jen-min jih-pao* editorial called for provincial and city Party committees to strengthen their leadership of the enrolment process even if the year's admission numbers were fewer and candidates many, but it was also clear that in practice the role of the Party was increasingly being subordinated to that of the State organs.[43] Certainly, Party bodies were exhorted to address themselves to raising the ideological and academic quality of candidates, especially those from outside the education system, but the increase in the number of prospective entrants from within suggested vertical control by State organs and academic authorities.

In theory, then, the changes of 1957 reasserted the traditional integration of education and society; enrolment according to local needs would make students address themselves to the problems of the areas in which they lived. But the implementation of the enrolment process produced the opposite effect. In the years 1949-56 candidate flow between the Large Administrative Areas, to some extent at least, benefited those areas less well endowed; enlistment of prospective students in their localities of origin in 1957 only perpetuated inequalities between areas. As a result, the limited decentralization of enrolment in 1957 came in practice to be justified in economic not political terms, and as such reflected the Liuist interpretation of the proletarian intellectual concept.

In spite of partial decentralization, however, the final authority for enrolment policies remained vested in the Central Government. During the years of unified enrolment the admission process chain of command was headed by the National Enrolment Committee *(Ch'üan-kuo kao-teng hsüeh-hsiao chao-sheng wei-yüan hui),* the membership of which was approved by the State Council. One source stated in 1953 that among members of the committee were representatives from the Ministries of Higher Education, Education, Health and Culture, the Second Ministry of Machine Building, the Youth League, and heads of certain institutions. Its chairman was the Minister of Higher Education, Ma Hsü-lun.[44] The committee was established annually but the nature of its composition was consistent; again, in 1956, it consisted of thirty members, including representatives from concerned departments of the Central Government and prominent Peking institutions of higher education. Similarly, its chairman was the Minister of Higher Education, Yang Hsiu-feng.[45]

However, although the committee's composition and tasks were determined by the State Council, prior consultation with a wide range of interested parties appears to have preceded its formation. In 1957 the Shanghai *Wen-hui pao* referred to an enrolment conference with the participation of a hundred delegates from educational administrative organs and institutions of higher education in the various areas. Discussion was carried out through small groups from the regions of North China, the North-West, the North-East, Central China, South China, Shanghai, Kiangsu, Szechwan, Yunnan, and Kweichow, a slight variation of the earlier Large Administrative Areas. Apparently this conference had only a technical advisory purpose, as it was stated that it reported to the State Council which would later approve and promulgate decisions concerning enrolment in 1957. Thus while the State Council formulated general manpower plans, the task of the conference was to determine what was possible on the basis of area needs and facilities.[46]

The National Enrolment Committee was designed to strengthen the leadership of enrolment work through vertical control, and it acted under the auspices of the Education Ministries. The committee established general guidelines for the enrolment process while the concrete tasks at local levels were dealt with by a hierarchy of enrolment work committees *(ti-ch'ü kao-teng hsüeh-hsiao chao-sheng kung-tso wei-yüan hui)*,[47] established at administrative area, province, and city levels. These committees were organized by local education bureaux, in cooperation with related government departments and institutions of higher education which fell within the scope of the various geographical divisions. They were usually established from April onwards.[48] The National Enrolment Committee devised regulations concerning which institutions would enrol in particular administrative areas for the purposes of candidate distribution, and these rules were later publicized for prospective students by the relevant enrolment work committees.[49] Those institutions conducting individual enrolment were to do so in accordance with their own circumstances, and the methods they adopted for this purpose were only to be put into effect after the approval of the National Enrolment Committee, presumably through the medium of the Administrative Area Work Committee.[50]

The enrolment work committees were also responsible for the acceptance and allocation of new students. This process was carried out in the area centres of Peking, Shanghai, Wuhan, Mukden, Sian, and Chengtu. The results were usually announced in mid-August, after approval by each area's enrolment work committee. Finally, while successful candidates were normally informed by the institution for which they had been accepted, unsuccessful applicants were issued rejection notices by their enrolment work committees.

This system of vertical control was also demonstrated by the formulation of subject matter for the enrolment examinations. Immediately beneath the National Enrolment Committee was organized the Enrolment Examination Topics Committee *(Ming-t'i wei-yüan hui)*. At the second session of the National Enrolment Committee in May 1956 members of the Topics Committee were selected and approved, and general principles regarding examination topics were passed. The latter were, of course, chosen within the scope of the Enrolment Examination

Outlines *(chao-sheng k'ao-shih ta-kang),* compiled and published by the Education Ministries.[51]

The administration of the enrolment process was based on a central unified plan and organizational leadership by the province (city), with institutions of higher education responsible for implementation and the original Large Administrative Area as the scope. In this way enrolment work committees in provinces and cities came under the overall leadership of the area and national committees, although they were also supervised by local education bureaux. Under this general supervision, province and city enrolment work committees were responsible for much of the actual implementation of the admission process: candidates' registration, the administration of examinations, the assessment of scripts, acceptance of new students, and their entry procedures.[52] The co-operation of government departments and educational institutions was also seen as crucial for the successful operation of the enrolment process.

Although the Youth Leagues were also mentioned in this context, the role of the Party appears to have been minimal. Undoubtedly, the Party membership of leadership personnel in enrolment organs would have meant that Party influence was by no means absent, but the emphasis on the function of government departments and the hierarchy of committees only underlined still further the importance of vertical control.

Institutions of higher education were especially enjoined to make a positive contribution to enrolment work and not complacently rely on government departments to carry it out. Unified enrolment was said to be extensive and had to be accomplished in a relatively short time. Institutions were therefore to dispatch high quality cadres who had previous experience of enrolment work to serve on the committees at each level.[53] The number of cadres to be sent was based on the ratio between the numbers to be admitted to a particular institution and the enrolment work as a whole. In this way institutions performed an advisory function in the work of unified enrolment;[54] they provided specialized assistance to Party and government functionaries in such tasks as the conduct of entrance examinations and the assessment of candidate performance.

Nevertheless, complaints were voiced in the press that institutions were failing to provide both facilities and personnel for unified enrolment. In Shanghai, academic authorities had in many cases apparently refused to make accommodation available. More importantly, the leadership of institutions was accused of assuming that enrolment processes were the concern of administrative departments; the *Kuang-ming jih-pao* claimed that some universities just waited for new students to be sent in. Far from dispatching experienced personnel, such institutions considered enrolment a burden and sent unsuitable junior staff instead to take part in the work of enrolment organs.[55]

One of the functions of the enrolment work committees was to deal with the process of examination registration. While the dates of examinations for unified enrolment were fixed by the National Enrolment Committee, being held between the 15 and 18 July in 1955, registration dates were laid down, for example in 1955 and 1956, by the Administrative Area Work Committees, and in 1957 also by provincial and city committees, in accordance with local conditions. In 1956 registration took place mainly in June and early July.[56]

The registration dates for those institutions conducting individual enrolment, like fine arts, were generally laid down by the National Enrolment Committee. In 1955 registration was to take place between 25 May and 25 June, but each institution chose a time within this period according to its own conditions. Similar criteria governed the timing of examinations.

For the purposes of registration, examination areas *(k'ao-ch'ü)* and their management offices *(k'ao-ch'u pan-shih ch'u)* were designated throughout the country under the auspices of the Administrative Area Work Committees. Their total number was provisionally fixed by the National Enrolment Committee, but could be increased where appropriate by Administrative Area Committees. Examination areas were located in provincial capitals, certain cities, and other major centres of population. There were 77 of these in 1954, 120 in 1956, and 110 in 1957.[57] Candidates were to register in the examination areas nearest to the schools from which they had graduated, their work units, or places of residence.

The registration process for fine arts and other similar institutions conducting individual enrolment differed from that prescribed for unified enrolment. Documentation and approval of registration were undertaken by individual institutions, although some general guidelines were presumably given by local enrolment committees. As early as 1955, institutions like Fine Arts jointly conducted their registration process, and in 1957 this seems to have taken place in cities where several such institutions were concentrated, for example, Peking, Shanghai, and Canton.[58]

In general, however, the registration process passed through the management offices located in examination areas. There were two main methods of registration: collective and individual.[59] The following were subject to collective registration: (i) a particular year's graduates from higher middle schools, worker-peasant rapid middle schools, and vocational middle schools, and (ii) specialist cadres. Before the registration process began, schools and work units were responsible for preparing a list of candidates' names. In the case of the higher middle and worker-peasant rapid middle school graduates, appended at the end of the list would be the names of those who were not able or not permitted to register for examination. The reason why such eligible graduates were not being permitted to take the examination was not indicated; nevertheless, it can be assumed that the work of composing the lists involved political screening of potential candidates. On this basis it would appear that schools and work units were required to give an opinion as to the suitability of candidates.

This was also suggested by the documentation needed before registration could be completed. In the case of collective registration, schools and work units appointed special personnel to present the following information at the examination area management offices: (i) candidates' academic records, (ii) references from teachers or superiors, (iii) forms filled up by the candidates themselves in requesting registration, (iv) record of medical examination, (v) four copies of a recent passport-sized photograph, and (vi) registration fees.[60]

Individual registration followed a similar pattern concerning the documents and formalities required of such other categories of candidate as serving cadres subject to "free application" and intellectual youth. It is therefore difficult to ascertain how the chances of acceptance varied between collective and individual registration, but the fact that those from within the education system and specialist cadres chosen for application only in certain fields were included in collective procedures suggests that the likelihood of entry was greater under this system. Their credentials and qualifications would already have been closely examined before registration, and they had been consistently exposed to academic and ideological preparation for a longer period of time. Furthermore, specialist cadres would have been particularly chosen for registration by work units.

On the other hand, intellectual youth, by definition, often had a dubious background which even ideological indoctrination might not have entirely erased. The reluctance with which leadership personnel consented to the registration of cadres eligible for "free application" has been explained earlier, and inadequate preparation might well have placed them at a disadvantage in the examinations.

Moreover, that the registration process was not merely a formality is indicated by references to investigation methods *(shen-ch'a he-ke)* in the 1956 Enrolment Regulations for the South-West Area: "Whether under collective or individual registration, candidates who do not pass the investigation will have returned to them their registration expenses and academic record documents."[61]

Investigation methods, carried out over a period of several weeks between the beginning of registration and the start of the enrolment examinations, would provide an opportunity to check on such matters as family origin, personal connections, and political history: such checking of candidates' background would support earlier information provided by agencies of socialization, like the Youth League. For example, even though not all applicants were members of the League, it seems unlikely that any candidate would have gained admission if he had been seriously objected to by that organization. Investigation was a continuous process.

Registration, therefore, was not automatic: granting of the examination entry document *(chun-k'ao cheng)* was apparently only given after exhaustive enquiries as to political reliability. Complaints that investigation methods had been deficient indicated that some candidates had been found wanting in the past. It is perhaps significant that these complaints were published in October 1957 during the anti-rightist campaign which followed the Hundred Flowers and were directed as much towards students who had already studied in universities as current candidates.[62]

Nevertheless, the seriousness of investigation methods was also underlined by provisions relating to the disqualification of candidates. Forgery of academic records, concealment of political history, and negative behaviour were punishable by abrogation of examination entry approval or prevention of admission to higher education.[63] Since under collective registration documents were processed by the relevant school or work unit before being forwarded to the examination area management office, forgery and falsification would more likely have occurred among those coming under the individual registration rubric.

Medical examination prior to registration took place, for example, between 1 April and 31 May 1957, even if it may well have been of a very general nature. Certainly, it was stated that candidates suffering from certain defects could not be registered for particular specialties: for instance, colour blindness would have disqualified applicants in various scientific and technological fields. Examples were also given of candidates who changed their specialty preferences on medical advice.[64] Those considered generally unacceptable on medical grounds were presumably included in the appendix to the list of candidates presented by school or work unit to the examination area management offices. Only a very small percentage appears to have been rejected for registration in all disciplines, however. Reviewing previous years' enrolment, the *Jen-min chiao-yü* stated that the percentage of the higher middle graduates in Szechwan who had originally intended to register for examination, but who were not permitted to do so for health reasons, fell from 3.97 per cent in 1955 to 2.96 per cent in 1956. But there seem to have been considerable regional discrepancies, as it was added that the equivalent percentage for the Fourth Middle School in Soochow was 10 per cent in 1953, falling to 0.5 per cent in 1957.[65]

Candidates were subject to both medical and political re-examination on admission to higher education, and it was clearly stipulated that those who failed on either of these counts would have their entry qualifications rescinded. Although figures concerning those who failed the medical examination are not available, health standards seem to have been flexible; if candidates, as a result of special treatment, were able to pass another medical test a year hence, they could continue their studies. But no such leniency seems to have been shown regarding political criteria. Even though no statistics have been given as to those rejected on political grounds, re-examination undoubtedly acted as a further check on potentially unreliable elements.

In any case, a brief perusal of statistics for registration and admission indicates that a greater selectivity, based on political and academic criteria, was becoming the norm by 1957. Taking the years 1952-56, the *Chung-kuo ch'ing-nien pao* stated that the total number of candidates registering for examination (that is, including individual, joint, and unified enrolment methods where applicable) was 73,000 in 1952, 81,000 in 1953, 134,000 in 1954, 177,000 in 1955, and 350,000 in 1956. In 1957 the *Kuang-ming jih-pao* mentioned that 250,000 had registered for enrolment examinations. These may be set against entrants to higher education during the same period. Orleans, again on the basis of the Chinese Communist press and *New China News Agency* sources, confirmed that those admitted numbered 65,900 in 1952, 71,400 in 1953, 94,000 in 1954, 96,200 in 1955, 165,600 in 1956, and 107,000 in 1957. For purposes of clarification these totals are computed in Table 5 below:[66]

TABLE 5: REGISTERED AND SUCCESSFUL CANDIDATES (1952-57)

Year	Those Registered for Enrolment Examination	Entrants to Higher Education
1952	73,000	65,900
1953	81,000	71,400
1954	134,000	94,000
1955	177,000	96,200
1956	350,000	165,600
1957	250,000	107,000

In both columns, the figures are rounded, but they indicate the increasing selectivity emphasized in the enrolment process.

Moreover, these numbers can be checked against those ratios between candidate sources (registration) and the enrolment plan (entrants) given in an educational newspaper: 1.9:1 in 1956 and 2.3:1 in 1957. In addition, a shift in the ratios between different categories of candidate registered for examination and the enrolment plan was becoming apparent. In July 1957 the *Kuang-ming jih-pao* claimed that of those registered for examination in that year, 180,000 or more (71.4 per cent) were higher middle school graduating students and rapid middle school graduates compared with 42.6 per cent in 1956. The ratio of these two categories registered for examination and the enrolment plan was 1.7:1. Not only were there greater numbers of higher middle graduates from whom entrants could be chosen, but these were also representing an increasing proportion of the total registering for examination.[67]

In conclusion, because of their longer and more consistent exposure to agencies of academic and ideological socialization, those subject to collective registration, especially higher middle graduates, were becoming increasingly advantaged in the competition for entry to higher education.

5

The Selection System

The selection system was designed to fulfil the enrolment plan. Central control required all institutions to select in accordance with the enrolment regulations and on the basis of three criteria: politics, health, and examination performance. But the central directives governing selection processes were broad and flexible and intended to take account of diverse candidates as well as different fields of study. Selection will therefore be considered under the following headings: (i) the designation of examination subjects, (ii) the allocation of candidates, (iii) the content of examinations, and (iv) the assessment of scripts.

During the years 1950-57 candidates took examinations according to the academic category into which their proposed field of study fell. These categories applied nationally but varied in number and size over time. In 1954, for example, there were two categories: the first encompassed the natural sciences, engineering, agriculture and forestry, and medicine; the second included the humanities, law, finance and economics, physical education, and fine arts. National language, political general knowledge, and foreign language (English or Russian) examinations were taken by both categories of candidate. But while those registering for fields of study in the first category were tested also in mathematics, physics, chemistry, and biology, applicants for the second category were additionally examined in history and geography.[1]

These categories underwent slight modification in 1955. In that year there were three of these: (i) engineering and natural science, (ii) medicine, as well as agriculture and forestry, and (iii) the humanities together with political science and law.[2] The first category, however, also included all natural science specialties in teacher training institutes, as well as the following subjects in the fields of agriculture and forestry: agricultural mechanization, forestry exploitation, mechanical engineering in wood resources, and the renovation of irrigation dykes. Similarly, the second category encompassed the biological sciences, including all biology specialties in teacher training institutes, together with psychology and physical education specialties. Finally, the third category also covered education specialties in teacher training institutes, together with specialties in finance and economics.[3]

In 1955 the examination subjects to be taken by those registered for the three categories were essentially equivalent to those established for the two categories in 1954. The examination subjects required for the first category in 1955 were identical to those laid down for the first in 1954, but with the exclusion of biology and foreign languages. The requirements for the second category in 1955 were similar to the first, except that mathematics was excluded, and the fundamentals of Darwinism (presumably a reformulation of biology) added. Finally, those registered for the third category in 1955 were to be examined in subjects identical to those prescribed for the 1954 second category, with the exception of foreign languages. With minor modifications, the categories of academic fields and their examination subjects remained substantially the same in 1956 and 1957.[4]

In summary, the enrolment examination subjects for relevant fields of study in 1955 may be tabulated as follows:

TABLE 6: ENROLMENT EXAMINATION SUBJECTS 1955

Fields of Study	*Enrolment Examination Subjects*
Category I Engineering and Natural Science	National Language Political General Knowledge Mathematics Physics Chemistry
Category II Medicine, and Agriculture and Forestry	National Language Political General Knowledge Physics Chemistry Fundamentals of Darwinism
Category III Humanities, and Political Science and Law	National Language Political General Knowledge History Geography

For purposes of analysis, the examination subjects can be divided into three kinds: (i) common, (ii) basic, and (iii) skill. All three would, to some extent, examine individual aptitude, as they tested the acquisition of specific knowledge. Even though they were the least specialized, the common subjects of national language and political general knowledge demonstrated the mastery of technical skills. Proficiency in one's own language was, after all, a sine qua non of successful study in higher education. While, in theory, the political general knowledge paper was principally designed to discover revolutionary commitment rather than specialized learning, it would, in practice, have been difficult to separate the two concerns. But, in general, it could be said that the function of the common subjects was to guarantee the quality of entrants in all academic disciplines.

The manpower needs in the enrolment plan of specialties and institutions did not necessarily correlate with either the quantity and quality of applicants or with the fields of study for which they had registered. Resulting disparities could only be resolved through the selection system. If the common examinations were designed to guarantee general standards, the basic subjects were the general foundation of all the specialties necessary for national construction. Thus the basic subjects of mathematics, physics, chemistry, biology (the fundamentals of Darwinism), foreign languages, history, and geography were related to the many types of proposed study for which candidates had registered. The basic examinations were testing breadth rather than depth, in order to discover candidates' suitability for a wide range of disciplines, as there was no certainty that they would be allocated to subjects for which they had applied. In fact, such basic subjects could not but test the intellect; in theory, however, determined study, fired by ideological fervour, received more attention than natural endowment. Nevertheless, the aptitude of individuals for particular subjects (whether because of production experience or personal preference) could not be left entirely out of account. The content, therefore, of the basic subjects was broad in scope and intended both to test knowledge already acquired and ascertain potential for further study.[5]

If the common subjects related to all academic disciplines and the basic examinations could be considered aptitude testing, the additional skill tests sought to discover personal excellence in specific fields of study. This carried concessions to aptitude one stage further. Skill examinations, like the common and basic subjects, were laid down centrally in the *Outline of Enrolment Examinations for Institutions of Higher Education,* published annually. These skill subjects did not apply to all academic disciplines, but only to those specialties which made particular demands of new students. Therefore, in addition to the common and basic subjects, certain candidates were to be examined in skills to discover special proficiency.

Skill examinations differed widely. But basic and skill subjects were not necessarily mutually exclusive. Although a foreign language (English or Russian) was not a basic subject in the years from 1955 to 1957, those registered for foreign language specialties had to take skill examinations.[6] The 1957 Enrolment Regulations stated that finance and economics, economic geography, and philosophy specialties required skill papers in mathematics. Certain specialties in forestry stipulated skill examinations in 1956, though not in

1957.[7] Skill subjects were not entirely different from those in the basic category, but they did stress academic excellence in certain specific areas.

Distinctive skill papers were to be found in disciplines like fine arts. For example, in 1957 skill curricula examinations in such subjects were both written and oral. Creative contributions were also demanded of candidates. For instance, those registering for music institutions were required to present their own compositions.[8] Finally, candidates applying for entry to teacher training had to take extra skill subjects, such as physical training, designated by the Education Ministries in accordance with the instruction given in institutions.[9]

Skill subjects confirmed the inequalities emerging in higher education. It has been earlier argued that applicants from outside the education system like "specialist" and "free application" cadres would have been well equipped to take skill subjects in fields associated with their former employment, but the narrowness of their academic experience would have precluded the required proficiency in other disciplines. The skill subject regulations thus favoured candidates from within the education system, especially higher middle school graduates.

The field of study an applicant chose determined the skill subjects in which he would be examined. At registration candidates selected preferences for institutions and departments, the number and nature of which varied over time and by area. This variation was especially marked in the years before the higher education system had been consolidated. In 1952 each candidate was required to name three departmental preferences under which five choices of institution were possible.[10] It was on the basis of these and their examination performance that applicants were distributed to higher education. The allocation decision was nevertheless final and prospective students were encouraged to follow it.

Attention will generally be focused on the selection of preferences during the years 1955, 1956, and 1957, as this was the period when unified enrolment was supposedly consolidated. It must be noted at the outset, however, that in practice, higher middle graduates had a greater range of choice in the selection of preferences, and it was against a background of candidate inequality that selection took place.

During the years 1952-57 the system of planned allocation was in operation. Because of the modification it underwent towards the end of the period under discussion, however, planned allocation, like unified enrolment, was really a misnomer. In fact, its only consistent feature was the allocation of students according to the central plan by the administrative area enrolment work committees.

Press sources claimed, however, that most candidates were being distributed according to their preferred specialties and institutions, very few being directed to academic areas not of their choice. It was the proud claim of the *Kuang-ming jih-pao* in July 1954 that the greater proportion of new students admitted to higher education had been granted their first preference, even if it also acknowledged that some entrants would not be so fortunate because of pressure of numbers and academic standards. At this point the competitive nature of the allocation process becomes significant. As there was an obvious discrepancy between the placing of candidates' preferences and the planned numbers to be allocated, the level of examination performance had to be the yardstick when excessive numbers had chosen the same preference. This criterion was a common theme in *Jen-min jih-pao* reports between September 1952 and August 1955.[11] In June 1955 it was emphasized that candidates whose political and health conditions were adequate and examination performance satisfactory would be accepted according to the preferences they had chosen.[12]

But, by September, when the selection process was nearly complete, it was being admitted that while the majority had been accepted according to their preferences, a small minority of candidates who were suitable in every way for specialties and institutions of their choice could not be admitted. This was because the latter had already taken in their full complement. The qualifications of these unplaced candidates were then looked at again by the area enrolment work committee not only considering their health, political conditions, and examination performance, but also their general scholastic record. Clearly, references from middle schools or other appropriate authorities came into focus. After this reappraisal they would have been distributed to institutions and specialties which lacked numbers. At the same time it was stressed that there were fewer such candidates in 1955 than in previous years.[13] Selection and distribution were based on examination performance; the allocation criterion was meritocratic.

Moreover, general guidelines for standards in enrolment examinations were given by the National Enrolment Committee but naturally varied from year to year and area to area. Local enrolment committees, in co-operation with institutions of higher education, judged candidates according to references from schools or units and the three conditions.

Those prospective students who satisfied the political and health conditions but fell just below the necessary examination standard were classified as provisional students *(shih-tu sheng)* and distributed to specialties and institutions which lacked their full complement. This meant that they would be admitted for a term or a year during which the institution in question would be able to ascertain whether or not they were suitable for further study. They would then either be transferred to the status of proper student or have their provisional entry qualifications cancelled. A special examination was usually given at this point. But although this provisional method was in operation during the early years of unified enrolment, it was stated in 1955 and 1956 that this system would no longer operate.[14] The provisional rubric appears to have been a temporary measure, designed to make up the slight deficit produced when accepted students failed to register for entry. This system was also closely related to sources of students, especially higher middle graduates. In 1955 the *Jen-min jih-pao* asserted that the standard at which students could be accepted had been raised, as there were enough suitable candidates to fulfil the enrolment plan.[15]

Planned allocation, then, was flexible. But early optimism of press sources concerning allocation according to candidates' preferences gradually gave way to a more sober appraisal, which underlined still further the meritocratic tendencies emerging in the enrolment process. In 1956, the *Chung-kuo ch'ing-nien pao* which, because of its potential readership, was more intimately concerned with the education of youth claimed that some candidates had been severely disadvantaged by planned allocation. The selection system, it said, was in dire need of reform, as those not distributed according to their preferences had found it difficult to study.[16]

1956 saw considerable modification in planned allocation and it was now asserted that all entrants would in future be distributed according to preference, as this was in the national interest. This placed further emphasis on aptitude and specialized proficiency, but press comment did not indicate how many candidates were given the first of their preferences.

These new measures only intensified meritocratic tendencies. It was now explicitly stated that once the three conditions of entry had been fulfilled, order of merit among candidates would be the criterion by which they were allocated. Those who performed best in the examinations were the most likely to be given their first preference.[17] In August 1956 the *Chiao-shih pao* outlined in detail the mechanics of the selection process: "When accepting candidates who are satisfactory in politics, health, and examination standard, we will arrange them on the basis of their total marks and accept them according to the order of preferences they have filled up."[18]

In spite of its modification in 1956, however, planned allocation was not entirely abandoned. It was frankly admitted that the country's need for certain types of manpower would be given high priority, and that the subjective wishes of some candidates did not always suit their own capacities, let alone the national plan. Thus, while the order of candidates' preferences would be a prime consideration, some applicants would necessarily still be directed to certain subjects.[19]

Increasing allocation according to preferences and a concomitant reduction in planned distribution were accompanied by a more detailed assessment of candidates. Earlier criticism that planned allocation to unsuitable specialties had caused students' study to suffer now gave way to a demand that background in general be appraised. In addition to examination performance higher middle graduates' academic references were to be considered; in the case of serving personnel, scholastic record, work experience, and special talent *(chuan-chang)* came into focus. The use of these criteria was not merely designed to eliminate biased evaluation; they indicated the attempt to tap talent everywhere. Reference to the term *chuan-chang* is itself significant for it implies aptitude. The wider consideration of the academic background of all candidates intensified the meritocratic tendencies already inherent in the preference system. The attempt to bring cadres from production into higher education was undeniably related to their experience in certain fields; the enrolment process appears to have given far greater weight to their specific talent per se than to their proletarian origin.[20]

This mixed system of selection contained within it the seeds of elitism. The new measures of 1956 brought greater flexibility in some respects, but planned allocation was still very much alive and now took on a new form. This involved a second session of selecting preferences and applied to those candidates whose political and health standards were adequate, whose examination marks reached the minimum acceptance level, but who could still not be admitted according to their preferences. They were required within a certain period to fill in new preferences for a second session of selection. These candidates had already been rejected once, and so the range of preferences now permitted was more restricted. Once again, institutions, through the local enrolment work committees, would conduct the acceptance process. This not only required further administration but, in view of the time limit, presented problems for candidates in isolated places where communications were poor. Such candidates could, however, express willingness to be distributed according to the State plan, as might those who were not given their place of preference even after the second session.[21] As a result, the *Kuang-ming jih-pao* could claim in August 1956 that the overwhelming majority of these candidates would be accepted.[22]

But allocation was being based more and more on quality of examination performance. Even if a candidate's personal record were taken into account, academic criteria were becoming increasingly important. The system of preferences produced a stratified selection process; there was a clear distinction between those given their choice in the first session, those awarded it in the second, and the remainder directed through planned allocation.

In fact, in candidate distribution, as in other aspects of enrolment, 1956 was a watershed, confirming previous trends. Comments in the press in 1957 on the operation of the selection system in previous years indicated that preferences were being concentrated in certain academic fields and as a result some institutions and specialties had had to rely on directed distribution to complete their enrolment.[23]

Announcing the abolition of planned allocation, a 1957 joint directive of the Ministry of Higher Education, the Ministry of Education and the Youth League elaborated a new concept of student preference which gave still more weight to personal aptitude: "Promotion preference reflects at a definite stage the interest and special talent of youth and its decision to serve socialist construction."[24] Conspicuously absent is any reference to the idea that interest can be trained and that special talent is in any case a product of the struggle of practice. The abolition of planned allocation was followed by a new preference system introduced in 1957. This was an attempt to give candidates a wider choice by greater co-ordination of specialty and institution preferences, being particularly relevant to engineering fields. From 1952 to 1956, for example, the engineering subjects were divided into fifteen large groups, each consisting of many specialties. A candidate selected for an institution according to a specialty group could well find himself in a field of study rather different from the one he had expected.[25]

In contrast, under the reform of 1957 candidates were permitted to register for twelve specialty and twelve institution preferences.[26] They would now be able to select several specialties in the same institution or several institution preferences for one specialty. This system was said to convey two main advantages: candidates would have a greater range of choice, and specialty and institution preferences would be better co-ordinated. For instance, a candidate who had a strong desire to enter a physics specialty would be able to opt for it in several institutions. If, on the other hand, a prospective student favoured a particular institution at all costs, he could select several specialties in the one institution.[27]

One notable feature of the 1957 preference system was its implicit emphasis on personal choice as a desirable end in itself; claims were made that it promoted better study. The retention of a second session of preferences in 1957, in spite of the abolition of planned distribution, indicated that State organs and enrolment committees were still not entirely satisfied with the operation of the selection system. Ever present was the problem of balancing the numbers registered for various specialties and institutions with those designated by the enrolment plan. But even the second session was now justified in terms of extending personal choice.

In August 1957 the *Jen-min jih-pao* reiterated that many of those rejected in the first session were of comparatively good quality and the second system was directed towards finding suitable places for them. The concrete methods for conducting the second session were outlined in detail. After the first session had been completed, those candidates rejected would be issued documents to that effect by local enrolment organs which were to assist candidates in their second selection of preferences. Subsequently, institutions which still lacked a full complement would be provided with details of rejected candidates. Afterwards these institutions would select a suitable number of comparatively high quality candidates and inform these of their opportunity to fill up new preferences within a given period. Thus candidates in the second session were only permitted to apply again for institutions and preferences which lacked their full complement. Rejected candidates were not, however, compelled to participate in the second session and it was implied that in cases where the choices still available were not suited to their preferences they would forego the opportunity of reapplication. The importance of personal interest was again being stressed.[28]

Although no detailed statistical breakdown is available, it is probable that many of the institutions and specialties participating in the second session were concerned with local needs. These would have included teacher training, agriculture, and some medical institutions which, as a general rule, took students from the provinces and cities in their areas.[29]

The changes of 1957 underlined the increasingly selective nature of the enrolment process. The second session of preferences was a reflection of the initial selection and represented stringency rather than leniency of standards. Selection of students under the first system was based on academic excellence, but as the number registered varied by specialty and institution, acceptance standards were adjusted accordingly. Those subjects with many candidates could raise the level of admission. Yet in order to guarantee the quality demanded by the enrolment plan, it was categorically asserted that specialties for which few had expressed preferences must not completely disregard academic standards, even though the admission level might be slightly lower than that of other specialties. Therefore, on no account could less favoured specialties and institutions take in applicants who were markedly inferior; here was another justification for the second session of preferences.[30] But only those who had been rejected for all their first preferences were eligible to apply for the second session.

Moreover, those who fell below a certain standard in the examinations were not permitted to select new preferences,[31] and as the actual numbers now needed were few, the second session was as selective as the first was competitive. In August 1957 the *Jen-min jih-pao* emphasized that those applying for the second session exceeded the numbers required by relevant institutions and specialties.[32] Clearly, the order of academic success remained the criterion for selection and distribution according to preferences, even in the second session.

These meritocratic tendencies were also strongly suggested by the attitudes of candidates. Complaints were voiced that some youth offered the chance of the second session were unwilling to select institutions in their own provinces and cities, on the assumption that the local specialties which lacked a full complement were, by definition, less prestigious. Candidates denied the second session of preferences and those again rejected were urged to take part in production and serve national construction to the best of their ability, but, signficantly, they also had the option of private study in their free time to prepare for future enrolment examinations.[33]

The criteria on which the selection system was based bring into focus the mechanical process by which candidates were allocated to specialties and institutions. The examination standard at which students could be accepted was determined by three factors: (i) the enrolment plan, (ii) the average academic level of prospective candidates, and (iii) the assumption that those admitted would be able to keep pace with the courses in higher education.[34] Two main conclusions can be drawn from this process: the examinations were tests of aptitude, and there was great flexibility of assessment. The question of aptitude has already been examined in some depth. Flexibility of assessment brought great variation in acceptance standards. The Education Ministries, through the National Enrolment Committee, did not impose any hard and fast rule but only a general minimum standard, below which institutions could not accept students. In the selection process, each institution therefore laid down its own standard in accordance with the nature of its specialties. Moreover, entry levels varied among specialties within an institution.[35]

Candidates were considered by institutions on the basis of preferences. If his first preference institution considered a candidate suitable, he would be accepted. If not, his case would be passed to the second, third, and so on to the twelfth if necessary, until he was accepted or finally rejected. The task of the preferred institution was to compare the candidates and select the best for acceptance.[36]

The method of comparison can be illustrated by reference to hypothetical cases. In the first instance fulfilment of the three conditions was the sine qua non of acceptance. The candidates' examination marks would then be arranged in order of merit and in turn co-ordinated with preferences. The question arose, however, as to the method to be adopted when there were two candidates, of whom A had a first preference and B a third preference for the same institution, when B's examination success was superior to A's. In accordance with the general guidelines in the enrolment regulations, provided that B had not already been admitted for his first or second preference institutions, he would be selected instead of A. In this case, the deciding factor was B's superior examination performance.[37]

Variations in acceptance standards were permitted because academic fields demanded different aptitudes. For example, engineering institutes required a good basis in mathematics and physics; their construction specialties demanded proficiency in drawing. The humanities called for high performance in the national language.[38] Thus the arrangement of candidates in order of examination merit had to take account not only of total marks but also success in individual subjects. This rubric applied to common and basic examinations. In a second hypothetical case if B's total marks were higher than A's but his mathematics, physics, and chemistry examination success was not as great as A's, then engineering and natural science subjects would favour accepting A rather than B.[39] It is noteworthy that in its attention to marks in specific examination subjects the Chinese selection process differed from the Soviet one.

In discussing the Soviet system Korol claimed that whatever a candidate's chosen field of study, his examination success in different subjects had equal value. The Soviet process did not distinguish between two candidates whose total marks were the same, even though one of them scored badly in mathematics while the other's deficiency was in a foreign language.[40] Therefore, although the enrolment process as a whole was modelled on Soviet organizational structure, even greater concessions to aptitude appear to have been given when assessing marks in the Chinese system.

But, although the common and basic subjects were of broad scope and designed to test aptitudes, the candidates had to revise within the specific framework prescribed by the Education Ministries. For example, *An Outline of Enrolment Examinations for Institutions of Higher Education for Summer 1956* was published for this purpose. The topics for the individual examinations were also selected from this outline. The Topics Committee, established under the National Enrolment Committee, was responsible for setting the examinations by taking into account the academic standard of candidates throughout the country.[41]

Analysis of the content of examinations will be confined to the two common subjects, national language and political general knowledge. The national language examination was characterized by both implicit and explicit political content. In its literature section, the candidates had to display understanding of the following points: (i) important political thought, (ii) literary style and special points of artistic merit, including details of plot, structure and linguistic ingenuity, (iii) historical background and social significance, (iv) the evolution of literary genres as exemplified by the works under consideration, and (v) representative writings of the authors concerned. Although several of them predated the modern period, the literary creations studied were selected for their political content, and the genres which they exemplified were considered suitable vehicles for the expression of revolutionary commitment. Even classical texts were to be understood within the Marxist-Leninist framework. While political criteria permeated every aspect of literary study, items (i), (iii), and (v) made them explicit. For example, one of the modern works selected, *Spring Silkworms* by Mao Tun, would have been politically analyzed on these three counts. The literary merit of the titles studied was seen in terms of their contribution to the revolutionary cause.[42] Finally, in the language section of the examination the essay topic represented 60 per cent of the total mark; half of this percentage was awarded for ideological content and the subject of the essay always carried a political theme. For example, in 1953 the essay subject was entitled "Recalling a Revolutionary Cadre Whom I Have Known".

The major objectives of the political general knowledge examination can be gauged from the reference books recommended: *The Social Science Basic Knowledge Reader, The Constitution of the People's Republic of China,* and *The Report on the Draft of the Constitution* by Liu Shao-ch'i. In addition to an understanding of revolution, factual knowledge of the State structure and economic construction was required.[43] But it was emphasized that political examinations were designed not so much to test the acquisition of knowledge as to discover personal standpoints on current issues. In fact, even as early as 1951 complaints were being voiced as to the candidates' attitudes to the political general knowledge examination: "Prospective students have recently bought books on terminology and memorized them. . . . Politics examinations are mainly to see . . . where we stand on particular issues.''[44] Thus the political general knowledge outline exhorted candidates to follow current internal and international affairs in order to better demonstrate their political awareness in the examinations. But even knowledge of present developments was of no use without personal commitment. This, of course, would be evaluated on the basis of the references from schools and units, but political general knowledge would also test how positively a candidate could express it. By its very definition, however, personal commitment must be expressed in practice. In discussing the role of philosophy and social science shortly before the enrolment examinations in 1956, the *Kuang-ming jih-pao* reiterated to prospective students that Marxist-Leninist theory was not just dogma but a guide to action; the positive role of the Marxist-Leninist teacher and the Communist cadre was a glorious one.[45] In summary, national language and political general knowledge were designed to test commitment as well as aptitude, but in practice, it may well have been easier to test the latter than the former.

Examination content brings into focus the assessment of scripts. Examination questions were set centrally by the Topics Committee, but the evaluation of answer scripts required much delegation of authority to the administrative areas, provinces and cities. The responsibility for organizing Script Assessment Committees *(shih-chüan p'ing-yüeh wei-yüan hui)* lay with the local enrolment work committees, with membership subject to the approval of the National Enrolment Committee.[46] In July 1956 one source referred to the appointment of nearly 10,000 university and higher middle school teachers as members of script assessment committees.[47] The Education Ministries required that each institution of higher education send experienced teachers to assist in examination marking; in the past the few teachers sent to mark and assess had been inferior and negligent. Assessment was to be considered part of the normal routine during the summer term.[48] In addition, higher middle teachers were recruited, primarily to co-ordinate standards at the two levels of education, but probably also because there were too few markers from the universities.

Unified guidelines for standards and methods of assessment were provided by the National Enrolment Committee, but the script assessment committees enjoyed considerable initiative. These were instructed by local enrolment work committees to formulate plans for reading scripts and allocating marks and were divided into sections for different subjects; answers to examination questions were determined by individual study and group discussion.[49]

In spite of only general supervision from the centre, however, there was nevertheless an attempt to maintain a consistent standard of marking and evaluation within each assessment committee's jurisdiction, in order to evaluate scripts fairly. An agreed system of mark allocation was in operation, but it proved more difficult to eliminate personal bias among members.

Moreover, while unanimity in assessment was easier to achieve in subjects like mathematics, physics, and chemistry, questions of interpretation were more likely to arise in national language, political general knowledge (in spite of its scientific nature), and history. These subjects often had several acceptable answers and the sections into which markers were organized played a crucial role in reaching a collective decision.

In the assessment of scripts, performance in subjects related to a candidate's preferences appears to have been more important than a rigid pass mark. In the early years when candidates were few, admission standards seem to have been extremely low: many entering engineering specialties in 1952 only scored an overall average of twenty marks for all examination subjects and consequently found study difficult.[50]

This average was presumably the lowest pass mark, but more significantly, it would have disguised both better and worse performance as well as aptitude in specific subjects. For example, in 1955 the *Jen-min chiao-yü* reported that of those higher middle graduates examined for natural science and engineering in 1954, 73 per cent failed in mathematics and 72 per cent in physics. Even in 1956 only 25 per cent of those higher middle graduates registered for natural science and engineering, and 26 per cent of humanities candidates, gained an average of 60 per cent in the required papers. At the same time Nanking Engineering Institute complained that new students' knowledge of such basic subjects as mathematics was woefully inadequate.[51] Exactly how many such students were admitted was not stated, but clearly the focus of assessment was the individual examination subject.

But, although aptitude in subject areas still remained a major criterion in 1957, overall averages, which had a bearing on acceptance standards, were becoming increasingly important as sources of candidates became more plentiful and their quality was raised.

Press sources indicated that examination performance improved during the years 1952-57, even though it varied markedly according to area, institution, and subject.[52] For example, in 1955 the average mark of successful candidates for all subjects in the enrolment examinations had reached 77 per cent in the case of Ch'inghua University and 72 per cent in that of Peking University.[53] Figures from other areas presented a similar picture: a survey of the examination success of higher middle graduates from two areas in Szechwan Province showed that the numbers of those with marks above 80 per cent in national language had increased by 10.62 per cent in 1956 as compared to 1954, and in mathematics the relevant figure was 12.6 per cent.[54] Taking a national perspective, the *Jen-min chiao-yü* asserted that the average mark of successful candidates for all examination subjects had been increasing by about 5 per cent each year since 1952 and in 1957 was 10 per cent higher than in 1956.[55]

While scattered statistics of this nature preclude any coherent tabulation of examination results, there is little doubt that the operation of the selection system was producing intense competition for entry to higher education.

6

The Elite-Mass Structure

The CCP leaders' educational philosophy compelled them to strike a delicate balance between the demands of a developing economy and their egalitarian social goals. Though the selection process was designed to widen educational opportunity as well as serve national construction, it resulted in the creation of those inequalities so often characteristic of development.

The results of selection may best be understood through an examination of the location of institutions. During the years 1949-53 attempts were made to ameliorate uneven distribution; the number of institutions in coastal provinces and cities was reduced from 118 to 113, while those in the hinterland increased from 87 to 114. As a result, hinterland engineering institutes grew from 11 to 22, agriculture and forestry institutes from 9 to 17, medical and pharmacy institutes from 7 to 18, and teacher training institutes from 7 to 31. At the same time the proportion of students in the coastal region fell from 61.49 to 55.9 per cent, while in the hinterland it rose from 38.6 to 44.1 per cent. Within this overall perspective student numbers in the North-East increased by 2.5 times and in the North-West Area by almost 7 times. Significantly, in the North-East Area the number of students enrolled in both engineering and teacher training quadrupled during the period 1949-57. Likewise, engineering recorded a twelve-fold increase in the North-West Area.[1]

These numbers indicated an attempt to spread educational opportunity more evenly. Thus academic priorities will be seen against the background of institution redistribution, even if the method of allocating successful candidates only produced further inequality within the education system.

The regional redistribution of institutions would have been irrelevant, however, unless the area student quotas were filled. Statistics show that this presented considerable difficulty; students favoured some areas less than others. For example, in 1955 a total of 5,965 students were to be enrolled in institutions in the North-West Area but only 6,456 registered for examination. As only 3,621 were considered suitable for entry, that area was left 2,344 short of its quota. In contrast, the East China Area's quota was 26,575 for the same year in which 56,559 applicants registered; the enrolment examination produced 36,621 acceptable candidates, 10,046 more than necessary.[2] These disparities meant that standards of enrolled students varied from area to area. Candidate examination performance, for example, was higher in East China than the North-West, and those of inferior calibre would have been distributed to areas lacking their full complement. Regional inequalities were being intensified.

It is against this background that overall national priorities must be seen. The three major emphases were engineering, teacher training, and medicine. Taking the years 1947 and 1957 as vantage points, the major changes in enrolment priorities are underlined. Figures for these subjects, with the addition of agriculture for comparative purposes, may be tabulated as follows:

TABLE 7: ENROLMENT PRIORITIES: PERCENTAGES (1947 and 1957)

Subject	1947	1957
Engineering	17.82	37.05
Teacher Training	13.47	24.50
Medicine (inc. Pharmacy)	7.66	11.38
Agriculture	6.56	9.10

The emphases laid down by the Kuomintang were reiterated by the Communists. There was, however, a dramatic drop in the percentage of students enrolled in political science and law as well as finance and economics which for the same two years showed a reversal from 24.37 to 1.8 per cent and 11.45 to 3.2 per cent respectively.[3] Absolute numbers, though not entirely consistent in their terms of reference, nevertheless confirm the patterns shown above for engineering and teacher training. For example, it was stated in March 1957 that between 1949 and 1956, 95,000 had graduated in engineering and 58,000 in teacher training. Additionally, the same source noted that there were currently 150,000 enrolled in engineering and 99,000 in teacher training. The total number of graduates for all fields in the same period was given as 302,500 while those enrolled for all subjects amounted in 1957 to 408,000.[4] Finally, the pre-eminence of engineering was indicated by the fact that of 148 new specialties established during the years 1952-57, 95 were in that field.[5]

Such priorities may be even more clearly analyzed by reference to the actual numbers enrolled in specific subjects during the years from 1949-56:[6]

TABLE 8: THE NUMBER OF STUDENTS ENROLLED IN HIGHER EDUCATION, BASIC
AND SPECIAL TRAINING COURSES. (THOUSANDS)
(1949-50 and 1952-53 to 1955-56)

Subjects	1949-50	1952-53	1953-54	1954-55	1955-56
Engineering	30.3	66.6	80.0	95.0	109.6
Agriculture	9.8	13.3	12.8	12.8	17.3
Forestry	0.6	2.2	2.6	3.1	4.0
Finance & Economics	19.4	22.0	13.5	11.2	11.4
Political					
Science & Law	7.3	3.8	3.9	4.0	4.8
Medicine					
& Pharmacy	15.2	24.7	29.0	33.9	36.5
Physical					
Education	0.3	0.3	1.1	1.9	2.3
Natural Sciences	7.0	9.6	12.4	17.1	20.0
Humanities	11.8	13.5	14.2	18.3	18.9
Teacher Training	12.0	31.5	40.0	53.1	60.7
Fine Arts	2.8	3.6	2.7	2.6	2.2
Total	116.5	191.1	212.2	253.0	287.7

In spite of a definite order of priorities, however, there appears to have been considerable difficulty in co-ordinating enrolment quotas and national construction needs. It was admitted in 1957 that only a general prediction of the latter could be made, with the result that it was not always possible to achieve a correlation between specialty student numbers and the minute divisions of expertise nationally required. Some specialties would eventually be found to have enrolled too many, others too few.[7]

Furthermore, however persuasive the ideological preparation of candidates, the preference system still allowed them considerable choice and their own tastes did not necessarily coincide with the State's wishes. Of the three major priorities, engineering, teacher training, and medicine, there were apparently few problems in persuading applicants to register for the first and the last, which were considered to offer lucrative rewards on graduation. But there is abundant evidence that teacher training was an unpopular field of study, owing to the limited career opportunities it offered. Concessions to candidates' preferences and aptitudes were exacting a heavy price in terms of the Party's wider social goals.

Meanwhile, vertical control was strengthening the Ministries' and academic authorities' influence on enrolment. During the Cultural Revolution it was claimed that Liu Shao-ch'i's supporters in the Education Ministries and "bourgeois'' intellectuals in the universities had jointly promoted this growing emphasis on expertise at the expense of revolutionary commitment. For example, Red Guard sources claimed that, at a national conference of representatives from comprehensive universities in September 1953, the Minister of Higher Education, Yang Hsiu-feng, praised emphasis on expertise, asserting that the basic function of universities and institutes was the cultivation of specialized personnel. He was also accused of speaking in a similar vein in 1956, when he ''frantically opposed Chairman Mao's instructions.''[8] But these accusations were exaggerated. In fact, the eventual polarization of the two interpretations was not so much the product of conflict between conscious personal wills as the result of the translation of educational philosophy into practice.

Thus, although a high ranking group of figures in education centred around Liu Shao-ch'i and the Ministries can be generally called Liuist, there is no evidence to suggest a clearly determined attempt to advocate a policy directly opposed to that of Mao Tse-tung. But by making expertise their central focus the Liuists did relegate politics to the background.

This stress on individual academic excellence prepared the basis for an intellectual elite. This was initially foreshadowed by a call in 1957 to raise the quality of entrants, and the factory analogy was used: ''If we see institutions of higher education as factories, then enrolling new students is like selecting raw materials; whether the raw materials are good or bad can influence directly the quality of products.'' This statement reflected the Liuist interpretation.[9] But more powerful invective was yet to come. The *Jen-min jih-pao* echoed this theme, placing a premium on the selection of higher middle graduates; this was clearly an indirect criticism of other candidates, especially those from outside the education system. In the past there had been cases of entrants who had either found study so difficult that they were forced to leave university or struggled desperately to master their subject. The article then tacitly admitted that expanding sources of candidates during the period 1949-56 had meant lowering entry standards.[10]

The new policy was elitist: candidates of academic quality were favoured, and this in practice meant those from within the education system. In his opening speech at the establishment of the 1957 National Enrolment Committee, Yang Hsiu-feng emphasized growing selectivity: ''The raising of quality is the central task of higher education from now on.''[11] Furthermore, as early as August 1956, the *Chung-kuo ch'ing-nien pao* emphasized that only a small minority of applicants would be admitted: ''If candidates think that only entry to higher education gives them a future, then thousands of youth throughout the country have no chance in life, because only a small minority can be accepted.''[12] Other sources reiterated that the large numbers in the 1956 enrolment plan were exceptional and that the situation would return to normal in 1957.[13] Compared to the early period of unified enrolment, competition for entry to higher education had by now become intense.

Further theoretical formulation for more rigorous selection was contained in a statement by the Minister of Education, Chang Hsi-jo, an intellectual outside the CCP, who used the treasure pagoda analogy:

> This summer not all higher middle graduates will be promoted to higher education. In no country in the world is it possible for all students at one level to go up. In all cases the primary school student numbers are the greatest, those in middle school are comparatively few, the figure for higher education is the smallest, and these together form a treasure pagoda. This is the common law of educational development, and the norm of social life. The reason for the promotion of the majority of higher middle graduates last year was the enormous development in socialist construction.[14]

In this connection, an educational journal quoted the example of the Soviet Union, where only one in ten of equivalent candidates could be promoted to higher education.[15]

The treasure pagoda analogy may be illustrated by reference to numbers enrolled at each educational level.[16]

TABLE 9: NUMBER OF ENROLLED STUDENTS (THOUSANDS)
(Pre-1949 and 1949-57)

	Higher Education	Vocational Middle Schools	Middle Schools	Primary Schools
Pre-liberation peak year	155	383	1,496	23,683
1949	117	229	1,039	24,391
1950	137	257	1,305	28,924
1951	153	383	1,568	43,154
1952	191	636	2,490	51,100
1953	212	668	2,933	51,664
1954	253	608	3,587	51,218
1955	288	537	3,900	53,126
1956	403	812	5,165	63,464
1957	441	778	6,281	64,279

Note: In addition, a large number of agricultural middle schools and other vocational middle schools were opened in 1958, with an enrolment of two million students. The figures for students in institutions of higher education given here do not include research students.

Finally, the female student ratio, with one exception, declined at each higher rung of the educational ladder:

TABLE 10: PROPORTION OF FEMALE STUDENTS TO TOTAL NUMBER OF STUDENTS (percentage of total in each category)

	Higher Education	Vocational Middle Schools	Middle Schools	Primary Schools
Pre-liberation peak year	17.8	21.1	20.0	25.5
1949	19.8	—	—	—
1952	23.4	24.9	23.5	32.9
1957	23.3	26.5	30.8	34.5

Nevertheless, even though the treasure pagoda was a common law of educational development, it was stated that "in the journey from socialist to communist society we must universalize not only primary but middle school education. Furthermore, in future we will gradually make higher education universal. But at the beginning of socialist society the treasure pagoda cannot be dispensed with, because production forces are not great enough."[17] What is significant here is the implication that universalization will be achieved on the basis of elevation. Primary and middle education would be improved and extended, as only then could the elevation and ultimate universalization of higher education be achieved. Thus these priorities meant "levelling up" rather than "levelling down"; the integration of education and society would be abandoned, at least for the short term, so that workers could be turned into engineers and peasants into agricultural experts.[18]

In fact, the resulting emphasis on expertise had made academic authorities so conscious of standards that educational administrative bodies in some areas ranked middle schools under their jurisdiction according to their graduates' performance in the enrolment examinations.[19]

When new educational policies were being debated in 1958 there were complaints of too much emphasis on candidates' scholastic attainments at the expense of their political quality; it was said that the "rightists" exposed in the struggles earlier that year had in many cases been considered academically exceptional prior to their exposure.[20]

The treasure pagoda analogy, however, merely placed the seal of legitimacy on trends already evident. Allocation of better candidates was enabling more prestigious institutions and specialties to maintain higher standards, thereby increasing inequality.

The mechanics of selection have been earlier outlined, and general principles adopted for the distribution of candidates who had not succeeded in being admitted according to their preferences formed the first link in the vicious circle of inequality. Those whose standard fell below that demanded by their preferences were sent to institutions and specialties which few candidates had chosen. For instance, applicants for engineering, medical, and natural science subjects were often directed to agricultural fields or scientific curricula in teacher training. Unsuccessful candidates in literature and history were allocated to humanities subjects in pedagogical institutions.[21] Unpopular fields like geology and mining also often received students of inferior quality.

Even when a candidate had been admitted to a department, the allocation process was still not complete. As departments consisted of a number of specialties, students had to state their preferences once more, although no examination was involved at this stage. This process, especially relevant to engineering specialties, existed, of course, prior to the reform of the preference system in 1957. It is a matter of conjecture how many applicants were actually given their preference by a department's administrative personnel, but some students seem to have been bitterly disappointed.[22] Once again the most reputable specialties received the most able students.

Elitist patterns were in any case already present in the institutional structure of higher education. Courses in universities and institutes were divided into two types: basic courses *(pen-k'e)*, and special training courses *(chuan hsiu-k'e)*.[23] While the basic courses in universities and institutes took four or five years, these special training courses were two years or less in length and especially numerous in such fields as engineering, teacher training, and agriculture and forestry. They were designed to train rapidly greater numbers of personnel at certain technical levels. This necessitated the co-operation of the Ministry of Education with other Ministries; for example, it collaborated with the Ministry of Agriculture in the establishment of a course in water conservancy at Ch'inghua University. In 1952 it was stated that a considerable proportion of new students was being accommodated in special training courses.[24] These were said to be equivalent in standard to the basic courses, differing only in their shorter duration and more concentrated curricula. Yet doubt was cast upon this claim when the Party considered it necessary to admonish students whom it accused of despising special training courses.[25] In fact, the rationale for their establishment suggested that their students were not equal to those in basic courses. An enrolment handbook, issued in 1955, stated:

> In order to satisfy the country's economic construction needs . . . very many institutions have set up specialties of special training courses. . . . Their aim is to train high level technical personnel with a definite theoretical basis. . . . After graduation they will all be able to lead production. . . . The special training courses will produce a great many cadres.[26]

Two main conclusions can be drawn from this examination of special training courses. Firstly, as these courses were usually concentrated in fields like teacher training, unpopular with potential students, it seems likely that they were of low quality. It was through the special training courses that the least able higher middle graduates were given a training which equipped them, for example, to fill posts in middle school teaching where demand exceeded supply. Moreover, numbers of primary school teacher applicants would have been sent to courses of this kind. Secondly, although cadres received preference in enrolment, they were not necessarily admitted to prestigious institutions and specialties. It seems likely that after instruction in the latest technology in special training courses, they would have returned to their original units.

The selection system and the distribution process promoted a meritocracy; the "basic-special training course" dichotomy brought inequality of opportunity. A third ingredient now confirmed the emergence of a stratification system within higher education: the concentration of candidates' preferences in certain academic fields and institutions.

Prospective students were later accused of listing specialties in order of merit when applying for enrolment examinations. Engineering subjects were especially favoured and in 1953 such specialty preferences, regardless of order, represented 55 per cent of the total number of applications, while teacher training, agriculture and forestry, and politics inspired less enthusiasm among prospective students.[27] This pattern recurred throughout the period 1952-57.

For example, in 1957 those registered in the Shanghai examination area included candidates from both within and outside the education system. Over 18,700 youth were to participate in enrolment examinations, including 14,404 graduating from middle education (the majority of whom came from ordinary general middle schools), 2,479 young workers, and 1,871 intellectual youth, some of whom had left school but not yet been employed. Of the preferences of such candidates, the natural sciences and engineering represented 61.1 per cent, agriculture and forestry, health, and physical education 21.8 per cent, and the humanities, law, and finance and economics 16.1 per cent.[28] The remaining percentage was not specified. What emerges from the Shanghai example is that engineering maintained its earlier popularity, while others such as agriculture and forestry continued to be low in candidates' estimation. Teacher training is not given a separate rating, but as it encompassed different disciplines, it is presumably included within the categories mentioned, though unfortunately its exact share cannot be determined.

The popularity of certain academic fields was clearly connected with candidates' perception of future material rewards. This perception would in turn have been a reflection of the ideological preparation candidates had been given prior to registration. The media played a part in this process and seem to have emphasized the importance of some fields, while neglecting to promote others adequately. For example, on 18 June 1952, the Hong Kong newspaper, *Ta-kung pao*, noted that numbers of women, influenced by Soviet films, had expressed a desire to enter engineering institutes. Similarly, on 11 July 1952 the *Jen-min jih-pao* claimed that many wanted to study water conservancy engineering, after hearing a report about an expert in that field. Perhaps some academic disciplines received too little advertisement in the media.

The *Jen-min jih-pao* feared that the failure of some teacher training institutes to enrol their full complement in 1951 would have an adverse effect on national construction. It happened that many candidates were reluctant to express preference for teacher training in view of its lack of prestige and low salary:[29] for instance, in July 1952 only 5 per cent registered teacher training as their first preference.[30]

Some students were said to be unwilling to enter agricultural studies because of a bourgeois attitude towards manual labour,[31] and politics was believed to be a haven for inferior students who could only hope to become minor cadres on graduation.[32]

Finally, while there was never any doubt about the prestigious status of such institutions as Peking University, many candidates nevertheless failed to understand the important role played by comprehensive universities. In fact, the function the latter performed was crucial. Their courses in natural science were the basis on which specialized study in the technical institutes rested; their courses in the humanities were the backbone of teaching in the rest of the education system.[33]

Thus, by 1957 the selection system, institutional structure, and the concentration of candidates' preferences were producing an elite-mass structure in higher education: the elite were those students of the best quality who, as a general rule, had originally come from within the education system; the mass consisted, firstly, of those enrolled in the least popular basic course specialties, and secondly, of those from outside the education system recruited for the special training courses. The elite-mass structure is a theoretical concept, but it provides a useful framework within which inequalities in higher education may be understood.

The elite-mass structure was analagous to social stratification, and like social stratification it did not preclude social mobility. Measures to increase the worker-peasant contingent in higher education were an integral part of the Party's policy of creating proletarian intellectuals. Brief reference has already been made to the direction of workers and peasants to certain institutions and specialties but their general situation now merits further analysis.

The enrolment opportunities of cadres were limited. Certainly, their status on return to production would have been enhanced as a result of retraining, but their chances of material advancement and upward mobility were considerably fewer than those enjoyed by graduates of higher middle schools. Cadres, however, were only one element among students of worker and peasant origin. It has been suggested that the policy aimed at increasing the numbers of workers and peasants in higher education was at least a partial denial of the Party's philosophy. The earlier analysis of *ch'eng-fen* and *ch'u shen* emphasized achieved as opposed to ascribed status. Performance was the crucial factor. Nevertheless, in January 1955 the *Jen-min jih-pao* defined students of worker and peasant origin *(kung-nung ch'eng-fen ti hsüeh-sheng)* as including children of workers and peasants and worker and peasant cadres.[34] The phrase "children of workers and peasants" would presumably have included the "five types of Red Youth."

By these criteria and under the enrolment regulations of 1955, 1956, and 1957, candidates of worker and peasant origin would have included the following: (i) a proportion of the graduates of higher middle schools, (ii) some of the graduates from vocational middle schools, (iii) personnel from Party bodies together with a major proportion of those from government organs, production units, and mass organizations like trade unions, and (iv) retired and seconded soldiers. Not all of these would have been successful in the enrolment examinations.

It was stated optimistically in 1955 that higher education had opened its doors to workers and peasants, with the result that they now represented 28.9 per cent of students, as opposed to 21.9 per cent in the academic year 1953-54.[35] In May 1958 the *Peking Review* surveyed past years' enrolment, and the following percentages for those of worker and peasant origin in higher education were provided, but excluded were the two academic years given above by the *Jen-min jih-pao*: 1952-53, 20.46 per cent; 1955-56, 29.20 per cent; 1956-57, 34.29 per cent; 1957-58, 36.42 per cent. Later in 1958 the *Kuang-ming jih-pao* confirmed the percentages for 1952-53 and 1957-58. These statistics generally correlate with the more comprehensive view of middle as well as higher education given in *Ten Great Years* (see Table 11).[36]

The Party's policy of increasing the proportion of worker and peasant students in higher education must also be seen within the context of primary and middle education.

TABLE 11: PROPORTION OF STUDENTS OF WORKER AND PEASANT ORIGIN TO
TOTAL NUMBER OF STUDENTS (1951-57)
(PERCENTAGE OF TOTAL IN EACH CATEGORY)

	Higher Education	Vocational Middle Schools	Middle Schools
1951	19.1	56.6	51.3
1952	20.5	57.1	56.1
1953	21.9	55.9	57.7
1954	—	58.8	60.7
1955	29.0	62.0	62.2
1956	34.1	64.1	66.0
1957	36.3	66.6	69.1

Note: Data for students in higher education include research students.

In giving two figures which tally with those later provided by *Ten Great Years*, the *Jen-min chiao-yü* proudly claimed that in the 1956-57 academic year those of worker and peasant origin in primary schools represented 80 per cent, those in middle schools 66 per cent, and those in higher education 34 per cent.[37] But as workers and peasants were 80 per cent of the country's population, the above figures are not very impressive.[38] Clearly, the hurdles of competitive entrance examinations and financial means were still operating against workers and peasants as late as 1957.

Moreover, these figures appear even less impressive when they are viewed against the background of student distribution. In 1956-57 when those of worker and peasant origin represented 34 per cent of those enrolled in higher education, their number in the comprehensive universities in the major cities was only 10 to 20 per cent, a proportion which was said to be decreasing rather than increasing. In contrast, the percentage of those of worker and peasant origin in teacher training and agriculture and forestry institutes in the provincial cities was considerably higher.[39] This may be seen as one aspect of the elite-mass structure in action.

In addition, the educational revolution of 1958 brought a more candid assessment of worker and peasant entry to higher education. In July of that year the *Kung-jen jih-pao* claimed that previously the children of workers and peasants, as well as those worker and peasant cadres who had knowledge of the class and production struggles, had frequently been denied entry to higher education because of their lack of scholastic success.[40] At the same time the *Wen-hui pao* added that slighting the importance of those of worker and peasant origin or doubting their qualifications were manifestations of "emphasizing expertise at the expense of politics."[41] These tendencies are all the more surprising in view of the political investigation of candidates, which barred those with unsatisfactory political records, and the preferential acceptance rubric, designed to facilitate the entry of those of worker and peasant origin. Clearly, these aspects of the enrolment process left much to be desired.[42] In any event, the proportion of workers and peasants was considered too low and the political quality of student bodies still inadequate.

This is not to say, however, that the special devices to assist worker and peasant applicants had been entirely neglected. They had not. Undoubtedly, they were succeeding in gaining admission but the special post-entry provisions designed for one section of them, worker-peasant cadres and production workers, suggest that their standards were often not comparable to the majority of students. These arrangements usually took the form of worker-peasant classes *(kung-nung pan)*; for example, it was stated that whereas the Department of Machine Building at Ch'inghua University ran only one worker-peasant class in the 1953-54 academic year, this had increased to three in 1954-55. The Department of Civil Engineering also conducted a worker-peasant class during the latter year.[43] The fact that these classes were actually in operation would tend to refute the charge of Cultural Revolution vintage that Liu Shao-ch'i and "bourgeois" academic authorities had acted to exclude those of worker and peasant origin. Although the success of the Ch'inghua classes has not been documented, a survey was carried out concerning similar classes in Shanghai's Chungshan Medical Institute and the Peking Railway Institute. This report argued that worker and peasant cadre students at Chungshan Medical Institute had hitherto been deficient in academic training but their practical experience more than compensated for this and ultimately helped them to understand theory. Moreover, the 35 students in the worker-peasant class at the Peking Railway Institute had, by the year 1957-58, completed, in three and a half years, curricula which the majority of students could only learn in seven to ten years. As a result, they had acquired the scientific knowledge necessary for socialist railway construction.[44]

Nevertheless, it would appear that the examples quoted were exceptional, as other evidence suggests that those of worker and peasant origin were not of uniformly high academic quality. Academic authorities were anxious to maintain standards, even if this meant the exclusion of many of those of worker and peasant origin. This was by no means a policy of social discrimination, but a refusal to compromise on academic excellence. For example, in late 1957 an assistant lecturer in the Department of Structure at Shanghai's T'ungchi University was accused of opposing the automatic entry, without examination, of a small number of the best students from worker-peasant rapid middle schools on the pretext that such a policy would hinder scientific development.[45] It is perhaps noteworthy that Ch'inghua and Chungshan were institutions of exceptionally high reputation and may well have been in some way able to attract the best workers and peasants.

That the success of the above students of worker and peasant origin is atypical is also suggested by the numbers who had to withdraw from higher education or repeat courses. This seems to have been especially common in the early years before the new system of higher education had been consolidated. It was stated that in the academic year 1953-54 about 7,000 students withdrew from higher education because of poor performance in courses; there were also considerable numbers of students who preferred to study for two years in the same class rather than withdraw. In some classes repeaters reached 30 per cent of the total.[46] There is much evidence to suggest that worker and peasant students would have been prominent among dropouts and repeaters.

A general summary may now be made of the social origin of enrolment. By 1957 only a third of those enrolled were of worker and peasant origin and such students were as a rule confined to the less prestigious specialties and institutions in provincial cities. But there is reason to believe, however, that a small number of workers and peasants of exceptionally high academic calibre had succeeded in entering famous institutions like Ch'inghua and T'ungchi. Given growing emphasis on academic excellence, the enrolment process became a channel of mobility for the very able among candidates of worker and peasant origin. Functional specificity needed every individual with ability. Meanwhile, a developing economy was creating new centres of power, and education had become a prime determinant of this new stratification. The Chinese Communist education system, like Imperial institutions, produced social mobility, though precisely in the act of doing so, limited its scope.

The extent of the mobility which those of worker and peasant origin were capable of achieving can be documented through the examination of (i) their elevation from special training courses to basic courses and (ii) their promotion from spare-time middle level to full-time higher education. In 1958 the *Chung-kuo ch'ing-nien pao* referred to examples of old worker and peasant cadres who, in the space of two or three years, had studied courses which took most youth five or six years. Thus it was shown that cadres with very little previous school education were able to acquire scientific knowledge. For instance, a Party committee secretary from a chemical factory in Mukden, studying in the third-year grade in the Department of Chemical Engineering at Tientsin Polytechnic Institute, had only received a lower middle second-year education, but only two months after entry had been promoted from a special training course to a basic course.[47]

In fact, the enrolment regulations were so phrased to take into account the widely different qualifications of candidates. In this context the role of spare-time education *(yeh-yü chiao-yü)* must not be underestimated. Chinese Communist sources were replete with instances of production cadres and workers of high political quality, extensive production experience, and exceptional scholastic achievement, who succeeded in being admitted to higher education through spare time study. Certainly, some famous production models appear to have been directly seconded to higher education in order to improve their theoretical technical knowledge, but graduates of spare-time institutions, often established in factories, took examinations for entry to technical institutes. In 1954 there were said to have been 119 graduates of middle level spare-time schools in production units in Shanghai who entered higher education this way. Later, in 1956, 42 spare-time middle school graduates from Shanghai were similarly examined for, and admitted to, Tientsin Polytechnical Institute and Peking Steel Institute. Furthermore, during the academic year 1957-58 it was claimed that in the Peking Mining Institute alone there were several hundred cadres and workers who had been promoted in this way from mines and factories. Finally, at the beginning of the 1957 academic year, courses at the three institutions of Ch'inghua University, the Peking Steel Institute, and Peking Petroleum Institute included 120 new students who had started out as worker and peasant cadres or production workers. These had formerly studied in spare-time schools and later took the enrolment examinations.[48]

Unfortunately, Chinese Communist sources are not always explicit as to the specific type of spare-time school which permitted worker and peasant mobility to higher education, but the scattered examples given seem to have been spare-time general middle schools. In conclusion, in the case of spare-time schools as in other channels, the upwardly mobile among those of worker and peasant origin had not only to surmount the academic hurdle of being as good, if not better than other candidates, but they also had to break down the barrier of reluctance to help them on the part of leadership personnel. Although there is little or no evidence to hand, it would be surprising if such opposition had not been as great or greater to cadres who came under the equivalent cultural level rubric.

In the formulation of enrolment policies according to manpower needs the State had always to strike a delicate balance between personnel to be trained and the utilization of those who had already been trained. But the overriding need to tap all available talent permitted a limited mobility for those of worker and peasant origin. The elite-mass structure was thus not incompatible with upward mobility. But the last selection of examples has been concerned mainly with those of worker and peasant origin from outside the education system; the next will focus on those both from within and without, but with marginally greater attention to the former.

Those of worker and peasant origin would have been disadvantaged in the education system because of financial circumstances and home environment. These two factors were naturally closely linked. Initially, the cost of higher education will be assessed in terms of State and familial expenditure. In an article implicitly defending the treasure pagoda system, the *Jen-min chiao-yü* stated in April 1957 that educational expenditure represented 7.14 per cent of the State budget and that this figure only referred to the three levels of the full-time education system, with the addition of various other teacher training institutions. But if expenditure on vocational middle schools and certain other ad hoc educational arrangements for cadres had been included, this figure would have risen to 10 per cent of the national budget.

Specifically, it was calculated that each student in higher education cost 1,200 *yüan* per annum. It was not recorded how this sum was arrived at, but the article significantly went on to explain that since peasants earned an average annual income of sixty *yüan,* then each university student must cost the combined earnings of twenty peasants. Similarly, a middle school student would require 360 *yüan* or the income of six peasants.

An examination of the familial expenditure incurred by education indicates the extent to which those of worker and peasant origin were disadvantaged. It was argued that while a middle school student needed an outlay of 260 *yuan* a year from the State and 100 *yüan* from his family, for the university student the equivalent totals were 1,000 and 200 *yüan.* [49]

The treasure pagoda system was defended in these terms. Here the great variation in individual incomes comes into focus, and the following tables, when read together with the statistics given immediately above, bring out in sharp relief considerable urban-rural discrepancies. [50]

TABLE 12: INCREASE IN AVERAGE ANNUAL WAGE OF WORKERS AND OTHER EMPLOYEES (1952-57)

| | Average Annual Wage *(Yüan)* | Index Numbers | |
		1952 = 100	Preceding year = 100
1952	446	100	—
1953	496	111.2	111.2
1954	519	116.4	104.6
1955	534	119.7	102.9
1956	610	136.8	114.2
1957	637	142.8	104.4

The average peasant's salary of 60 *yüan* seems slight indeed when a familial contribution of 200 *yüan* was required to maintain a student in higher education. Although urban salaries appear to have been appreciably higher, the cost of higher education would nevertheless have placed a considerable burden on families of production workers.

TABLE 13: RAPID INCREASE IN INCOME OF PEASANTS (1952-57)
  (index numbers, 1952 = 100)

1953	106.9
1954	110.7
1955	120.7
1956	124.3
1957	127.9

Against this background, the provision of financial aid would only have alleviated, not solved, the problems which students of worker and peasant origin, especially, faced in higher education. In general, tuition fees were not charged but a student's expenses, particularly at the more famous institutions in Peking and other major cities, would have placed a heavy burden on children from poor peasant families and those of factory workers. As in the case of middle schools, assistance took the form of financial aid rather than scholarships. In the early years of the regime financial aid was dispensed to all students, regardless of personal circumstances, but this did not cover all expenses. In January 1955, however, this policy gave way to a more selective one whereby aid was given according to need. Ostensibly, there were two main reasons for this: the need for economies in State expenditure, and to eliminate waste as well as complacency among students.[51] According to these new provisions local governments would, under central guidance, determine the number of scholarships and the amount of aid available for their particular areas. The funds would then be allocated to an area's educational institutions, and students were required to obtain verification of their need from the authorities of the area in which they lived. Verification would have given specific details about number of persons in the family, parental occupation, political background, and economic conditions. The information would be enclosed with a candidate's application for financial aid, later being assessed by the educational institution concerned. Institutions thus enjoyed a certain initiative, and the dispensation of aid varied accordingly. But, in general, the principle adopted was that all who needed assistance would receive it.[52] But as there were only limited funds available for financial aid and these were dispensed under an elaborate system of subsidies for various items of student expenditure, it seems probable that the assistance given by no means fully solved the problem of need, especially in the case of those of worker and peasant origin.[53]

These changes of 1955 brought not only greater attention to need in specific cases but also further incentives to certain students and academic fields. For example, in 1955 and 1956, special assistance, called transferred cadre financial aid *(tiao-kan jen-min chu-hsüeh chin)* and production worker financial aid *(chan-yeh kung-jen chu-hsüeh chin),* was given to relevant categories. The former applied to all serving cadres who had taken part in national construction for three years as well as retired and seconded soldiers who had worked for a similar period, subject to verification by their original units. Production worker financial aid referred only to the one category. In addition, students in teacher training institutes were all given financial aid, apparently without recourse to a means test, and primary school teachers with three years' service received assistance under the transferred cadre rubric.[54]

To the extent that the new system addressed itself to cases of need it enabled poor worker and peasant youth to receive higher education. Moreover, transferred cadre financial aid assisted mature students of worker and peasant origin. But this support for production cadres and workers must be seen in the context of the limited purposes for which they were recruited; because they were allocated to certain fields associated with their former employment, their opportunities were restricted. Admittedly, there were "free application" cadres who theoretically had great choice in their field of study, but they appear to have been the exception rather than the rule. The new regulations of 1955 must thus be seen not as significantly widening educational opportunity but rather as providing incentives for specific academic priorities.

In 1957, however, a directive from the State Council to the Education Ministries announced the abolition of transferred cadre financial aid, the rationale being that cadres' study was preparation for employment and their life style while at university should not be too far removed from their future worker and peasant subordinates. Transferred cadre financial aid was said to have been equivalent to the living expenses of six peasants, presumably per annum, implying a sum considerably above that awarded to other students. It was argued that if cadres were treated so generously, divisions would arise within student bodies.[55] In future, cadres in economic difficulties would be able to request the financial aid available to other students.[56] In the long run, however, the effect of this would be to reduce incentive for cadres to register for higher education, as in doing so their financial aid would be less than their normal remuneration. Assuming that cadres had some choice in their transfer, this would have applied to specialist as well as "free application" cadres. Eventually, the abolition of special treatment for cadres would of itself tend to decrease rather than increase the worker and peasant contingent in higher education. Therefore, by 1957, yet another aspect of policy had come to favour those within the education system rather than those outside it.[57]

Financial aid did little to increase the worker-peasant ratio in higher education, and inequality of opportunity emerged as clearly in the destination of unsuccessful candidates. After their failure to enter higher education at the first attempt, candidates from outside were disadvantaged in comparison to those from within the education system. There were two main alternatives open to rejected candidates: preparation for a second attempt to pass the unified enrolment examinations and participation in production.[58] In fact, however, the private study at home needed for a second examination was only feasible for those whose families could forgo a youth's earnings.[59] Moreover, only higher middle graduates and intellectual youth were mentioned in connection with examination re-registration.[60]

That cadres had only one alternative if rejected in the enrolment process was implicitly stated in the *Kuang-ming jih-pao*. Government organs, production units, and educational institutions were urged to encourage cadres (including primary schoolteachers) successful in the examinations to follow allocation and to ensure that unsuccessful candidates returned to their original work. There were apparently cases where organs refused to accept the services of those rejected in the examinations; this was strongly condemned by State Council directives. Similar regulations were in force for rejected retired and seconded soldiers who had to go back to their units.[61]

As a rule, vocational middle school graduates had been sent by their production units to register for examination; if rejected, they would return to them and be allocated suitable work.[62]

Thus, in conclusion, the most cadres could hope for, once rejected, was study in spare-time schools run by enterprises, further underlining the inequality of opportunity open to rejected candidates.

The elite-mass structure had come to permeate every aspect of higher education; it was also reflected, for example, in the allocation of graduates and the recruitment of postgraduate students. A policy of unified allocation of graduates, according to central planning, was adopted in 1950. In 1952, for example, the Ministries of Personnel and Education formulated plans in co-operation with other government departments, and by 1953 the allocation system was being consolidated. Because of disparity between manpower supply and demand, graduates were assigned work, ideological preparation being conducted to ensure their compliance.[63] Graduates were then collectively dispatched, and Party as well as Youth League activists mobilized to guarantee that they followed the State Plan by taking up the posts assigned to them.[64] Ideological preparation was said to have been so successful in 1955 that many students volunteered for construction work in Tibet, where demand was great but conditions not always hospitable.[65] It seemed that young graduates were determined to go wherever the State needed them.

But other sources suggest that the reality was very different. Certain production units did not draw up their graduate requirements satisfactorily, and these in turn were insufficiently scrutinized by government departments. In addition, although graduates were allocated according to the expertise they had acquired, departments to which they were assigned sometimes failed to make adequate use of it.[66] There is no doubt, however, that experts in crucial specialized fields were appropriately allocated, while those graduates sent to inhospitable areas were frequently the least qualified.

Furthermore, by 1956 there were indications that control of graduate allocation was not as effective as had been claimed. Precisely because certain types of
expertise were in short supply, of crucial national importance, and attracted com-
mensurate material rewards, measures had to be taken to prevent graduates from
trying to sell their qualifications on an open market, albeit within a State sector.
However, it seemed that all who enjoyed higher education were to a greater or
lesser extent increasingly able to bargain with society for the price of their services.

In order to place these growing social inequalities in perspective, the numbers
of graduates at the three levels are outlined in Table 14. Table 15 shows numbers
of graduates from higher education by subject.[67]

TABLE 14: NUMBER OF GRADUATES (IN THOUSANDS) (Pre-1949 and 1949-57)

	Higher Education	Vocational Middle Schools	Middle Schools	Primary Schools
Pre-liberation peak year	25	73	326	4,633
1949	21	72	280	2,387
1950	18	75	296	2,829
1951	19	57	284	4,232
1952	32	68	221	5,942
1953	48	118	454	9,945
1954	47	169	644	10,136
1955	55	235	969	10,254
1956	63	174	939	12,287
1957	56	146	1,299	12,307

It must be emphasized, however, that there was some discrepancy between
planned and actual numbers of graduates. For example, the 269,000 students
who were reported to have graduated during the First Five-Year Plan period were
between 4 and 5 per cent fewer than the plan target, even if in the two fields of
engineering and economics and finance the projected numbers were exceeded.
This disparity appears to have been due to two factors: the failure to make allowances for dropouts, and the extension of course length in some comprehensive
universities and engineering institutes from four to five years.[68]

The academic elite among the graduates was destined for postgraduate study
in higher education. The postgraduate study period was generally four years

TABLE 15: NUMBER OF GRADUATES FROM INSTITUTIONS OF HIGHER EDUCATION (MAIN SUBJECTS) (Pre-1949 and 1949-57)

	Engineering	Agriculture	Economics and Finance	Medicine	Natural Sciences	Pedagogy	Liberal Arts
Pre-liberation peak year	4,792	2,064	2,969	1,236	1,701	3,250	2,736
1949	4,752	1,718	3,137	1,314	1,584	1,890	2,521
1950	4,711	1,477	3,305	1,391	1,468	624	2,306
1951	4,416	1,538	3,638	2,366	1,488	1,206	2,169
1952	10,213	2,361	7,263	2,636	2,215	3,077	1,676
1953	14,565	2,633	10,530	2,948	1,753	9,650	3,306
1954	15,596	3,532	6,033	4,527	802	10,551	2,683
1955	18,614	2,614	4,699	6,840	2,015	12,133	4,679
1956	22,047	3,541	4,460	5,403	3,978	17,243	4,025
1957	17,162	3,104	3,651	6,200	3,524	15,948	4,294

Note: Data include only the main faculties of institutions of higher education. In the pre-liberation peak year series, the faculty of agriculture includes the faculty of forestry, and the faculty of pedagogy includes the faculty of physical culture.

during which students carried out research under the supervision of leading scholars.

Postgraduate study was intended to train teachers for higher education and personnel capable of independent scientific research. Provision for postgraduate research was, however, confined to a small number of institutions: the comprehensive universities and some of the engineering, agriculture and forestry, and medical institutes.[69] The number of postgraduates to be enrolled by specialties and institutions was laid down centrally by the Ministry of Higher Education. For instance, in 1956 it was stated that the country's comprehensive universities would enrol 293 postgraduates *(fu po-shih)*[70]. Although no higher degrees were awarded by name, postgraduates were referred to as "candidate doctors" in the 1956 regulations and as four-year researchers *(ssu-nien yen-chiu sheng)* in 1957. Prominent institutions enrolling postgraduates were Peking University, Ch'inghua University, Peking Petroleum Institute, Peking Railway Institute, Tientsin Polytechnical Institute and Peking Agricultural Institute. It was announced that in 1956 Peking University would enrol 157 candidate doctors, the highest total for any institution.[71]

Postgraduate students were therefore a small academic elite found in a few key institutions. This was clearly demonstrated by the regulations concerning those eligible for examination registration. In 1956 these were divided into three categories: (i) graduates of basic courses in higher education who had taken part in scientific, educational, or other associated work for a period of two years, (ii) graduates of basic courses in higher education who had not so worked for two years, but who had verification of their exceptional academic calibre from their original institutions or work units, and (iii) those who were not graduates of basic courses but had verification from scientific organs, institutions of higher education or work units, confirming that they had worked for three years, were of a standard equivalent to that of basic course graduates, and had potential for scientific research. These statutes varied slightly according to field of study; for examination registration in medical fields, basic course graduates were required to have three years work experience and those of equivalent level five years of the same.[72]

Each candidate was only permitted to register for one specialty in one institution, and this had to be the subject he had previously studied. Requests to enrol in a new, though closely related, specialty would be assessed by the enrolling institution.[73] Postgraduates would not necessarily study at their alma mater.

Earlier practical experience was seen as beneficial to future theoretical study and the third eligible category did offer a channel of mobility for those of exceptional calibre who had hitherto enjoyed little formal education.

None were denied the opportunity of postgraduate study through lack of means, as all postgraduates received financial aid. The regulations were as follows: basic course graduating students as well as those who had not worked for two years each received 45 *yüan* per month and were given extra assistance by cost of living adjustments according to area. All those who had taken part in production for two years were awarded financial aid amounting to 80 per cent of their former salary, and where this did not reach 45 *yüan,* it was increased accordingly. Two main observations may be made: postgraduate financial aid was considerably above the income paid to the average peasant or worker and appears to have been roughly comparable to the salaries enjoyed by high level scientific personnel.

Individual institutions enjoyed considerable initiative in the postgraduate enrolment process. The general outlines of examination subjects were formulated by the Ministry of Higher Education, and on this basis institutions set the topics for each specialty's papers, devised according to current teaching curricula. Once topics had been determined, information concerning relevant reference texts was sent to candidates.[74]

The examination subjects were divided into three sections: (i) specialty studies, (ii) political knowledge, and (iii) foreign languages. In the specialty section, one to three papers, or at most four, were taken. Candidates could choose one of the four political knowledge papers: dialectical and historical materialism, the fundamentals of Marxism-Leninism, political and economic studies, and the history of the Chinese Revolution. Similarly, applicants selected one foreign language from those stipulated by the enrolling institution. There is no doubt that the examinations favoured basic course graduates, who were well-equipped to take specialty papers. Their greater powers of expression were a distinct advantage in all examination papers, and few candidates in the third category would have been proficient in the required foreign language.[75]

Finally, references from a candidate's university or work unit were of primary importance. Postgraduates were carefully selected on the basis of the three aspects of politics, scholarship, and health. But however rigorous the political criteria, conditions of entry to postgraduate study placed a premium on academic excellence. This academic emphasis was even more explicit in 1957. Basic course graduating students now formed a new category and those of exceptional academic quality could be immediately selected for postgraduate work by their institution.[76]

The elite-mass structure was also reflected in the unified distribution of postgraduates after the completion of their studies. Those admitted to postgraduate study under the work rubric were in most cases allocated to their former units. In contrast, graduating class students who had been immediately accepted for postgraduate study were given preference when teaching posts in higher education were filled. Some of the latter were also distributed to scientific research work in the comprehensive universities and the institutes under the Academy of Sciences.

In conclusion, the inequalities being produced by enrolment processes would ultimately be felt in society itself.

7

Revolution and Counter-Revolution

In the context of enrolment the CCP had used institutional means in its attempt to create proletarian intellectuals during the years 1949-57. Rapid middle schools were established and enrolment regulations formulated to facilitate worker and peasant entry; candidates from within the education system underwent ideological preparation. But even as late as 1958 students of worker and peasant origin still remained a minority in higher education. Meanwhile the events of the Hundred Flowers period served as a grim reminder that ideological education had been far from adequate in ensuring revolutionary commitment to the Party's goals.

An article in the July 1958 issue of the *Jen-min chiao-yü* claimed that some teachers in higher education had imparted technique *(chi-shu)* but neglected students' political thought; this became known as "teaching books but not teaching people" and was said to be a manifestation of capitalist class thought.[1] There were also concrete examples of student rightists. A graduate of the Fifty-First Middle School in Shanghai had excelled in the university enrolment examinations in 1954, but was later exposed as an enemy of the Party. His disgrace was placed squarely at the door of his middle school teachers who did not properly understand the term "good student," as they had stressed "expertise" and slighted "politics."[2] Moreover, the majority of the teachers and students in his school were of bourgeois origin; their thought had not been sufficiently reformed, and political classes and activities had become perfunctory.

The Joint Directive of the Central Committee of the CCP and the State Council, issued on 19 September 1958, sought to counter these trends.[3] This directive was a return to the fundamentals of the Party's educational philosophy, as Mao Tse-tung had expressed it in the 1930's, and in its ultimate implications it called for nothing less than the reconstruction of the education system. The CCP now aimed to reforge the link between education and society, placing politics in command. It was almost as if, in order to create proletarian intellectuals, the rules of the game had been altered and class warfare was to take place on a different battlefield.

One of the first salvoes of the 1958 educational revolution had been fired in August when Mao Tse-Tung inspected Tientsin University and stressed three points: Party committee leadership, the mass line (the CCP's close relationship with the masses), and the combination of education and productive labour.[4] Subsequent developments, however, indicate that it was the last of the three which had the greatest significance. Party committee leadership and the mass line had long been features of educational policy, but they were now to be re-emphasized.

In fact, the directive of September 1958 placed the seal of respectability on experiments already taking place. Part-time work part-time study institutions were established at the higher and the middle levels, the implication being that full-time education would gradually assume the part-time form. Meanwhile, a more thoroughgoing element of productive labour was to be introduced into full-time higher education. In July 1958 the Shanghai *Wen-hui pao* stated that polytechnical institutes, especially the new foundations, had as their basis the three unities: (i) education and politics, (ii) education and productive labour, and (iii) theory and practice.[5] The first of the unities was the most important; egalitarian social goals took precedence over the demands of a developing economy.

The admissions process felt the full impact of these new policies, on which enrolment regulations were based for the years 1958-65. Especially emphasized was the distinction between "old" and "new" intellectuals: "old" academics and experts could become loyal to socialism, while "new" ones of worker and peasant origin were trained. These twin goals were the "glorious duty of higher education."[6] This was not a major break with the previous period but a shift of emphasis was nevertheless descernible, and greater attention would now be paid to the enrolment of those of worker and peasant origin. Significantly, in July 1958 the *Kuang-ming jih-pao* quoted Lenin's injunction that the first enrolment priorities were the proletariat and the poor peasantry.[7]

It was against this background that the *Jen-min jih-pao* surveyed the defects of enrolment work during the period 1949-57. Enrolment organs and institutions of higher education had neither sufficiently relied on Party leadership nor placed politics in command. For example, the political quality of candidates had not been made the principal condition of entry. There was a general trend towards considering performance in the enrolment examinations as the main criterion; even the political general knowledge papers had been given a purely academic bent, and this resulted in candidates memorizing political books in "a life or death" struggle. Assessment and allocation of applicants had been based on numbers of marks obtained,[8] and this emphasis on academic excellence had operated against the entry of those of worker and peasant origin and had failed to remould those from other social classes.

The following three principles were therefore outlined in the 1959 Enrolment Regulations: (i) Party committee leadership, (ii) class tradition (that is, preference given to worker-peasant elements), and (iii) the responsibility of each institution for ensuring the quality of its own enrolment.[9]

The last of these principles also related to decentralization, a major characteristic of policy during the period of the Great Leap Forward. Its broader implications were that students' training would be directed to area needs, and 1958 saw the opening of locally run institutions of higher education.[10]

For this reason, there was a devolution of authority to local enrolment organs and individual institutions in 1958 and 1959; this was, however, limited to implementation, and the formulation of policy remained firmly in the hands of the Central Government. This new system was an amalgam of separate and unified enrolment, entailing greater freedom of action to provincial bodies and institutions of higher education. The Party believed that the unified admission system operating in the previous period had stifled local initiative and disregarded regional conditions. Local authorities now determined such concrete matters as the number of examination areas within a province and the actual organization of examinations, and established enrolment organs in conjunction with institutions of higher education; institutes in a given province, *hsien,* or city carried out enrolment work jointly through mutual consultation concerning the admission and distribution of students. Certain exceptions, however, like fine arts, physical education, and foreign language institutes continued to carry out individual enrolment, although special provision was made for these to carry out joint enrolment where appropriate. But this local initiative had to operate within the framework of the allocated numbers in the national plan, which reflected the country's overall needs. Moreover, any variation in academic qualifications demanded by particular provinces had to be reported to, and approved by, the Ministry of Education.

Finally, such crucial matters as examination subject outlines and candidate eligibility were still determined by the Central Government. Central leadership guaranteed plan fulfilment; decentralized management permitted local flexibility.

During the years 1949-57 different types of enrolments, unified, joint, and individual, were designated for various categories of institution. Inequalities, leading to an elite-mass structure, emerged within higher education. The period 1958-65 saw extensive modification of unified enrolment, but once again special regulations for different institutions only intensified the inequalities emerging previously. Furthermore, the years 1960-65 saw partial recentralization, as a greater number of institutions could enrol throughout the country, even if the implementation of enrolment was still carried out within the scope of provinces and cities. Unified leadership from the centre was now combined with regional management; provinces and cities managed admissions work by establishing enrolment organs for institutions of higher education under their jurisdiction. This task was undertaken according to unified regulations laid down by the Central Government. The words "unified enrolment" were being heard again,[11] and any devolved initiative fell to provinces and cities rather than institutions. Moreover, criteria for the selection of students, similar to those for the years from 1949 to 1957, remained in operation, and by 1959 there was a call to guarantee the quality of different categories of institution, the best of which would enrol the best students.[12] Thus, although continuing demand for manpower required the expansion of candidate sources, academic excellence was not to be sacrificed. In fact, in 1962 the *Kuang-ming jih-pao* combined a discussion of political quality with a renewed emphasis on more rigorous standards of academic selection "where our country's long-term profit lies."[13] Even under the decentralization of enrolment in 1958, unified guidance from the centre was given concerning acceptance of candidates, which was still based on examination performance and order of preferences.[14] In addition, the economic retrenchment of the early 1960's once again produced rival interpretations of the CCP's educational philosophy. The experiments of 1958 now gave way to a policy of regulation *(tiao-cheng)*, consolidation *(kung-ku)*, completion *(ch'ung-shih)*, and elevation *(t'i-kao)*.

Realizing that enrolment implementation was now diverging from his own thinking on education, Mao Tse-tung called in 1964 for extensive reforms in the examination system. The 1964-65 Enrolment Regulations accordingly emphasized the training of "proletarian successors," a veiled reference to the CCP's wider social goals, but simultaneously mentioned the creation of "cultural workers with socialist awareness and talent" *(jen-ts'ai)* for national construction, thus confirming continuing emphasis on individual academic excellence.[15]

In fact, decentralization of enrolment administration not only brought greater differentiation between institutions and increasing emphasis on academic criteria but a two-tiered system of central and local ad hoc planning. In general, however, the order of individual academic priorities within the Central Government's enrolment plan did not significantly change from the pre-1958 period. For example, the *Chung-kuo ch'ing-nien pao* stated that out of those to be enrolled in 1958, teacher training would take 52,500, engineering 46,000, and agriculture 10,300.[16] These priorities were similar in 1960.[17] The justifications given for placing engineering and teacher training in a premier position were the expansion of local industry, and the staffing needs of middle schools. Moreover, the enrolment plan numbers, 148,000 in 1958, 250,000 in 1959, and 280,000 in 1960, were considerably in excess of the 107,000 admitted for 1957 and apparently reflected the leap forward in national construction.[18] But central planning was now only part of the overall picture. In response to the call for local self-sufficiency, provinces and cities were to enrol additional students, over and above the number in the national plan, in order to train locally needed specialized construction personnel. The extra numbers would, however, necessarily have been limited because of staffing, buildings, facilities, and financial resources.[19]

The separation of national and local enrolment plans was followed by division of labour both between and within institutions. For example, in the case of Chungshan University, one of the most prestigious comprehensive universities, a number of departments and specialties were being altered to a five- from a four-year system. Similarly, the Chungshan Medical Institute changed its academic system from five to six years.[20] Meanwhile, at the Canton Teacher Training Institute, established in 1958, the four departments of Chinese language and literature, mathematics, physics, and chemistry had four-year basic courses, but special training courses were provided in the first three of the above, as well as in biology. This division of labour meant that the basic courses trained higher middle, and the special training courses, lower middle teachers.[21] While an increase in the length of courses was not necessarily confined to prestigious institutions, it was more prominent in academic areas related to national priorities. Special training courses were often designed to cater to local needs.

This intensification of the elite-mass structure was also shown in the allocation of graduates by the Central Government. While the majority of graduates were distributed to basic units in provinces and cities to work in industry and agriculture, a minority was sent to Central Government departments. The Shanghai *Wen-hui pao* stated in July 1958 that graduates from specialties directly related to Central Government needs would be so allocated, and others from natural science and engineering subjects would undertake scientific research or teaching in institutions of higher education.[22]

A similar pattern was evident in subsequent years; in 1963, of 77,000 engineering graduates, over 50,000 were to be distributed to departments of the Central Government, to strengthen the industrial base in such areas as Shanghai, Tientsin, and Liaoning. Over 90 per cent of the 17,000 graduates in agricultural fields would be employed by the State farms, *hsien* agricultural organs, and scientific research units. Graduating students in economics and finance numbered over 3,000 and were sent to serve the needs of national construction at various levels. The 25,000 who had studied medicine were allocated mainly to hospitals in cities, factories or mines. The 10,000 graduates in the natural sciences were to be divided between middle schools and scientific research organs. Finally, the 46,000 teacher training graduates would have been distributed to posts in middle schools. As in 1958, only a minority was allocated to Central Government organs and scientific research.

These statistics for the major academic fields in 1963 are now combined with the more limited data for the other years of the period from 1958 to 1965 in Table 16:[23]

TABLE 16: GRADUATES OF INSTITUTIONS OF HIGHER EDUCATION, 1958-65 (MAIN SUBJECTS)

	Total	Engineer-ing	Agri-culture	Economics Finance	Medicine	Natural Science	Educa-tion
1958	72,000	17,499	3,513	2,349	5,393	4,645	31,595
1959	70,000	—	—	—	—	—	—
1960	135,000	—	—	—	—	—	—
1961	160,000	54,000	10,000	—	20,000	—	53,000
1962	170,000	59,000	20,000	—	17,000	11,000	56,000
1963	200,000	77,000	17,000	3,000	25,000	10,000	46,000
1964	200,000	—	—	—	—	—	—
1965	170,000	—	—	—	—	—	—

Note: A dash indicates that statistics are not available. Also, graduates in other subject areas are not listed separately.

Finally, the regulations for the enrolment of researchers and the very limited social mobility they provided followed the pattern established in the pre-1958 period. The competition for postgraduate study is suggested by a report in 1963 that there were 10,000 applicants for 800 places.[24] The elite-mass structure was being perpetuated.

This intensification of inequality took place in spite of changes in the enrolment process, which will now be examined in greater detail. The reforms of 1958 were also a reflection of changing jurisdiction over higher education. At the height of the Great Leap Forward many institutions were being handed over to provincial and city authorities, and new ones were being established under local jurisdiction.[25] To cater further to local needs and decrease the flow of candidates between regions, the principle of "accepting talent according to area" *(chiu-ti ch'ü-ts'ai)* was adopted. This meant, with the exceptions outlined below, that a candidate would register for a local institution in the area where he lived.[26] But the decentralized administration of 1958, like its unified predecessor, was a mixed system. The balance of priorities between central and local ad hoc planning ultimately undermined the policy of decentralization; institutions were placed in order of rank on the basis of national needs.

In 1958 authorities in each province and city were ordered to ensure that, in the first instance, students of the best political quality and outstanding scholarship were sent to institutions which came under the Central Government. Requisite numbers were laid down after discussion between the Central Government, local authorities, and the institution concerned. During the years 1960-64 central control was even greater, however, with the determination of relevant numbers firmly in the hands of the Education Ministry. Mutual consultation was not mentioned. In 1965 the equivalent body was the Ministry of Higher Education.[27] Secondly, local authorities had to guarantee the enrolment of principal institutions in outside provinces and cities in terms of numbers from their own areas, as previously decided by mutual consultation. Thirdly, attention had to be paid to enrolment in the important institutions within the jurisdiction of the particular province and city in question. Fourthly, the enrolment needs of other local institutions were to be satisfied.[28] These four categories applied to the year 1958 but provisions for subsequent years were similar.

Thus, institutions in the first three categories above were able to enrol students from outside areas. Certain other institutions, by virtue of their special needs, were also not restricted to enrolling in their localities and could cross over provincial and city boundaries.[29]

In contrast, higher teacher training, medical, and agricultural institutes which prepared students to be cadres in particular provinces and cities, would, in principle, enrol within those areas.[30]

Finally, because of the continuing uneven distribution of candidates in the country as a whole, institutions in North China and the North-West, where sources were few, would enrol some students from East China and the Central South. Additionally, some of the institutions in the North-West would accept students from the provinces of Szechwan and Honan.[31]

In summary, as institutions were divided into priority categories, special provision had to be made for those candidates who wished to register for both individual and joint enrolment. These were similar to equivalent arrangements in the pre-1958 period. A candidate was permitted to go to an outside area to register for an institution conducting individual enrolment, for example, a fine arts institute, after having registered for joint enrolment in his own area.[32] This rubric also applied to candidates registering for the above mentioned categories of institution which took the whole country as their enrolment constituency.[33] In summary, institutions under the Central Government were allocated the best students and maintained their high standards.

Moreover, in 1959 the elite sectors of higher education were being identified with greater clarity. Vague references to "principal" and "important" institutions gave way to the new classification of "key point" *(chung-tien)*. These would have included such prestigious names as Peking University, Futan University, and the newly founded National Scientific and Technological University. The key point institutions, however, were only a proportion of those which came under the Central Government.

In June of the same year the *Kuang-ming jih-pao* explicitly stated that the first task of enrolment work was to guarantee the quality of new students in key point institutions.[34] The Shanghai *Wen-hui pao* further underlined the importance of key point by implying that fulfilling their quota was the sine qua non of completing enrolment as a whole. To give priority to key point was to give politics priority:

> Every revolutionary class and every aspect of national construction . . . must have a key point, and if we do not divide phenomena into light and heavy, and slow and rapid, but instead spread strength evenly, no matter what time or what question, the effects will be most damaging. In the development of higher education we must have "key point."[35]

Statements such as these had two basic implications: firstly, that elitist tendencies in higher education were to be encouraged for an indefinite period, and secondly, by extension, that universalization *(p'u-chi)* should proceed on the basis of elevation *(t'i-kao)*. The high quality of the key point would thus be maintained: they would enrol the best students, who would enjoy the most favourable staff-student ratios and the most up-to-date facilities. Key point institutions would both further national construction and provide high quality teachers for the rest of the higher education system. Some sources likened China to a chessboard with key point including three major categories of institution: the old-established universities of national eminence, other important bodies in areas where the development of higher education was less advanced, and the newly-established schools which were to be consolidated.

The policy of key point was "walking on two legs"; only elevation could guarantee universalization.[36] What this meant in the context of enrolment was that special efforts had to be made to mobilize high quality candidates to apply for key point. The quality of key point institutions could only be ensured if the catchment area was as large as possible. Nevertheless, their main enrolment target was higher middle graduates, considered the most desirable source of talent. Time and again were such candidates admonished not to be reluctant to apply for key point through fear of not being accepted, as registration did not preclude their application for ordinary institutions. Clearly, individual middle schools and enrolment organs were to encourage high calibre middle graduates to register for key point.[37] In addition, while key point institutions were urged to concentrate on increasing the ratio of students of worker and peasant origin, past experience rather suggested that this group would be poorly represented. Moreover, the fact that those applying for key point were not exempt from foreign language examinations would have worked against the entry of workers and peasants.[38] Only by emphasizing key point institutions could the country's cultural and scientific standards reach the advanced levels of the rest of the world. They formed the skeleton of the country's higher education, and in the short term the quality of lesser institutions would, if necessary, be sacrificed.

This increasing stratification of higher education will be illustrated by reference to two of the key point institutions, the Shanghai Scientific and Technological Institute and the University of Hunan, both newly founded. The task of the former was to train scientific research personnel for the institutes of the Academy of Sciences and instruction was closely co-ordinated with the Shanghai branch of that body. Education and productive labour were integrated by using the most up-to-date technical equipment, provided in the factories and laboratories of the research institutes. This was said to bring together the much vaunted three aspects of teaching, production, and research. But two caveats must be added. Firstly, productive labour took place in factories with exceptional conditions far removed from the majority of industrial enterprise. Secondly, practical study was directed towards scientific theory.[39] The role of productive labour was instrumental; it was subordinated to scientific expertise rather than a value in itself.

The establishment of the University of Hunan also indicated the intensification of the elite-mass structure in higher education. This comprehensive institution embraced the humanities, the natural sciences, and engineering. The first two fields were designed to train scientific research personnel and teaching staff for middle as well as higher education. The task of the engineering section was to produce high level national construction personnel.[40]

The ongoing process of stratification, therefore, was indicated even within the comprehensive universities, as the tasks of scientific research and university teaching were conceptually separated from the vocational skills required for industrial development.

The administration of enrolment was thus the background against which the educational revolution was to take place. Moves towards the integration of education and society were to be implemented on two fronts: the institutional and the ideological. The first operated within the higher education system as currently constituted, the second was designed to change the system itself. The first sought to create proletarian intellectuals by increasing the worker-peasant contingent in higher education, the second by linking education and productive labour.

Institutional devices used to facilitate worker and peasant entry will be seen within the framework of candidate eligibility for the years 1958-65, the categories of which were similar to those of the previous period. In 1958 the overall requirement of higher middle graduation or a cultural level equivalent to it was retained. The upper age limit was thirty but could be extended to thirty-five in the case of workers and peasants, worker and peasant cadres, retired and seconded soldiers, and certain other categories of cadre who had taken part in revolutionary work for ten years.[41] In 1959 it was stated that the age stipulation could be suitably relaxed according to local conditions. The categories of eligible applicants in 1958 were as follows: (i) graduates from higher middle schools and worker-peasant rapid middle schools, (ii) those graduating from vocational middle schools whose promotion was approved by either the departments in which they had been serving or local education bureaux, (iii) personnel in Party and government organs, and commercial and mass organizations, subject to the approval of their work units, (iv) seconded and retired soldiers who held verification letters from local authorities in their native *hsien* or the Party committees in their military units, (v) Overseas Chinese and Hong Kong and Macao students who had returned to China and held verification letters from the Overseas Chinese Affairs organs or their Promotion Guidance Committee in Canton, and (vi) various kinds of intellectual youth who held verification letters from their local authorities. Candidates in the first three categories had to submit graduation documents as well as introductory letters.[42]

These regulations underwent slight modification in the following years but did not change in conception. Significantly, however, the upper age limit was reduced to twenty-five in 1964 and could only be extended to twenty-seven in the case of such categories as workers, peasants, Party and government personnel, and retired soldiers.[43] This younger upper age limit indicated that greater attention was being focused on those from within the education system as enrolment targets; it would have worked against the entry of those from outside.

These categories of eligible applicant do not of themselves give any more weight to the entry of those of worker and peasant origin than the regulations of the pre-1958 period. But two stipulations which governed the operation of eligibility were designed to increase the worker and peasant contingent: guaranteed entry and preferential acceptance. In July 1958 the *Chung-kuo ch'ing-nien pao* called for the raising of political quality; greater concessions would now be given to workers and peasants.[44] Preferential acceptance *(yu-hsien ling-ch'ü)* had been used in the previous period but guaranteed entry *(pao-sung ju-hsüeh)* took the process a stage further. Under this latter rubric, workers, peasants, and worker-peasant rapid middle school graduates, together with worker and peasant cadres who had taken part in revolutionary work for a long period, could be admitted without undergoing the enrolment examination, subject to scrutiny of their qualifications.[45] But this did not mean that all in these categories would automatically enter higher education: they still had to pass through a screening process. It appears that those to be accepted were specially selected by work units and took academic examinations held by individual institutions. This test was designed to ensure that they would be able to keep pace with course work after entry, a stipulation enforced, no doubt, in reaction to past experience with the low quality of entrants of worker and peasant origin. In the case of worker-peasant rapid middle school graduates, assessment of ability was undertaken by their previous work units and the institutions of higher education for which they had been selected.[46]

For those not screened under the guaranteed entry rubric, the old device of preferential acceptance was maintained, and those eligible to take advantage of it sat for enrolment examinations. The categories of those eligible generally followed the pattern of the previous period and included not only guaranteed entry targets but retired and seconded soldiers, the national minorities, children of revolutionary heroes, Overseas Chinese, Hong Kong and Macao students, and significantly, intellectual youth who had worked in industry or agriculture for two years.[47] When such candidates' political and health conditions were satisfactory, they would be preferentially accepted, provided that their achievement in the academic enrolment examination was equivalent to that of most candidates.[48] Again, one of the determining factors appears to have been candidates' potential to maintain the standard required of them after entry.

But while the avowed aim of increasing the worker and peasant contingent remained, the methods of guaranteed entry and preferential acceptance were gradually abandoned. The 1960 Regulations repeat the 1958 preferential acceptance rubric for the relevant categories but omit guaranteed entry; the 1961 stipulations exclude both measures. In 1961, however, the *Jen-min jih-pao* asserted that only if cadres and Party and government personnel were admitted could quality of enrolment be ensured. But the paper added that such applicants "would, in the same way as other candidates, take part in enrolment examinations";[49] the academic criterion was still predominant. These tendencies were even more in evidence in 1962, when it was stipulated that Party and government personnel would be selected according to examination performance. Their entry was not guaranteed nor could they demand that acceptance levels be lowered.[50] The years 1963-65 produced similar emphasis.

The guaranteed entry and preferential acceptance methods must not, however, be seen in isolation, and within the general context of enrolment policies they appear as little more than a half-measure. The needs of national construction greatly outweighed the importance of facilitating worker and peasant entry.

In practice, the admission of such elements was also related to the shortage of candidates. As the number of students graduating from higher middle and worker-peasant rapid middle schools in 1958 was said to amount only to 220,000, it was imperative that all those eligible, both within and outside the education system, apply for registration. Furthermore, because of the new high tide in industrial and agricultural production, the number of intellectual youth registering for examination had been drastically reduced. Cadres were in short supply owing to the secondment *(hsia-fang)* campaigns (ideological remoulding through manual labour). In effect, the main enrolment targets were those graduating from higher middle schools and worker-peasant rapid middle schools, together with intellectual youth.[51] Higher middle graduates, numbering 300,000, were still the major enrolment source in 1959. There was a search for talent from all sources, however,[52] and the Education Ministry ordered government departments and communes to select cadres and peasants for registration. Undoubtedly, the screening process paid as much attention to academic as to political quality.[53] The entry of candidates from outside the education system was not a foregone conclusion, and if unsuccessful, they were to return to their original work units.[54]

In summary, as in the period 1949-57, a balance had to be struck between manpower already trained and that to be trained. The leadership of a work unit was empowered to give approval for registration, but with the proviso that production needs were not prejudiced. Those personnel studying in spare-time education were only allowed to register for examination with special leadership approval,[55] but where factories and mines had reduced labour needs by technical innovation, the possibility of members of the work-force being admitted to full-time education was greater.[56] The admission of such personnel to higher education, like spare-time study, provided only a limited channel of social mobility for the exceptionally able, however.

Academic entry standards were being enforced with increasing vigour. Cadres, like those who studied at Wuhan Surveying Institute, often acquired retraining rather than intellectual depth, and on graduation returned to their original units.[57] One category under the cadre rubric, middle and primary schoolteachers, could only apply for academic fields closely associated with their employment, and registration was in any case at the discretion of local education bureaux.[58] Moreover, while cadre and other "outside" applicants were eligible to register for institutions of national importance, like the National Scientific and Technological University, the latters' main enrolment targets were higher middle graduates.[59] Again, candidates from outside the education system were usually allocated to less prestigious fields of study.

Thus, in practice, equality of opportunity was denied, and those higher middle students who wished to join the work-force on graduation were criticized for missing the significance of higher education. But motivation was crucial for the high academic standard required. Furthermore, only those of outstanding calibre could hope to be admitted to prestigious key point institutions. This emphasis on personal excellence was also reflected in the policy of individual revision, which contrasted with the collective type characteristic of the years 1949-57.[60]

But the full blast of this academically meritocratic offensive did not come until 1962 when competition to enter higher education was more rigorous than ever. Moreover, in 1964 a broadcast from Kiangsi asserted that the greater proportion of higher middle graduates would have to find employment, as only a small percentage could be promoted to higher education; it was the duty not only of teachers but parents and the Youth Leagues to make this message clear.[61] It was an excellent situation from the State's point of view, as new students of better quality could be enrolled and academic standards raised.[62]

This stress on academic excellence was reflected in the operation of the enrolment process, the main features of which did not change fundamentally during this period. Such aspects as registration, examination areas and centres, dates, subjects, and methods of assessment have been discussed for earlier years. They will be mentioned again only in the context of the selection process.

There were subtle changes in the preference system, however. Previously, a candidate had only been able to register in one category of subjects, but in 1958 he was permitted to "cross over" two categories and required to take examination papers prescribed for both, together with any additional skill papers. This new preference system had the advantage of giving institutions a wider choice of candidates, but because it meant too much examination preparation, very few applicants availed themselves of it and crossing over categories was abolished in 1959.[63]

Preferences must be understood within the context of the examination subjects prescribed for 1958; with minor changes, these followed the earlier pattern, and may be tabulated as follows:

Field of Study	*Examination Subjects*
I. Natural Science	National Language
Engineering	Politics
	Mathematics
	Physics
	Chemistry
	Foreign Language
II. Medicine	National Language
Agriculture and Forestry	Politics
	Physics
	Chemistry
	Biology
	Foreign Language
III. Literature	National Language
History	Politics
Politics	History
Finance and Economics	Foreign Language
Fine Arts	

Foreign language examinations were in Russian or English, depending on which a candidate had studied. Significantly, exemption from such papers would not be granted to candidates applying for admission to key point institutions. Naturally, the same rule applied to those intending to study in foreign language specialties. In addition, all students would be given political and health re-examination on admission; failure to reach the requisite standard would result in withdrawal of eligibility for entry. Finally, skill examinations were to be taken by those wishing to enter such fields as fine arts and physical education.

In 1960 reference was made to the raising of examination standards: among graduating higher middle students being examined in Kwangtung Province, those passing numbered over 12,000 and of the latter there were 1,100 candidates with an overall average mark above 80. The number passing had increased five-fold compared to the previous year.[64]

Even more pertinent was the information relating to Fukien Province. On the basis of official *New China News Agency* sources in Foochow, the Hong Kong *Wen-hui pao* stated in 1960 that Fukien, first in order of success in the 1959 enrolment examinations, had maintained its position, even in the face of a general improvement in higher middle education throughout the country. In Fukien in 1960 there were over 10,000 higher middle graduate candidates being examined and their overall average mark for all subjects reached 85.49 per cent. In addition, 2,161 gained an average of 90 per cent and above. Subjects where standards had been especially raised included mathematics, physics, chemistry, and Russian; in these fields 588 scripts attained 100 per cent. Furthermore, schools and areas within the province were ranked in order of merit: the premier position was occupied by Foochow First Middle School where the overall average, for all subjects, of its higher middle graduating class reached 90 per cent.[65]

This ranking of schools according to enrolment examination results was producing an elite-mass structure in middle education. Earlier, reference was made to the establishment of special schools for orphans of revolutionary heroes and children of high ranking cadres. In defiance of a State Council directive calling for their abolition, some provinces and cities retained a few such schools. Even after one of them, the August the First School in Peking, was handed over to the local authorities, it still enrolled throughout the country rather than just in its locality. Red Guard sources claimed that in 1965 most of its students were the children of important cadres from other areas and only a minority were local; children born in worker and peasant homes accounted for merely 15 per cent of those enrolled.

The combination of parental pressure and an extensive catchment area enabled the August the First School authorities to maintain a high rate of entry to higher education. In addition, they allegedly illegally awarded gold and silver medals entitling their best graduates to automatic entry to prestigious institutions of higher education without examination. This was like the former Soviet system.[66] Finally, a Red Guard source claimed that the student-teacher ratio in schools for children of cadres was 6 to 1 as opposed to the equivalent figures of 28 to 1 and 35 to 1 for middle schools in general.[67]

But the condemnation of the August the First School appeared during the heat of the Cultural Revolution. While the majority of students were undoubtedly children of high ranking cadres, those from worker and peasant homes had not been entirely excluded, even though rigorous academic standards undoubtedly worked against their entry.

Meanwhile, inequalities among middle schools in general were being given official sanction. At a 1961 Central Committee work conference the Director of the CCP's Propaganda Department, Lu Ting-yi, ordered that certain middle and primary schools be selected as key point. A special investigation group went to such famous and academically successful institutions as the Nank'ai Middle School in Tientsin and the Foochow First Middle School, which were now to serve as models for the key point system. In 1963, under the guidance of local authorities, these schools concentrated on the selection and training of outstanding students, and they were given better facilities financed by the State. These policies accelerated the hierarchical ranking of middle schools. [68]

Student success in the enrolment examinations became the main criterion of efficiency for middle schools; the acceptance of candidates on the basis of marks and preferences was even more crucial in selection than in the period 1949-57. By 1962 candidates were being evaluated according to specific levels of performance: the overall average of 85 per cent and above represented the first stage, 80 to 84 per cent the second, and so on. Simultaneously, preferences were examined. First of all, those in the first stage would be accepted, and only after they had been selected for their preferred institutions would those in lower mark stages be assessed for entry. Academic criteria were even more explicit than in the previous period. [69]

In condemning this policy which "placed grades in command," a Red Guard source at Peking University surveyed principles of enrolment adopted in 1962. At a Party meeting in the Ministry of Education, over which the Vice-Minister, Chiang Nan-hsiang presided, it was reportedly decided that

> Examination grades are not only the standard for measuring degree of academic accomplishment; through grades one can also discern the students' political character. Hence, those candidates whose examination grades are above 80 should generally be accepted. If for any special reason there are some who cannot be selected, this will have to be approved by our Ministry. [70]

Stress on academic excellence in the evaluation of examination results would necessarily have had a bearing on the entry of workers and peasants. It was nevertheless not the intention of Liuists and "bourgeois academics" to exclude those of worker and peasant origin at all costs, as the Red Guard sources quoted above implied;[71] the failure of such students to enter higher education or stay the course could be attributed to home background, financial means, and previous training. Certainly, however, many educators and Party figures in the Ministries did see academic quality as paramount.

In any case, both the interpretations of the CCP's educational philosophy precluded a policy of deliberately excluding those of worker and peasant origin. In July 1958 the *Chung-kuo ch'ing-nien pan-yueh k'an* reasserted the concept of proletarian intellectual in the context of enrolment: "Political qualifications for entry are not entirely based on candidates' social origin and performance in the political general knowledge examination, they must be determined primarily by the quality of applicants' everyday thought." Personal performance was clearly the criterion of acceptability.

Moreover, Chinese Communist statistics concerning the social origin of students also provide a picture very different from the one painted by Cultural Revolution sources.[72] In September 1958 the *Kuang-ming jih-pao* claimed that of those candidates accepted for entry by institutions enrolling students in Kwangtung Province that year, 60.3 per cent were of worker and peasant origin. The paper then gave a more detailed statistical breakdown for individual institutions elsewhere in the country. For example, 86 per cent of new students at Nanking Aviation Institute and 57.7 per cent of those accepted for the University of Nanking were workers and peasants.[73]

Statistics quoted for Fukien Province in 1960 by the Hong Kong newspaper, *Wen-hui pao,* presented the same overall picture; 72 per cent of those graduating from higher middle schools were of worker and peasant origin, and this would have been reflected in the background of entrants. In addition, the academic authorities at universities like Peking and Ch'inghua had written to the Fukien Education Bureau, praising the students from that province.[74]

In 1961 a news item referred to advanced production workers entering the Shanghai Scientific and Technological Institute. Their entry underlined the importance of spare-time education as an agent of social mobility, as it was there that they had attained the cultural level necessary for enrolment registration.[75] Workers and peasants direct from production were also prominent in the student bodies of Shanghai institutions in 1963, notably Futan University and the Scientific and Technological Institute.[76] Finally, a report from Canton in 1964 indicated that production workers as well as soldiers of poor and lower middle peasant origin who had retired from the ranks had been admitted to such institutions as Peking University, the Chinese People's University, and the Peking Steel Institute.[77]

It is not possible to make a definitive statement concerning the social origin of entrants on the basis of such fragmented information, as isolated figures of this nature may well have referred to exceptional cases, but four main general conclusions can be drawn. Firstly, however unusual the examples quoted may have been, those of worker and peasant origin were not being denied entry. Secondly, registration figures indicated that those of worker and peasant origin were a majority among Fukien higher middle graduates applying for higher education in 1960; the worker-peasant ratio of accepted candidates in Kwangtung in 1958 presents a similar picture. These two provinces may have been exceptional but any increase in the number of workers and peasants among entrants would eventually be reflected in enrolment as a whole. Thirdly, the sparse figures given for Nanking in 1958 suggest that those of worker and peasant origin were more numerous in technical institutes than comprehensive universities. Fourthly, the entry of production workers to prestigious institutions underlined the importance of spare-time education as an agent of social mobility for the exceptionally able.

If candidates of worker and peasant origin were succeeding in gaining entry to higher education, the organization of preparatory classes *(yü-k'e)*, mainly for entrants previously involved in production, suggested that at least one section of them was less advanced than other students.

Worker-peasant classes had existed in the period 1949-57, but they took a new form in 1958, presumably to accommodate those admitted under the guaranteed entry and preferential acceptance regulations. These classes were of two types: those attached to, and those established within, an institution; in both cases study conditions and course length were flexible. By 1960 the first students in these classes had graduated.

In the same year graduates of the preparatory class attached to Hua Nan Agricultural Institute were being promoted to basic courses in various departments after a qualifying examination.[78] No mention is made of the drop out rate in preparatory classes but it may well have been considerable, in view of the study difficulties which those of worker and peasant origin seem to have faced.

The preparatory classes established within Chengtu Engineering Institute to help worker and peasant students who had come straight from production were discussed by the *Kuang-ming jih-pao* in May 1959. These classes appear to have been established on an ad hoc basis by specialties. Instruction, led by experienced teachers and senior students, took the form of collective study.[79] Another example was Kiangsu Teacher Training Institute, where special personnel were delegated to help newly enrolled students deficient in mathematics to revise higher middle curricula. There were similar cases in the foreign language field.[80]

Preparatory classes were an institutional method of facilitating worker-peasant entry to higher education and creating proletarian intellectuals. Simultaneously, however, the 1958 revolution stressed ideological means, implying fundamental structural changes in the education system.

While organizing the rural masses in the late 1920's, Mao Tse-tung wrote of the establishment by the peasantry of evening classes which contrasted with the "foreign-style" schools of the cities.[81] These provided the inspiration for the new integration of education and society in 1958, and part-time work part-time study institutions *(pan-kung pan-tu)* were established, initially at the higher and middle levels, serving as models for the reform of the full-time system.

The many forms that part-time work part-time study institutions took and the different categories they enrolled make any definitive analysis difficult, but their function may be gauged from an examination of certain models. One important type was the labour university *(lao-tung ta-hsüeh),* designed to satisfy local needs. Perhaps the most famous was the Kiangsi Communist Labour University; this will be considered in conjunction with two others, the Kwangtung Province Labour University and Canton City Farm Labour University. The students at the Kiangsi institution came from both inside and outside the province; they were of worker and peasant origin, usually primary school graduates, and apparently possessed a pioneering spirit for serving the masses and production. The university offered courses in agronomy, farm machinery, stock breeding, forestry, fisheries, and sericulture. Theory and practice were linked; students were engaged in both mental and manual labour. Courses generally appear to have been four years in length and prepared students to contribute to the economic development of the countryside.[82]

Likewise, Kwangtung Province Labour University had four-year courses. Its two major enrolment targets were (i) those graduating from higher and lower middle school, and (ii) intellectual youth. But while the first category was exempt from academic entrance examinations on the recommendation of their schools, the second group had to take them.[83]

Entry conditions were similar in the case of Canton City Farm Labour University, and students' competence in national language and political general knowledge were examined, mainly orally.

In both the Kwangtung and Canton institutions the students undertook agricultural labour; academic study was secondary and related to local needs. Subjects taught included fruit-growing and livestock rearing, as students returned to people's communes or were directed to other work on graduation, even if theoretically their personal preference would then be taken into account.[84] General curricula were also taught, however. Teaching staff in these two cases were apparently faculty members seconded on a part-time basis by full-time institutions or cadres provided by basic units.

The part-time work part-time study system could be justified in both political and economic terms. There was an acute shortage of schools; many were denied an education, and those who could not be promoted to the next rung of the educational ladder were increasing. The general concentration of middle schools and universities in the cities meant inequality of opportunity.[85] Liu Shao-ch'i, on a visit to eight provinces and cities in 1964, praised the part-time system as the only way in which increasing demands for higher education could be met. Lower and higher middle graduate urban youth were reluctant to go to the countryside; the promise of further education might serve as an inducement.[86] The part-time system would diminish inequality, pay its own way without need of public expenditure, and make it be possible to train vitally needed technical manpower for the countryside. Finally, but most important of all, the political goal of eliminating differences between mental and manual labour would be furthered.

But, in the last analysis, it has to be concluded that the part-time system was a very poor substitute for full-time education. The enrolment targets of the labour universities suggest that part-time institutions would generally have been filled with the less able students, who were now to be retrained for rural construction needs.

Part-time education, however, was also the ideal form which the full-time system should emulate. By 1965, of sixty-six institutes under the jurisdiction of the Ministry of Agriculture and Forestry, more than forty had been reorganized into the part-time form.[87] But some institutions of higher education began factories and experimental plots without reorganizing academic study.[88] Especially notable were the factories opened at Ch'inghua and Futan Universities where students were instructed in the classroom and at the bench. The full-time universities were said to be creating "all-round worker intellectuals"; the new Ch'inghua was described as "a living blueprint for the future development of higher education."[89] But even as early as 1960 the Liuist-controlled CCP Propaganda Department, which had considerable influence over the implementation of educational policy, was calling for a guarantee of academic quality, and if necessary, strict limitation over the time spent on productive labour.[90] In fact, the function of practical study was already contentious.

This conflict also affected part-time schools at the middle level. Like their counterparts in higher education, part-time middle schools took many forms. Attention here will be focused on two main types: those run by the masses *(min-pan hsüeh-hsiao),* and agricultural middle schools *(nung-yeh chung-hsüeh).*

Schools run by the masses were established in, and funded by, factories, mines, and communes. Information received from eighteen provinces and cities indicated that by April 1958 there were 2,487 such schools teaching 441,548 students. Their enrolment targets were workers and peasants who would be retrained in new production techniques: the schools' organizational structure and curricula were flexible and adapted to local conditions. But the aim was to raise cultural as well as technical levels; national language and political general knowledge were also taught, and where conditions permitted, history and geography would follow.

While the main purpose of the schools run by the masses was to provide local technical personnel, promotion of their graduates to full-time higher education was not precluded. But, although graduates would in theory have been eligible to register for university enrolment examinations, in practice few would have been competent enough to pass them. Information on promotion is sparse, but in this respect the schools run by the masses probably provided only a limited channel of mobility for the very able.

Discussion of these schools brings into focus the question of universalization *(p'u-chi)* versus elevation *(t'i-kao)*. These two processes were likened to a person walking on two legs, without one of which it was impossible to walk properly. The schools run by the masses were said to reflect universalization; the full-time system, elevation.[91] But opinion in the Party differed as to the relative emphasis to be accorded to each.

Similarly, the agricultural middle schools were addressed to special local needs. They were first established in the province of Kiangsu in 1957, operated and financed by people's communes. Study timetables were flexible and their academic level was usually equivalent to junior, but in some cases, senior, middle school. They were designed to train middle level agricultural technicians in five-year courses. Significantly, in addition to local students, intellectual youth who had been sent down to the countryside were enrolled. As in the case of the schools run by the masses, graduates were eligible to advance to higher education, but frequent modifications in study programmes and numbers enrolled suggest great flexibility, reflecting the needs of production rather than student promotion. They provided an education different from that of the full-time middle schools. In May 1958 the *Jen-min chiao-yu* claimed that formerly there was only the ordinary middle school; this was like a person walking on one leg and not going very quickly. Now the agricultural middle schools and the full-time system were analogous to a person walking on two legs and running fast. But, ultimately, there would be rival interpretations as to the function which agricultural middle schools should perform.[92]

The revolution of 1958 sought to forge a direct link between study and productive labour in both full-time and part-time institutions. But the evolution of full-time education to a new form would be a long-term process, and meanwhile the function of part-time schools could be subject to more than one interpretation. This conflict hinged on the respective weight to be given to universalization and elevation. The Maoist view emphasized the former; the Liuist, the latter.

A series of Ministry of Education conferences in the early 1960's assessed the experiments of 1958 and 1959. New institutions with poor conditions which had mushroomed during the Great Leap were to be closed down and enrolment of new students in higher education reduced; it was in any case tacitly admitted that earlier figures had been exaggerated and inconsistent.

Although taken from various sources, the following statistics nevertheless provide a general picture of enrolment in full-time higher education during the years from the Great Leap to the eve of the Cultural Revolution.[93]

TABLE 17: ENROLMENT IN INSTITUTIONS OF HIGHER EDUCATION, 1958-59 TO 1964-65 (IN THOUSANDS)

Academic Year	Enrolment
1958-59	660
1959-60	810
1960-61	955
1961-62	819
1962-63	820
1963-64	680
1964-65	700

Chinese Communist sources have never adequately defined the types of higher education covered in statistics for this period but a Red Guard newspaper claimed that, after two years of adjustment, in 1963 the total number of institutions had been reduced to two-thirds of that for 1960.[94] An outside source, on the basis of other Chinese Communist materials, calculated that by 1961 their number had been pruned to 227 from a 1960 total of 839. But in an address to a convention of student representatives from part-time institutions in October 1966 Chou En-lai disclosed that there were then about 500 institutions of higher education in China. While inconsistent statistics often bring confusion rather than clarity, they do at least suggest varying interpretations concerning the function of higher education and the order of its priorities.

This reduction in institution and student numbers reflected a growing concern among Party figures in the Education Ministry with the consolidation of the gains made during the Great Leap. These tendencies were confirmed by the formulation of the "Sixty Articles of Higher Education," drafted in the Education Ministry and the Party's Propaganda Department, which proposed a new system of leadership. This strengthened the authority of heads of institutions and departments, with the Party's role relegated to that of supervision. It also meant great weight being given to the views of so-called bourgeois academics, resulting in alleged collaboration between these and Liuists to subvert the revolution of 1958.[95]

Consistent with these changes in academic authority patterns was the call to raise teaching quality on the basis of well-tested curricula materials, abandoning, where necessary, the experimental methods used during the educational revolution. This was in many respects a return to the *status quo ante*.[96]

Moreover, these principles were forcefully expressed at Education Ministry conferences in 1962 which reaffirmed the need to train high level construction personnel. This in itself implied elevation, as it downgraded the role of productive labour in the theory-based specialized curricula now being prescribed.[97] Thus there were differing interpretations concerning not only the function of part-time institutions but the place of productive labour in full-time schools.

By March 1964 Mao Tse-tung was remarking upon the excessive academic orientation of the education system and its emphasis on examinations. In short, the implementation of policy by the Education Ministry was a very real denial of the Party's educational philosophy, as restated in the revolution of 1958, which demanded the integration of education and society through the political, academic, and physical development of the proletarian intellectual.[98]

It would be inaccurate, however, to suggest that those associated with Liu Shao-ch'i were opposed to part-time education and productive labour in full-time institutions; they merely placed a different interpretation on their function. For example, in 1957, Liu Shao-ch'i inspected schools in Hopei and Honan, directing them to institute productive labour as part of the curriculum.[99] Moreover, in 1964 Liu Shao-ch'i supported the establishment of agricultural middle schools.

Essentially, the Liuists saw full-time and part-time institutions as serving separate functions. On the one hand, there was the State education system, on the other, the various part-time schools. The part-time system provided education for those who would otherwise have been denied it, without need of heavy State expenditure. While the technical and cultural standards of the masses were thus being raised, crucial investment in production would not be jeopardized by an excessive diversion of funds to the education sector.[100] Faced with the day-to-day implementation of policy, Party leadership in the Education Ministry and its local bureaux tended to conceive part-time education in utilitarian economic terms. To this extent the Liuist interpretation gave preference to elevation over universalization. Academic standards in the full-time system had to be raised and the part-time institutions gradually improved, for only in this way would China be able to attain the advanced cultural and scientific levels of the rest of the world.[101] The Liuists, then, saw part-time education as essentially supplementary and a separate system in its own right. In general, the part-time system would train those not in a position to enter full-time institutions, even if there was always a possibility of promotion from part-time to full-time for students of exceptional calibre.

In contrast, Mao Tse-tung believed in the integration of education and productive labour as a value in itself. The education system would ultimately cease to exist as a separate entity; society itself would be a vast educational process. The political, not the economic, imperative should be in command.

The logical conclusion of the Liuist interpretation was the advocacy of two education systems. The clearest statement to this effect was that of Lu Ting-yi, a

Vice-Premier and Director of the CCP Propaganda Department, who fell from grace during the Cultural Revolution: "This dual education system was called 'walking on two legs' in the past; some students went on to further studies and became officials, while others were employed as workers or peasants. We must walk on both legs during the Socialist period."[102]

As it stands, this statement is watertight, permitting no mobility between the two systems. But a very different picture emerges when these sentiments are read in conjunction with other ideas attributed to Liu Shao-ch'i and Lu Ting-yi. Liu Shao-ch'i admitted the right of all, whatever their social origin, to receive education. This right, however, had always been implicit in the Party's educational philosophy; what distinguished the Liuist interpretation from its Maoist counterpart was its pre-eminent emphasis on academic achievement criteria rather than those of political commitment. But the achievement-oriented social mobility implicit in the Liuist interpretation was an ideal; not all aspirants actually attained it. Furthermore, Lu Ting-yi was reputed to have said: "Education consists of the transmission of knowledge and academic study."[103] The individual became the frame of reference; this implied recognition of aptitude and personal academic excellence. This argument was reinforced by Liu Shao-ch'i's statement that "knowledge is privately owned" *(chih-shih ssu-yu)*, which came under attack during the Cultural Revolution.[104]

Individual aptitude, achievement orientation, and academic excellence had their logical extension in Lu Ting-Yi's conclusion that "schools have the task of making people competent in various fields of knowledge," which echoed Liu Shao-ch'i's call for intellectuals to devote themselves to utilization of special skills and scientific expertise. Not only were those in science and technology to have a special role; humanities graduates would serve as the backbone of the power structure at local levels.[105] Moreover, in time, political knowledge, especially crucial for Party and Youth League members, might be relegated to the status of an expertise among other specialties. It would then be no longer in command, but just another skill.

In conclusion, during the years from 1958 to 1965 the two education systems confirmed the elite-mass structure which had been emerging in the previous period. In the Maoist view, the revolution of 1958 had turned into counter-revolution.

8

Beyond the Cultural Revolution: Reform and Reaction

The revolution of 1958 had brought a restatement of the Party's educational philosophy in terms of the fundamentals expressed by Mao Tse-tung in the 1930's. Its real significance had lain in the ideological means employed to place politics in command and achieve the integration of education and society, but the ensuing policies were subject to rival interpretations. For example, part-time education did not become the model for full-time institutions; its introduction instead brought into being two education systems. By 1965 it was clear that the Liuist interpretation, which saw productive labour in full-time institutions as economically instrumental and part-time education as essentially supplementary, had triumphed over its Maoist protagonist.

In its final implications the 1958 revolution would have meant that the education system would cease to exist as a separate entity when it became one with the part-time system, itself integrated with society. The way that the full-time system was then constituted, however, meant that there was built-in resistance to its evolution into a part-time form. This resistance was also a result of a conflicting interpretation of the 1958 restatement of the Party's educational philosophy.

By 1965 it had become clear to Mao Tse-tung and his supporters that the only way in which the Liuist subversion of the Party's educational philosophy could be prevented was by the closure of universities and institutes, with the concomitant destruction of the education system. The new enrolment policies and processes, mooted in 1966 but only gradually implemented in subsequent years, reflected the integration of education and society.

The Party's educational philosophy, as articulated by Mao Tse-tung, had inherited the traditional relationship between education and society, especially in its assumptions concerning the nature of man and knowledge. Under that relationship the intellect had never been considered very highly for itself; it was essentially an instrument directed towards the betterment of society. Moreover, since man was naturally good, all could be moulded by education and thereby discern the correct ordering of human relationships. Similarly, inherent in the Party's educational philosophy has been the contention that ability is not innate, but created in the struggle of practice.

Because of this, quality of personal commitment and politics was emphasized. By extension, the human will could mould material forces. This idea was succinctly summarized by the *Kuang-ming jih-pao* in January 1972:

> We have again and again studied the teaching of Mao Tse-tung and know that education is an organizational part of the superstructure and that it must rely on and serve the economic base, but it is also able to play the great role of moving forward the economic base. The expansion of production necessarily fosters the educational revolution and the promotion of the latter in its turn moves forward the central task.[1]

Thus, on these terms, the correct ordering of human relationships became paramount, and since ability could only be created by practice, the link between education and productive labour was of crucial importance. In order to achieve the integration of education and society, full-time institutions would eventually take on a part-time form, for education would have to be combined with productive labour, and this unity would become a value in itself rather than the means to an end.

During the years immediately following the Cultural Revolution several institutional models were adopted to attain this integration, and from these, two examples will be chosen to illustrate the new measures: Ch'inghua and Wuhan Universities.

In order to strengthen proletarian leadership in the universities after the Cultural Revolution, worker, peasant, and soldier specialists were recruited to undertake teaching, guarantee political quality, and promote academic reform. At Ch'inghua, by 1970, the link between education and society through production was being forged in three ways: (i) by worker participation in the university, (ii) by teacher participation in production, and (iii) by student participation in labour. The implementation of these policies demanded changes in academic organization.

In the Ch'inghua model, not only did the university establish its own factories, but students were also dispatched to outside enterprises to carry out production work. A new type of specialty emerged in which teaching, scientific research, and production were brought together.

The unity between these three components was formed in three different ways according to the nature of particular specialties. The majority of specialties based most of their activity in the factories run by the university, some generally focused their work on the co-ordination between the university and outside factories, and others used the university laboratories as their sphere of operation. But the Party emphasized that the university-run factories and laboratories were not a substitute for the essential co-ordination between outside enterprises and the university. The ideal towards which the specialties were to move was the integration of the three components in order to create a two-way link between education and society.[2]

Although the integration of education and productive labour at the University of Wuhan was achieved on the basis of similar principles, certain emphases, absent in the Ch'inghua model of 1970, were becoming apparent by 1972. As at Ch'inghua, the two methods of institutions running factories and factory-institution co-ordination were an important organizational part of establishing the three-way unity of teaching, scientific research, and production. Similarly, while each of these methods had some advantage over the other, a preference was expressed for factory-institution co-ordination. While the production process in the institutions' factories benefited both teaching and scientific research, factory-institution co-ordination re-educated staff and students, both politically and academically, at the same time furthering the expertise of the workers, peasants, and soldiers appointed as teachers. Factory-institution co-ordination was said to be more important, precisely because the system whereby institutions ran factories was not able fundamentally to change the separation of education from proletarian politics, the masses, and production.

The key to success in factory-institution co-ordination was selection of suitable specialties; in the years 1970-72 there were said to be eighteen natural science specialties which had established long-term co-ordination links with twenty-three factories. Under this rubric three short-term training classes had been conducted with factory co-operation and thirty-two technical innovation projects completed. While faculty members taught within the factory context, thirty or more workers had also been selected as teachers.

Additionally, it was emphasized that co-ordination was not a temporary but a long-term measure. The integration of education and society was to be achieved through the interchangeability of roles of teachers, students, and workers.

In order to ensure the organizational permanence of co-ordination, a "three unities" small group, consisting of cadre, worker, and teacher representatives, was established under the leadership of the institution's Party committee. This was designed to plan political thought reform, educational revolution, and technical innovation; in so doing it co-ordinated the leadership of factory and institution.

In spite of this apparent success, however, one significant reservation was expressed. Criticism of the institution and factory leadership was directed against a tendency ''to use labour to replace learning.'' Learning was the main objective:

> In the institution we must ''use teaching as the main objective'' and in going down to the factory we must also use ''learning as the main objective.'' We must bring together production and scientific research for the sake of teaching, and co-ordinate the creation of model products with systematic theoretical study. In connection with scientific research, it is not appropriate to demand too much of students at the lower levels, but they can be trained in technical innovation to prepare them for independent work. Of those at higher levels, we must demand that they undertake scientific research work under teacher guidance.

Thus an examination of the integration of education and productive labour at the University of Wuhan indicates that by 1972 this policy was increasingly being justified in terms of technical innovation, political study, and scientific research.

While unified leadership of factory and institution was intended to maintain long-term co-ordination, the policy of integrating education and society, which it represented, had become an instrumental means to a specific end rather than an end in itself.[3]

Attention has been focused on the natural sciences, but since Wuhan was a comprehensive university, it also taught arts and humanities. While sources are not available regarding the integration of education and productive labour in the latter fields at that university, information concerning other institutions' humanities subjects indicates an increasing stress on expertise similar to that of the Wuhan natural sciences.[4]

Finally, the creation of proletarian intellectuals, the cornerstone of the Party's educational philosophy, was again being interpreted as synonymous with the demands of national construction. Earlier, in February 1972, the *Kuang-ming jih-pao,* again with reference to natural science in Wuhan, saw the responsibility of a university as developing the country's science and technology in order to reach the advanced levels of the rest of the world. To this end, students were not only to be adept at technical innovation, but had to obtain a definite scientific theoretical level. Moreover, only then would they be able to achieve ''the dictatorship of the proletariat'' over the capitalist class in the fields of culture and science.[5]

From this increasing stress on expertise it was but a short step to the emphasis on individual academic excellence in specific fields of study. Thus, even after only four years of educational revolution, the implementation of new policies to integrate education and society was moving dangerously close to the interpretation formerly associated with Liu Shao-ch'i.

Ironically, on an institutional level, where the position of the so-called Party revisionists had been strongest, Mao Tse-tung and his supporters had emerged victorious. Such Red Guard sources as *Pedagogical Critique* charted what was described as "the seventeen year struggle between the two educational lines." Liu Shao-ch'i's "On Self-Cultivation" had been attacked. By mid-1966 the counter-measures of Liu Shao-ch'i and Chiang Nan-hsiang in the form of the work teams and academic criticism had been defeated; in May of that year Nieh Yüan-tsu's "big character poster" had been hung at the University of Peking and the first Red Guard unit had been formed under cover at the middle school attached to Ch'inghua. On 27 July 1968 the first Workers' and Peasants' Mao Tse-tung Thought Propaganda Team entered Ch'inghua, serving as the model for later teams at other institutions.

But in spite of this apparent proletarian victory, the above analysis suggests that elements of the former elite-mass structure had been re-emerging. While the protagonists of Liu Shao-ch'i's Soviet-style revisionist line had been defeated, the Party's educational philosophy was amenable to more than one interpretation in its implementation. In order to achieve the integration of education and society, the full-time system was to evolve into the part-time form. But the instrument to this end, productive labour, was increasingly being justified in the interests of expertise, and this represented a direct denial of the educational revolution which had taken place in the years 1966-69.

Discussion of changes in the former full-time system brings into focus the development of part-time institutions, which was also a yardstick against which the integration of education and society could be measured. It followed that differences in function between the full-time and part-time systems would gradually disappear; but their functions once again proved capable of differing interpretations, which were to have a significant effect upon their respective enrolment targets.

While the Ch'inghua and Wuhan examples were the models for the evolution of polytechnical and comprehensive universities into a part-time form, other experimental methods were being employed which tended to perpetuate the division between part-time and full-time education. Thus, while part-time institutions like the labour universities continued to run on lines similar to the pre-Cultural Revolution period, more significant were the experimental part-time programmes being conducted within full-time institutions. Because of their small scale and enrolment targets, the 7 May classes are to be distinguished from the Ch'inghua and Wuhan models.

As in the case of the part-time institutions of higher education established in the period 1958-65, the 7 May classes, named after Mao Tse-tung's famous directive, were oriented towards local needs and integrated with productive labour. Unlike the former, however, they were not separate entities, but branches of full-time institutions. Chinese Communist sources are replete with examples of 7 May classes initiated at universities and institutes during the period 1969-71.

The 7 May classes were physically separated from their controlling institutions and usually recruited workers, peasants, and soldiers from local areas. One exception to this general rule was the University of Futan, where thirty worker, peasant, and soldier students, recruited for a 7 May literature course in 1969, underwent a two-year course in that institution itself.[6]

But other examples indicate that instruction was usually given in a form of branch institution in local areas, the 7 May classes being initiated by the relevant parent institute, in co-operation with *hsien* revolutionary committees. For instance, the Chungshan Medical Institute in Canton sponsored a 7 May experimental class for worker, peasant, and soldier students in a mountain village in Kwangtung during May 1969. The institute accepted sixty-five students of middle school level for a one-year course. Similarly, the Peking Medical Institute operated five short-term classes in pharmacology during 1970 and 1971. Students were identified as grassroots pharmacological workers in factories, rural areas, and military units, and on graduation returned to their original posts.[7] But the most explicit statement as to the social origin of students and the function of the 7 May classes they attended was given in a *Jen-min jih-pao* report in April 1970 concerning the North-West Agricultural Institute. For this 7 May class over a hundred peasants were selected from a *hsien* in Shensi Province. Twelve teachers from the parent institute were assigned to the class, and lower middle peasants were employed as part-time instructors. Over three-quarters of the students were Party and Youth League members or commune and brigade cadres.[8]

Two main conclusions emerge from these four examples. Firstly, while no details were given as to the nature of equivalent courses in the parent institution, it seems likely that the 7 May classes were at a considerably lower level of expertise, providing not intellectual depth but retraining for cadres in connection with the specific needs of the local *hsien*. The second, derived from the first, shows that while such classes were conceived as experimental sites leading to the reform of their parent institutions, the actual function of the 7 May courses suggests the maintenance of the two education systems of part-time and full-time which had come into being during 1958-65. When analysed in conjunction with details regarding enrolment targets in former full-time institutions, the 7 May classes appear to have provided training for local cadres at a lower level of expertise than that taught in the parent institutions. The implementation of the 7 May experimental classes would seem to have had much more in common with the Liuist interpretation than its Maoist counterpart. The elite-mass structure was being perpetuated: there were still two education systems.

This perpetuation of the elite-mass structure was not, however, confined to higher education. In spite of changes of jurisdiction over middle schools, the two education systems of full-time and part-time continued to exist at that level. In November 1968 the *Jen-min jih-pao* discussed the Party's policy of transferring schools run by the State to the authority of local organs. From the winter of 1969 to the summer of 1970 many middle and primary schools were placed under the jurisdiction of communes and production brigades. Similarly, in the cities the principle that the middle and primary schools should be taken over by factories was debated, but it does not always appear to have been carried out as extensively as in the rural areas.[9] Nevertheless, local control of education did not prevent the re-emergence of the elite-mass structure. Full-time institutions at the middle level, like those in higher education, organized special classes related to local production needs. In December 1971 the *Kuang-ming jih-pao* quoted an example of a Hupei middle school, founded in 1970, which had established specialized classes in agricultural machinery and veterinary medicine, in addition to full-time courses. The timetable of these classes was flexible, ranging from nine months to a few days, since they were organized in response to local demand. Students appear to have been of poor and lower middle peasant origin and selected from production brigades. The low academic standard of these classes, in contrast with their full-time parent middle schools, can be gauged from the students' stated entry qualifications of primary school graduation. Moreover, in addition to the assignment of certain teachers from the full-time middle school, experienced poor peasants also gave instruction.[10] In short, these specialist classes were ad hoc arrangements, designed to fulfil local needs at a particular time, and were neither in enrolment nor academic standard comparable to their full-time parent institutions.

Furthermore, by 1972, implicit references to two education systems paralleled the growing stress on expertise. In a report from Hunan in April of the same year the ''walking on two legs'' analogy was again used to explain the need for universalization; to this end both the State and the masses had been running schools.[11] Thus evidence would suggest that the Party was relying on two systems to universalize education, with a growing tendency for schools in the full-time system to remain as separate entities, while part-time institutions were provided for those unable to attend regular schools. The role of this supplementary part-time system is graphically illustrated by figures given for school attendance. In 1971 one source claimed that the operation of the two systems had increased the number of children of school age in primary and middle education to 80 per cent in the cities of Peking, Shanghai, and Tientsin, and the provinces of Hopei, Kwangtung, Shensi, Kirin, Liaoning, Kiangsu, Shantung, Hupei, Chekiang, Shansi, and Szechwan. Finally, the *New China News Agency* stated in October 1975 that about 95 per cent of school aged children in China were enrolled.[12]

While the two goals of universalization and elevation were being simultaneously pursued, universalization was itself subject to different interpretations.

Stress on two education systems and the pre-eminence of expertise were being confirmed by a reassessment of the function of part-time schools. These schools were frequently criticized for their low academic quality, and in calling for an improvement in their academic standards, the *Kuang-ming jih-pao* advocated that part-time schools be made equal to the full-time system in terms of staffing, curricula, and timetable. While it is important not to exaggerate isolated examples of changing emphasis in part-time education, this call for regularization was, in its ultimate implications, in direct contradiction to the evolution of the full-time system to a part-time form. This meant that the order of priorities was being reversed: the model was no longer the part-time but the full-time system.

The reform of higher education set the stage for new enrolment policies and processes at the reopening of institutions. The relationship between full-time and part-time education would necessarily be reflected in admissions qualifications and methods.

In July 1967 the Chinese press reported that the Peking Aeronautics Institute had reopened, the first institution to do so since the Cultural Revolution. By the end of 1971 it was stated that ninety institutions of higher education in sixteen provinces and cities were conducting "experimental enrolment." But the reforms of the Cultural Revolution did not appear to have eradicated the hierarchical ranking of institutions in the enrolment context. On the contrary, Chinese provincial radio broadcasts in 1971 indicated that more than thirty leading institutions, including Peking and Ch'inghua, had been designated as national bodies which would enrol their students from throughout the country, with each province receiving a fixed quota. Other institutions, however, were to accept students from the provinces in which they were located. This catchment area system echoed the key point policy of earlier years; there was apparently still to be a two-tiered structure of national and local priorities.[13]

On 13 June 1966 a Joint Directive of the Central Committee of the Chinese Communist Party and the State Council announced the abolition of the entrance examination system. The year's enrolment work would be delayed for six months in order to carry out the Cultural Revolution and to prepare new admission procedures. Significantly, the joint directive acknowledged that, although enrolment methods had undergone reform since Liberation, they were still contained within the pre-1949 examination system. As a result, these methods had not furthered the Party's educational policies, especially the admission of workers, peasants, soldiers, and revolutionary youth. The goal of creating proletarian intellectuals had not been furthered.

Since enrolment was now said to be a process in which students and faculty participated, higher middle students made suggestions to the Party's Central Committee concerning the reform of higher education entry requirements. The main substance of these proposals was the idea that graduates of senior middle schools should first go among the workers, peasants, and soldiers, to be tempered in the storms of the three great revolutionary movements: class struggle, production struggle, and the struggle for scientific experiment. After this remoulding they would receive "ideological diplomas" for entry to higher education.[14]

In addition, the students urged that large numbers of steadfast revolutionaries from among the workers, peasants, and soldiers tested in class struggle be enrolled. Not only were higher middle school graduates with a firm proletarian stand to gain entry, but others with the requisite class background and political quality were also to be admitted.

There is no doubt that the way in which these ideas were discussed reflected the enthusiasm of early Cultural Revolution days, but the rationale for them had already been provided by Mao Tse-tung, in his talks on the peasant movement during the 1920's. At that time he had called for the reform of enrolment, the backbone of the capitalist class education system.

The new methods of enrolment were based on a system of recommendation and selection. Students were to be chosen from among those recommended by the masses for their outstanding moral (read political), intellectual, and physical qualities. The same criteria were to be used to enrol students for higher middle schools. By 1970 four categories of eligible applicant were being laid down with greater clarity and the *Kuang-ming jih-pao* gave the main enrolment targets for scientific and engineering institutions: (i) the best elements among workers and peasants, who had come to prominence in the three great revolutionary movements, possessed three years or more of practical experience, were twenty years of age, and had reached a cultural level equivalent to that of lower or higher middle school; (ii) intellectual youth who had taken part in productive labour in the countryside or had returned to their native places; (iii) members of the People's Liberation Army, and (iv) young cadres. Old workers and poor and lower middle peasants were not subject to the entrance restriction of age and cultural level.[15]

These categories do not appear to have changed fundamentally during the early and middle 1970's, but subtle shifts of emphasis were nevertheless discernable in 1975 and 1976. According to broadcast reports of the enrolment process in local areas during 1975, candidates were still required to have a cultural level equivalent to that of middle school, but the associated factor of age was more specifically outlined. One source stated that applicants should be aged between twenty and twenty-five and single, even if such stipulations might still be waived for old workers and poor and lower middle peasants as before, and now additionally, in the case of certain revolutionary cadres. Based on past enrolment regulations, the tightening of the age stipulation would have tended to suggest reemphasis on academic criteria.

Nevertheless, considerable liberality concerning educational background, age, and marital status had become evident in attempts to secure the admission of national minority students. Additionally, greater attention was to be given to the enrolment of women in various specialties.

It is significant, however, that while these categories of applicant remained generally consistent during the early and middle 1970's, the term ''workers, peasants, and soldiers'' was increasingly being used in a normative rather than an objective sense. This normative aspect was at least implicit in enrolment terminology during the period 1949-65, but sources published in the mid-1970's appeared to be carrying stress on the performance factor one stage further. A Kwangsi Conference on Student Enrolment in June 1975 spoke of the need to consider class background but not to regard it as the sole criterion. While precedence should be given to the admission of workers and peasants and their children, attention was at the same time to be paid to the enrolment of those sons and daughters of ''dubious elements'' (presumably the five non-red classes) who were capable of being educated. References to background indicated that social origin was still a factor in enrolment during 1975, but the phrase ''dubious elements'' could well be interpreted as a reference to those of revisionist tendencies rather than an indication of objective class status.

Two conclusions emerge from an examination of 1975 enrolment criteria. The first is an even stronger tendency than in the immediate post-Cultural Revolution period to stress the political performance of applicants; the second concerns a growing re-emphasis of academic ability.

It was now being stipulated that candidates should have two or more years of practical experience as opposed to the three required in 1970. Provincial sources also stated that care should be taken to ensure the assignment of students to suitable specialties. Moreover, reference was made to relaxation of age and cultural standard regulations in the case of ''outstanding'' workers, peasants, and soldiers whose experience covered a longer period of time. This rule could well have meant that the worker, peasant, and soldier category was being more rigidly limited. This did not, however, preclude the normative use of that category in a more general context.

Finally, while national minority applicants must clearly be regarded as special cases, the inclusion in the 1975 and 1976 regulations of Overseas Chinese strongly suggests a continuing attempt, as in the years before the Cultural Revolution, to utilize talent everywhere. The conduct of the enrolment process in these years leads to the conclusion that academic criteria were already coming increasingly into focus.[16]

But, in spite of these shifts in emphasis, the general framework of categories outlined in the immediate post-Cultural Revolution period remained. This was itself based on the integration of education and society, whereby the former would eventually cease to exist as a separate entity. Enrolment, however, was still a medium through which education and society were linked. Moreover, under the terms of the 1970 regulations, participation in the selection of students had now been carried one stage further. In theory, at least, it was no longer confined to the educational authorities, faculty, and students, but had been extended to society as a whole, to the masses. Thus enrolment itself had become a vast educational process in which both rulers and ruled participated. Party and revolutionary committees were to lead the masses in criticism of the so-called revisionists and in the propagation of Mao Tse-tung's educational line. Although the Party's role was pre-eminent and its leadership the key to maintaining reform of the admission system, only if the masses were mobilized to participate could the enrolment task be fulfilled. Selection of students was not merely the responsibility of the education bureaux. Just as education itself was to serve proletarian politics and be combined with productive labour, so should enrolment not be seen in isolation, but co-ordinated with other social and economic activities. Selection was not to be performed perfunctorily. Mobilization of the masses was designed to ensure that those responsible did not employ a purely professional viewpoint, where enrolment was conceived of as an institution admitting, and a unit sending, a certain number of prospective students. The enrolment process was designed to propagate Mao Tse-tung's educational line: it was an educational process in itself. Thus, under Party guidance, the masses were to perform two functions in enrolment. On the one hand they could offer themselves for registration, with personal interest directly subordinated to national interest; on the other they were to recommend suitable candidates, thereby guaranteeing the successful completion of the selection process. Enrolment became a social laboratory, in which both those selecting and those selected were being continually retested.

In addition, broadcasting stations as well as literary and fine arts propaganda teams were mobilized to proclaim the significance of the new enrolment policies and processes.

While the Party guided the masses, however, cadres were trained in the actual process of administration and implementation. In preparation, enrolment work conferences were held to apprise cadres of the great importance of workers, peasants, and soldiers being admitted to higher education.

The selection process was carried out with the *hsien,* or where relevant, the city, as the basic unit, through the initiative of the masses, and under the leadership of Party committees at various levels. Enrolment work was divided into four stages: (i) voluntary registration by individuals *(tzu-yüan pao-ming),* (ii) recommendation by the masses *(chün-chung t'ui-chien),* (iii) the approval of the leadership *(ling-tao p'i-chun),* and (iv) re-examination by institutes of higher education *(hsüeh-hsiao fu-shen).* Press sources provided detailed information on the first three of these stages. The process was said to be based on the four satisfactions: those of the individual, the masses, the leadership, and the institutions of higher education. First of all, a candidate's case was discussed by members of the production team to which he belonged. If his qualifications were deemed satisfactory, his case was handed to the next higher level, that of the production brigade, for consideration. After such cases had been further assessed by brigade cadres, a short-list of candidates was presented to the commune, which in turn made a further choice from among those remaining, for recommendation to the area *(ch'ü)*. After the area had made a preliminary examination, the qualified applicants were reported to the *hsien* for re-examination. When this process had been completed, the list of candidates was returned to the three levels of commune, brigade, and team for reconsideration. In some cases this reassessment procedure was repeated several times, so that under the maxim ''from the masses to the masses'' the opinions of the latter could be further ascertained, thereby ensuring the selection of the best candidates for enrolment.

Thus enrolment work was not to be performed perfunctorily, as a matter of each production team sending a certain number of names for the consideration of higher levels. Enrolment was a vast educational process in which all participated: the integration of education and society was thereby achieved.

One major conclusion emerges from the above description. While the new enrolment policies demanded the participation of the masses, the selection process and acceptance decision began as early as assessment by the production brigade. Therefore, the list of candidates presented to the commune had already passed through a screening process. Moreover, it was at commune and area levels that enrolment leadership groups *(chao-sheng ling-tao hsiao-tsu)* were established; most of these appear to have been led by Party committee secretaries and also included leading cadres from worker propaganda team offices. It was under the unified leadership of the Party committees that group members went to the various localities in order to make known to the masses enrolment policies, the qualifications required of candidates, selection methods, and the numbers to be enrolled. Group members helped the masses to conduct all round assessment of the candidate's political performance, practical experience, and cultural standard. Sometimes Party secretaries appear to have played a more explicit and personal leadership role. In the case of one commune, a Party committee secretary undertook his own investigation of eight production brigades, in order to interview those who had registered. This example, quoted for emulation, stated that it was only when enrolment work was carried out in such depth that the quality of selection could be guaranteed. In another instance, the Party secretary of a *ch'ü* in Hunan discovered that certain youths whose names had been put forward by communes were not of a satisfactory standard, while some outstanding candidates had not been recommended. He immediately contacted commune Party secretaries to remedy the situation.[17]

Therefore, in spite of the masses' participation in achieving the integration of education and society, the actual task of selection began with the brigade and was further formalized at the commune and area levels. The masses were to transform the enrolment process into a study session, where Liu Shao-ch'i's revisionist policy of emphasis on expertise was to be criticized and the proletarian educational line upheld. Education and society were one. Nevertheless, it is to be noted that, at the stage of re-examination by the *hsien,* those candidates who had been recommended through the screening process were to be organized to participate in further ideological preparation under the guidance of Party committee members.

Additionally, further education in political line was carried out among applicants immediately prior to their departure for higher education. Thus ideological work continued even after their entry to university, and basic level Party and Youth League members maintained contact with students by letter, encouraging them to study for the revolution. In this process the Party's role was pre-eminent.[18]

To this extent the role of the masses was more limited than it appears at first sight. The main task of selection was undertaken at the commune and area levels, where leading personnel were presumably more cognizant of the political and academic standards required of candidates. While the masses in the production teams were aware of an individual's practical experience and political quality, they were undoubtedly much less equipped to judge academic standard. Nevertheless, even though the recommendation of the masses would not have guaranteed a candidate's final selection, it was certainly crucial if he were to be considered at higher levels for entry to a university or institute.

By 1972 academic criteria were being reasserted. In discussing the three conditions required of candidates, the *Kuang-ming jih-pao* stressed that to uphold the primacy of political quality was not in any way to deny the importance of intellectual education *(chih-yü).*[19] It was equally wrong to neglect either. After the initial period of educational reform had passed, academic criteria again came into focus. An examination of categories of eligible applicants for 1975 and 1976 suggests even more strongly that the new enrolment policies of 1966 did not replace the academic quality demanded in previous years, but rather provided additional conditions for candidates to fulfil.

The fourth stage of the selection process, re-examination by institutions of higher education, varied over time and according to area. In general, however, institutions either sent delegates to interview candidates or communicated with local units by post. By 1973 a coherent pattern was emerging, together with a more formal system of academic assessment; re-examination was carried out by an institution's enrolment personnel in collaboration with the Party dominated local leadership groups. In the same year the *Jen-min jih-pao* described how an institution's representatives went down to basic units to ask Party cadres and the masses about candidates' overall quality. In return, these academic personnel assessed prospective applicants in the light of specialty needs, giving the local leadership a balanced idea of enrolment targets and an institution's requirements. In summary, the Party once again guided the masses and academic criteria were becoming increasingly crucial in selection. Finally, on these terms a university or institute could reject candidates selected by local units, and this prerogative may well have been exercised to the full by the elite national institutions.[20]

In the past the pivotal element of academic assessment had been the enrolment examinations. Although no unified nationwide entrance examination system was yet in force in 1972, isolated references were already being made to academic tests. In addition, discussion of enrolment reform in 1977 referred to the temporary revival of entrance examinations in 1970 and their formal reintroduction two years later. Examinations continued in 1973 but most universities did not hold them in the following three years, suggesting considerable disagreement over educational policy.[21]

The years 1972-76 witnessed a growing power struggle between the Gang of Four, inspired by Mao's wife Chiang Ch'ing, and the moderate bureaucratic faction in the State Council, led initially by Chou En-lai, and later by his protégé, Teng Hsiao-p'ing. Educational policy reflected this wider conflict and once again rival interpretations of the Party's philosophy. During the years 1973-74 the Anti-Lin Anti-Confucius Campaign was in full swing, and Lin Piao was accused of advocating the revisionist educational policy of Liu Shao-ch'i. Simultaneously, campaign articles categorized any new reactionary tendencies in the cultural and educational field as inevitably linked to the survival of Confucian learning. As Lin had stressed production forces rather than relations at the Ninth Party Congress in 1969, he was an elitist; by definition, he had implied the desirability of emphasizing individual aptitude and personal excellence.

But the Gang of Four, firmly in control of the media, now saw their main target as not the already discredited Lin, but more significantly, Chou En-lai and his associates in the State Council. The Gang's control of the media may well have exaggerated their influence over educational policy, but there is little doubt that the operation of enrolment in the mid-1970's was deviating considerably from the spirit of the 1966 Maoist reforms. Patterns of elitism were reappearing and in September 1973 the *Jen-min jih-pao* claimed that, in spite of emphasis on the role of the masses under Party committee leadership, politics had been separated from vocational work and selection decided according to examination results. From the radical point of view this was tantamount to the revisionist policy of "equality before marks."[22]

The views of the Chiang Ch'ing group were not, however, shared by China's academic world. Chou's "moderates" were not alone in believing that an accurate measurement of academic ability was indispensable; in late 1975 faculty members at Ch'inghua were criticizing the low standard of worker, peasant, and soldier graduates. As late as 1977 graduates being tested for employment in Shanghai lacked even a basic knowledge of middle school curricula; such an indictment can be seen as retrospectively justifying Chou's call for the formal reintroduction of entrance examinations.[23]

Against this background it is possible to trace the evolution of the new examination system. Because of China's coming diplomatic offensive Mao Tse-tung directed in 1971 that study of foreign languages be intensified; a year later Chou En-lai ordered that students in those fields be directly admitted from the current year's higher middle graduates. A similar rubric was to apply to science and engineering faculties, and these measures were the initial moves in Chou's campaign to raise academic standards.[24] Thus a tentative emphasis on cultural tests and direct entry of higher middle graduates finally led to the formal revival of entrance examinations, as outlined in a State Council directive of 1973.

The gradual way in which the new policies were being debated indicated an undercurrent of disagreement in Party circles. The pre-1966 examinations had been condemned for placing marks in command; the Gang saw their reintroduction as a reversal of the Cultural Revolution reforms. They did not, however, entirely reject the need for cultural assessment, but differed with the moderates over the weight given to academic criteria and how examinations were conducted.

Strident radical criticism in the media was directed at the reassertion of academic excellence implied in the 1973 State Council directive. A policy of "marks in command" had allegedly resulted in candidates revising behind closed doors and the selection of "pace-setters." To the radicals the real issue at stake was the emphasis to be placed on written and practical tests. In July 1974 their mouthpiece, the *Kuang-ming jih-pao,* implicitly accused the moderates of conducting cultural tests in 1973 which stressed book knowledge and rote learning but neglected political behaviour and practical experience.[25]

In summary, the radicals valued personal revolutionary commitment more highly than individual academic excellence and believed that written examination marks should not be used as the principal basis for judging cultural standard. Preference should be given to candidates who applied academic study to production practice, not those who merely remembered theoretical formulae. This combination of theory and practice expressed Mao Tse-tung's educational philosophy: there were two kinds of knowledge, one was from books, the other perceptual, and each by itself was incomplete. Only if they were combined could the true ability of candidates be assessed. This was the correct way to conduct enrolment examinations.

A closely related question was who should conduct cultural assessment. Following the Cultural Revolution reforms, the radicals saw the masses' part in the enrolment process as crucial. But, in surveying the 1973 admissions work, the *Jen-min jih-pao* bemoaned the fact that the masses' task had been reduced to supervising the political examination, when the educational revolution demanded that they have the final word in the investigation and evaluation of candidates.[26]

The Gang was using the issue of practical tests to resist the reassertion of individual academic excellence inherent in the revived written examination.

Ironically, however, the radicals' emphasis on the practical aspects of examinations only intensified the new inequalities arising in the education system. The trend towards expertise was also accompanied by a hierarchical structure of enrolment organs, reflecting increasing differentiation in standard and function within higher education. Practical testing might well have been suitable for lesser institutions specializing in applied science, but written examinations would necessarily have been more appropriate in the case of comprehensive universities like Ch'inghua and Peking which concentrated on pure science and the humanities. One obvious result of the conflict over assessment in 1973 and the temporary abandonment of formal examinations a year later was the greater initiative enjoyed by individual institutions. The fourth stage of the enrolment process, re-examination, meant in practice that elite universities were employing their own criteria in the selection of students.

In conclusion, methods of examination varied from place to place, but specific examples provide a general picture of how assessment was being conducted.

In November 1973 the Hong Kong *Wen-hui pao* gave a brief outline of the enrolment process as it affected young workers of the Shanghai Steam Turbine Factory. Here, practical learning seems to have been the main criterion of assessment, as the "cultural examination" was held at the factory itself. Small examination groups, consisting of leading cadres, old workers, and technicians in the factory, were organized to conduct this part of the selection process. The examination was based on the Yenan principle of collective study. The candidates who had been recommended were divided into small discussion groups, according to the nature of their work. They were permitted to consult reference materials and encouraged to confer among themselves. The small examination groups placed emphasis on practical problems in production, raising points themselves to clarify the candidates' arguments. Thus the cultural examination was designed to test an applicant's intellectual power through the solution of real problems.[27] This is how the selection process was conducted by a factory in the city of Shanghai, but similar methods were no doubt employed by enrolment leadership groups in the rural areas.

Radical attacks in the media suggested the growing respectability of expertise, individual academic excellence, and assessment according to written examination marks. This was especially true of Ch'inghua, where a specific quota of exceptionally able candidates in the natural sciences were by now exempt from the normally required two years of productive labour, thereby passing directly from middle school to university. Foreign languages applicants enjoyed similar concessions,[28] and a new system of academic priorities was emerging. In any case written examination subjects followed the pre-Cultural Revolution pattern. Science applicants, for example, were tested in politics, Chinese language, mathematics, physics, and chemistry, and judged on the basis of marks for individual papers. In contrast, practical examinations were regarded as an additional, but not a crucial, factor in the selection process.[29]

Radical opposition to these elitist trends must nevertheless be seen in the wider context of their struggle with Chou's moderates for political power. Control of the media exaggerated their strength at the centre, but they had much less influence in the country as a whole, even though events since Mao's death have suggested provincial pockets of predominance. It was from one of these, Liaoning, that the radicals sought to propagate their own model of the proletarian intellectual, the "blank sheet candidate," who later became a barometer of the struggle between the two educational lines.

In August 1973 the *Jen-min jih-pao* reprinted an article from the Liaoning Daily, entitled "A Thought Provoking Test Sheet Answer," by an enrolment examination candidate, Chang T'ieh-sheng, who had handed in a blank paper and appended a note protesting against the predominance of academic criteria and neglect of practical learning. To the radicals, his refusal to leave production work for examination revision vindicated the Cultural Revolution reforms and implicitly condemned the moderates for placing marks in command; in his willingness to sacrifice a university place for the sake of revolutionary construction he had struck a blow for the abolition of examinations.

Thus during the mid-1970's the Gang popularized the "blank sheet candidate" as a model youth and forced written examinations to be temporarily abandoned. Yet their victory was short-lived and the trend towards expertise continued under the tutelage of the State Council moderates and China's academic world. By November 1976 the radicals had fallen and the *Jen-min jih-pao* reversed the verdict on the Gang's protégé. Chang T'ieh-sheng now became a negative example, whom the radicals had cynically used in their campaign to sabotage the educational revolution. The 1973 enrolment process had, after all, been conducted fairly, there were no unfair questions, and candidates were allowed to refer to books during the examinations. Chang had not handed in a blank answer paper and his attack on written tests was merely designed to conceal his poor academic performance, for which he had gained only 38 marks in Chinese language, 66 in mathematics, and 6 in chemistry. In addition, far from sacrificing personal for collective interests, he had shown a desire to enter university at all costs by pleading his special status as a production team leader. Finally, he had lied about family background; his father had been a prosperous grain merchant in the service of the Kuomintang.

But whatever the substance of these charges and countercharges, Chang T'ieh-sheng became the symbol of the struggle between the two educational lines.[30] He was, however, far more than just a model youth, and his later elevation to the Standing Committee of the National People's Congress suggested that the radicals sought to fill not only the universities, but the higher councils of Party and State, with their own nominees. For the Gang, Chang T'ieh-sheng served a dual purpose: he vindicated the Cultural Revolution enrolment reforms, but more importantly, he and others like him could be used to create a power base in the universities and in the country at large.

The "blank sheet" was not, however, the only tactic employed to bypass the selection system, and soon a new phenomenon, "the back door," was widespread. "The back door" was first highlighted by the case of a soldier applicant, Chung Chih-min, and suggested that the recommendation process was especially amenable to corruption. In this instance a father had successfully influenced the cadre section of a military district to recommend his son for university entry in 1973. Chung Chih-min was initially prepared to accept this as perfectly natural, but on contact with the masses during study, he began to re-examine his political attitude and finally concluded that it was immoral for revolutionary successors to rely on parental influence. Thereupon he requested re-enlistment in the army.[31]

Conflict over written examinations was providing ample opportunity for high-ranking cadres and military officers to help their children avoid the various stages of the admission process. It is hard to believe that the radicals would have been reluctant to adopt similar methods, but they were quick to make political capital; Chung Chih-min's application to withdraw from Nanking University, like Chang T'ieh-sheng's "blank sheet," was a useful weapon with which to beat their opponents in the wider context of the emerging power struggle.

In 1977, however, the new Chinese leaders reversed the verdict and placed the blame for "back door" corruption on the Gang of Four. The radicals had denied the authority of Party and State in the admission and distribution of candidates; their own nominees had been accepted, but other more politically reliable and academically competent applicants had been excluded, resulting in a fall in academic quality.[32]

In no way did the temporary abolition of enrolment examinations signal a reversal of the long-term trend towards individual excellence and academic elitism.

Furthermore, changes elsewhere in the education system were pointing in the same direction. For example, references to student promotion and curricula subjects in middle schools during the 1970's suggested growing stress on expertise. This in itself was likely to lead to assessment of applicants based on academic criteria. In fact, just as additional rather than new qualifications were required of aspiring candidates for higher education, so was the reform of curricula in middle schools involving the compilation of additional materials rather than abolition of the old. By 1971 five basic courses were being taught in middle schools: (i) education in Mao Tse-tung's thought (including contemporary history, the politics of modern China, and a record of the two-line struggle in the Chinese Communist Party), (ii) the fundamentals of agriculture (encompassing arithmetic, physics, chemistry, and economic geography), (iii) revolutionary literature (incorporating language), (iv) military physical education (with Mao Tse-tung's doctrine of people's war and concepts of war preparation), and (v) productive labour.[33] In October 1975 a *New China News Agency* report used different terminology but referred to substantially the same basic subjects, with the addition of elementary hygiene and knowledge of the arts.[34] The conclusion must be drawn that these curricula did not differ markedly from those taught in the pre-1966 period, and generally paralleled the former enrolment examination subjects.

Even more significant was the establishment of an examination system to govern promotion and retention of students at various stages in middle schools. This system, taken in conjunction with the reintroduction of teaching research guidance groups for each academic subject, also condemned as incurably revisionist at the height of the Cultural Revolution, indicated that at the middle level, academic criteria were becoming increasingly important.[35] If this was the case, then the period of productive labour required of middle school graduates before entry to higher education would have been regarded as an additional, though not the only qualification required.

The new enrolment processes mooted in the Joint Directive of June 1966 did not operate on a significant scale until the years 1970-71, except in the case of such model institutions as Ch'inghua. Under guidance from the Central Government, a series of educational work conferences like that convened by the Hupei Provincial Revolutionary Committee in January 1971, laid the groundwork for the first enrolment since the Cultural Revolution. Additionally, by the mid-1970's, central planning was being more consistently applied to enrolment, and in 1976 for example, the Central Ministries issued directives concerning quotas and manpower, even if there was still considerable devolution of initiative in policy implementation. As all these related developments, in conjunction with the reintroduction of entrance examinations, pointed to stabilization of the enrolment process, those admitted to higher education during the early and mid-1970's will be assessed within the categories debated in 1966.

The four categories of eligible applicant outlined in that year were to be selected on the basis of their political quality, as demonstrated in the three great revolutionary movements. The distinction between candidates from outside and those inside the education system had ceased to exist, and all members of society participated in the enrolment process. Candidates were not to take their selection for granted. Mao Tse-tung thought-study classes were organized by local revolutionary committees to prepare prospective students ideologically; at the same time their applications were being considered at the relevant levels. Political education never ceased, as even those of the purest worker and peasant origin were capable of walking the "revisionist road."[36] Moreover, both applicants and those recommending them participated in a study session. Enrolment was a vast educational process: the integration of education and society had been accomplished.

But the announcement of catchment areas, the creation of enrolment organs, and the revival of planned targets by the Central Government produced once again a conflict between educational philosophy and organizational structure, even if in a new guise. Certainly, on the surface the enrolment work was being conducted according to the target categories and selection processes outlined in 1966. In July 1972 the *Kuang-ming jih-pao* reported that, of seventeen intellectual youth who had earlier been sent to the countryside from Nanking for productive labour, six had been recommended by the masses for entry to higher education.[37] Intellectual youth, however, represented only one of the target categories. A call for individual production units to overcome "vested-interest-ism" and to see correctly the connection between the "part and the whole" indicated that all was not well in the selection process, especially in relation to the entry of the worker, peasant, and cadre categories. Just as leading personnel had been reluctant to allow cadres to register lest the efficiency of a unit be prejudiced, certain *hsien* authorities were accused in 1972 of treating the enrolment task perfunctorily. There were cases cited where local leaders considered enrolment a matter of having a particular number enrolled from a certain *hsien*; in their view this did not require the effort of mobilizing the masses to undertake the task of selection.[38] These tendencies, if unchecked, could quite easily have defeated the object of recommendation and selection by the masses. Moreover, coming into focus was the old fundamental question of balancing the need for those already trained to certain levels of competence with the demand for personnel with still higher expertise.

Such trends were given further momentum by the adoption of a quota system, in response to a national enrolment plan. One of the perennial problems faced during the period 1949-65 was the uneven development of education in China; by the early and mid-1970's the quota system was being designed to equalize opportunity for entry to universities and institutes, especially through concessions to the rural areas.[39]

The Peking Steel Institute may be cited as an example to illustrate the operation of the quota system. In March 1972 it was stated that the institute would enrol one student from a local foundry. This system did not, of course, preclude the participation of the masses who, in the event, decided in favour of a lower middle graduate worker, but it would be more likely to promote routinization of enrolment in the hands of leadership personnel.[40] A certain number would have to be chosen; this in itself limited freedom to select any number of politically and academically qualified applicants.

An institution's part in the final acceptance of candidates has already been briefly discussed, but fuller detail concerning this process was provided by reports of provincial enrolment conferences, bringing into even sharper relief the growing differentiation of function within higher education. For instance, a Shantung meeting on student enrolment in July 1975 expounded the principle of "from the commune to the commune," whereby agricultural and teacher training institutes in that province would enrol students to be trained for the specific needs of local areas. The model for agricultural institutes was that of Chaoyang in the province of Liaoning, which ran both three-year basic courses and special training classes. In contrast to the institutions serving local needs were the prestigious bodies, equivalent to the key point of the early 1960's, which enrolled students throughout the country and trained them as highly qualified manpower for national needs.[41] Thus graduates of basic courses at the latter institutions came under the unified assignment of the State. For these reasons, institutions like Peking and Ch'inghua Universities had greater initiative in the final stage of re-examination than those institutions serving local needs. The different roles played by universities and institutes in student selection and manpower training bring into focus the function which the enrolment of designated categories of candidate was to perform.

While recent developments have reaffirmed their privileged position, such universities as Peking and Ch'inghua were nevertheless initially selected in the early 1970's as the models for other institutions, their enrolment reforms setting the tone for the rest of the country. The purpose of workers', peasants', and soldiers' admission to university was not merely symbolic; in the words of the Cultural Revolution they entered the university, managed the university, and used Mao Tse-tung's thought to reform the university, thus bringing the educational revolution to a new stage.[42]

Nearly 600 worker, peasant, and soldier students with practical experience were admitted to Ch'inghua from March 1969 onwards, while a later report announced the entry of 2,800 candidates from the same sources during the latter months of 1970.[43] But in spite of the importance of their political mission, the academic standard of at least some of these entrants was apparently very low. The old device of special study classes was used to make good the academic deficiencies of old workers being admitted to Ch'inghua.[44]

During 1971 the Party reported on the resumption of enrolment in the following provinces and cities: Hupei, Hunan, Anhwei, Kiangsi, Hopei, Shantung, Kwangtung, Kwangsi, Chekiang, Kiangsu, Szechwan, Peking, and Shanghai. A few examples from the areas listed will indicate how the enrolment process operated.

Radio broadcasts from Shantung in April and Szechwan in November of 1971 indicated that the four major enrolment target categories were all represented among new entrants to higher education. The Shantung source stated that institutions in the province, including its comprehensive university and a range of technical institutes, had enrolled over 6,000 students. Firstly, these encompassed workers, peasants, soldiers, *hsien* and provincial cadres, as well as primary schoolteachers of exceptional calibre who had come to prominence in the three great revolutionary movements. Secondly, the list also included intellectual youths who had been re-educated through productive labour. Thirdly, Overseas

Chinese were mentioned. The Szechwan source also pointed out that soldiers were selected directly by their units rather than through the recommendation of the masses and that youth from the national minorities were also enrolled, but it nevertheless followed a pattern similar to the Shantung example.

Three major conclusions may be drawn from these enrolment details. Firstly, since it was stated that certain institutions were admitting students from outside provinces and cities, the hierarchical ranking of institutions had re-emerged. Secondly, the categories accepted did not differ vastly from those of the pre-Cultural Revolution period. Thirdly, the two sources gave figures for Party and Youth League members. In the Shantung case, of the 6,000 workers, peasants, and soldiers, more than 85 per cent were children of workers and poor peasants. More significantly, however, 75 per cent of the 6,000 were Party members. According to the Szechwan source, entrants to Chengtu Telecommunications Institute consisted of workers, peasants, and soldiers together with intellectual youth, and no fewer than 80 per cent of them were members of the Party or the Youth League.[45]

In summary, it may be observed that the categories presented in these sources are by no means inflexible, and the conclusion emerges that no great change had taken place in the composition of enrolment during the early and mid-1970's, in spite of the Party's claims that workers, peasants, and soldiers were being admitted. Numbers for each category enrolled were not given. The information provided, however, did suggest that there was still an opportunity of social mobility for the very able. Party and Youth League membership, while no doubt identifying the high political quality demonstrated in the three great revolutionary movements, nevertheless indicated a privileged position, not typical of the vast majority of workers and peasants. Furthermore, higher education itself was again conferring social mobility; 1975 reports stated that many graduates had been admitted to the Party or Youth League while still at university.

In addition, by 1972 a new emphasis on academic criteria was in evidence. In March of that year the *Jen-min jih-pao* criticized the previous two years' selection of older students, whose personal responsibilities were said to have adversely affected their study. In future, younger candidates would be favoured, the implication being that intellectual ability rather than practical experience would be at a premium. This emphasis became so marked that a Hupei conference on enrolment in 1975 accused some local authorities of pursuing the following revisionist policies in enrolment work during 1973: (i) the exclusion of workers, peasants, and soldiers, (ii) exclusive concentration on candidates' cultural records, and (iii) placing marks in command in enrolment examinations. Certainly, in assessing the validity of these charges, radical control of the media must be taken into account, but it is nevertheless clear that by 1972 opportunities for entry to higher education had in practice become more circumscribed than the extensive categories formulated earlier would have implied.[46]

Precisely because they had been inadequately defined, enrolment categories are difficult to evaluate. Nevertheless, brief biographies of intellectual youth admitted in 1972 are especially illuminating in this context. In discussing the entry of worker, peasant, and soldier candidates to Nank'ai University in May 1972, an example was cited of the daughter of a poor peasant who had worked initially in a production brigade and then in a Peking factory.[47] She had been recommended by workers for entry to Nank'ai, but as she had graduated from a lower middle school in 1968, she could equally well have been classified as an intellectual youth. Thus while such biographies do not necessarily identify the differences between categories, they nevertheless indicate that enrolment targets, like Chinese Communist statistics, have often been normative rather than factual.

The enrolment statistics available for the early and mid-1970's are few and relate mainly to model institutions. Figures for both different categories and the destination of students within academic disciplines are sparse. On a national level, information concerning quotas is not readily accessible, but a few scattered statistics for countrywide enrolment merit consideration. Chinese Communist sources stated that 153,000 students were admitted to institutions of higher education in the academic year 1973-74 and 167,000 during the following session. In addition, at the beginning of the 1973-74 academic year total enrolment had reached 400,000; the equivalent figures for 1975-76 and 1976-77 were 500,000 and 600,000 respectively. Increasing numbers of entrants in 1973-74 and 1974-75 suggest an estimated enrolment of 450,000 for the missing year 1974-75; by the autumn of 1974 over 80,000 students had graduated.

Three main points may be noted in connection with these statistics. Firstly, they only include those studying basic courses in full-time institutions of higher education, thereby leaving out of account part-time and spare-time institutions run by factories and rural districts. Secondly, enrolment had been steadily increasing since the Cultural Revolution, even if the figure for the academic year 1975-76 was considerably below the 700,000 given for the 1964-65 period. Thirdly, both the above points suggest the consolidation of the educational revolution.[48]

When taken together with details concerning courses held by universities and institutes, these figures give a fair indication of the hierarchical structure which was re-emerging in higher education by the mid-1970's. This elite-mass structure could be readily seen in the different courses to which the candidates were being allocated.

Their own practical experience would have been of inestimable advantage to workers and peasants directed to study in certain academic fields. Practice would have helped them to understand theory. Moreover, although detailed evidence is lacking, it seems likely that the majority of workers and peasants were being sent to study subjects closely associated with their former employment, and many of them to vocational classes which instructed them in special skills. This would have been particularly true of those workers and peasants academically inferior to higher middle graduates; such candidates would have been sent to training classes expressly designed to popularize new expertise and solve crucial questions arising in production.[49] Although terminology describing such courses was not always consistent, reference will be made to two examples of the 7 May classes, cited above in the context of the relationship between full-time and part-time education.

On 2 June 1970 a broadcast from Kwangtung Province disclosed that Chung-shan Medical Institute had admitted eight hundred new students from among workers, peasants, and soldiers with practical experience. Again, this category was not clearly defined. The report added that those selected were well versed in medical work, and 80 per cent of them were Party and Youth League members. Finally, but most significantly, six hundred students were admitted to the five-year system at Chungshan, while the remaining two hundred entered the 7 May one-year course.[50]

Similarly, in August 1971 the *Kuang-ming jih-pao* carried an article by the revolutionary committee of the North-West Agricultural Institute concerning the 7 May one-year veterinary classes organized at that institute.[51]

The conclusion must be drawn, then, that the former two-tiered structure was already re-emerging within individual institutions by the early 1970's. Higher education still had two main tasks: the creation of research personnel, and the training of technical manpower. Both elevation and universalization were being given a place in a higher education supposedly reformed during the Cultural Revolution. The old dichotomy between basic courses and special training courses was appearing in a new guise; some entrants were still academically more equal than others. By extension, differentiation on the basis of catchment areas was already confirming the hierarchical ranking of institutions. Neither the initiation of new enrolment policies and processes nor the reorganization of specialties and curricula had prevented the re-emergence of the elite-mass structure in higher education.

The few details available concerning the operation of the enrolment process in the early and mid-1970's did not as yet suggest that any significant changes had taken place in the composition of entrants to full-time institutions of higher education. The composition of entrants to model institutions like Ch'inghua indicated that the two basic principles of the new regulations, recommendation by the workers and peasants of intellectual youth together with the selection of the best workers and peasants, had certainly been followed.[52] But it is doubtful whether the substance, as opposed to the form, of the new regulations was being observed. For example, recommendation by the workers and peasants of higher middle school graduate intellectual youth may well have raised the political quality of university entrants, but it had not necessarily altered their social composition. The criterion of experience in productive labour had supplemented, not replaced, the academic qualification of higher middle graduation. A considerable proportion of entrants were still higher middle graduates, as they had been before the Cultural Revolution.[53] The Party claimed that entrants to higher education were coming from factories and people's communes; but this was not a radical departure from the old enrolment system. The numerous devices in the pre-Cultural Revolution regulations to facilitate worker and peasant entry always provided a channel of mobility for those of exceptional calibre.

The new enrolment policies and processes of 1966 meant a return to the fundamentals of the Party's educational philosophy, as they assumed that all could be correctly moulded through the requisite training, productive labour. But although all categories of entrant were on this count theoretically eligible to be selected for higher education, in practice their chance of entry was still based, at least in part, on their early opportunities to receive not only political but also academic training. They were, moreover, restricted in the categories of higher education to which they might be admitted. Thus, a reformed structure and new selection criteria provided only a limited channel of mobility for a few of those of worker and peasant origin who had shown exceptional promise in the three revolutionary movements. The limited social mobility and the fostering of outstanding talent, associated with Liu Shao-ch'i's interpretation of the Party's educational philosophy, had reappeared in a new guise.

For purposes of analysis these enrolment categories have been separated, but close examination of the material available suggests a blurring of distinction between them. However, as the Party's educational philosophy in both its interpretations had always stressed achievement rather than ascription, these categories may be considered normative, as statements of intention rather than concrete facts. Moreover, the passage of time and generational change were already producing students who had lived all their lives under the Communist regime; the literal distinction between "bourgeois" and "worker and peasant" origin would eventually lose its meaning.

This would not, of course, preclude the appearance of new unorthodox tendencies formerly associated with the "exploiting" classes. In fact, press sources gave details of undesirable attitudes even among those of the purest worker and peasant origin. To some extent, however, these attitudes were actually being promoted by the shift in emphasis towards expertise.

Unlike the early post-Cultural Revolution period, the mid-1970's were seeing a new stress on academic criteria. Even though the radicals had attacked the reintroduction of formal written examinations and forced their abandonment in 1974, the Gang's power and influence rested on a very narrow base. Meanwhile, the moderates' call to raise academic standards steadily gained ground and earlier, in

1972, Chou En-lai had already directed that theoretical research in the natural sciences be strengthened. 1975 was high tide for the moderates; Teng Hsiao-p'ing was rehabilitated and the way prepared for China's technological breakthrough. In the following months Teng compiled his "Outline Report on the Work of the Chinese Academy of Sciences" and delineated education's role in China's modernization. In his view, it was incorrect to disregard politics, but equally so to neglect science and technnology; intellectuals should not be divorced from the masses, yet full rein must be given to experts. These emphases required organizational change in the Academy which would set the tone for the rest of the education system. Party leadership in the Academy's research institutes would be downgraded and that of experts raised; directors were again to come into their own, thus ensuring specialist control over key sectors. Teng's fall in 1976 initially delayed these reforms, but in the long term has not prevented their implementation, because only in this way can China's national ambitions be realized.[54]

In fact, Teng was merely expressing views increasingly held in China's academic world concerning declining standards, and his policies, especially the proposal that "cultural aces" be directly recruited from higher middle graduates, were partly in response to student reaction to theoretical subjects. Attacks on technique divorced from practice and politics in the Cultural Revolution years had been the main cause of this reaction.

In early 1971 the *Kuang-ming jih-pao* criticized the reluctance of students to study theoretical subjects: "In the past a few people spread the notion that if one studied mathematics, physics, and chemistry, one had nothing to fear; now they have moved to the other extreme, and do not want to be associated with those three subjects."[55] Later in the year the same newspaper spoke of the remedy: "We have taken measures to enable the students to devote 70 per cent of their time to professional study, thereby encouraging them to improve their technique."[56]

The rich experience which the worker, peasant, and soldier students had acquired in the revolutionary movements was invaluable; but once they had entered the universities they were urged to concentrate on the study of theoretical subjects.[57] Theory was still to be linked with practice, but never neglected.

This new move towards expertise appeared closer to Liu Shao-ch'i's than Mao Tse-tung's interpretation of the Party's educational philosophy. Experience in production still fulfilled an important function in helping students to understand theory, but that role was now being conceived as instrumental rather than a value in itself. This meant that in the last analysis workers and peasants were as likely to be chosen for their vocationally oriented production experience as for their political quality.

Nevertheless, students of worker and peasant origin were from time to time being accused of excessive attention to specialized study. This may in part have reflected the growing struggle between radicals and moderates, but it suggested at the same time that students were becoming more and more career oriented. A report from the Kwangtung Chemical Engineering Institute in February 1972 admonished them for neglecting the second and third aims of the dictum. "Enter the institution, manage the institution, and use Mao Tse-tung's thought to reform the institution." These entrants considered that they lacked the requisite academic background and believed that it was in their best interests to attend to study rather than expend their energies on management and reform. This attitude was criticized as being "tantamount to abandoning the base."[58] It was indeed ironic that those chosen to place politics in command had conceived of their duty in terms of vocational function.

The Party's educational philosophy, in its Maoist interpretation, suggested a need for continual struggle. Differences in home environment and academic opportunity would always be likely to create new centres of privilege and unorthodox political tendencies. How expertise served politics and the class composition of student bodies were both important criteria for judging the success of the new enrolment policies, but even more crucial was the question of whether the ideological purity of students' thought could be maintained. Cultural Revolution sources cited cases of students from worker and poor and lower middle peasant families who had entered higher education and then had begun to despise their labouring forbears.[59] The elaborate measures taken since 1969 to prevent those enrolled from "changing colour" had been only partially successful: by the early 1970's even students of proletarian origin were being accused of incorrect political attitudes.

The Party had always reserved the prerogative of awarding class status, which was not naturally endowed but moulded through revolutionary struggle. But productive labour and work-study integration had failed to preserve students' ideological purity. For instance, the *Kuang-ming jih-pao* attacked students at Ch'inghua for giving expertise priority over politics and quoted them as saying: "Politics really amounts to insurance, but technique is different; if you do not study well, you will not be given a cheque".[60] Student attitudes were increasingly reflecting the Liuist interpretation. No doubt they had the collective as well as their own individual interests at heart, but they appeared more concerned with economic realities than the egalitarian implications of Mao's thought. In this vein they had continued: "To be favourably compared in technique to capitalist expertise, that is what the promotion of politics is all about." Moreover, many students of worker-peasant background saw themselves as revolutionary successors, a new elite, and believed that they had no need of continual thought remoulding. Social origin was their passport to political correctness; all they lacked was specialized knowledge. Productive labour had become instrumental, the university system remained a separate entity, and the integration of education and society was being achieved on Liuist terms. The Maoist vision had not been realized, for Teng Hsiao-p'ing's stress on expertise at the expense of politics would ultimately create a society very different from the one which Mao Tse-tung had envisaged. The accession of Hua Kuo-feng and Teng's second rehabilitation were to give this modernization programme the final stamp of legitimacy. The prophet had been reinterpreted.

9

The Prophet Reinterpreted

Mao Tse-tung's death was certainly a watershed in the politics of modern China, but in educational policy it merely provided a catalyst for changes already in evidence. The Hua Kuo-feng leadership moved swiftly to discredit Chiang Ch'ing's radicals and to intensify China's modernization programme, earlier formulated by Chou En-Lai. Since the second rehabilitation of Chou's protégé, Teng Hsiao-p'ing, economic priorities and manpower requirements have been outlined in greater detail. Considerable shifts of emphasis in China's academic world have been designed to satisfy the need for specialized personnel in national construction, and the much vaunted arrival of the slogan "Let a Hundred Flowers Bloom, Let A Hundred Schools of Thought Contend" aimed to stimulate scientific innovation rather than literary creativity. Education has the narrow focus of producing functional manpower for economic development. The West has often cast the intellectual as society's critic; China still sees him as the servant of the ruling orthodoxy. Both the Maoist and Liuist interpretations of the Party's educational philosophy follow this heritage, subordinating individual to collective interests.

China's present development strategy, however, reflects the Liuist view in its call for qualified manpower, echoing the economic priorities of the 1950's. But the new order is not merely a replica of the regime's earlier years; many Maoist ideas from the 1958 Great Leap and the Cultural Revolution have been redeveloped and incorporated in China's new Liuist style education system.

Education has been accorded a key role in the "four modernizations": agriculture, industry, national defence, and science and technology. Pursuing this technocratic theme at the April 1978 National Educational Work Conference, Teng Hsiao-p'ing saw education as an integral part of the national plan, structured to serve the production forces of the socialist economic base. He summarized these priorities as follows: (i) education's growth would coincide with the pace of the economic plan, (ii) personnel training would relate to the needs of economic sectors, and (iii) curricula content would raise scientific and cultural levels. Co-ordination between the State Planning Commission, the Education Ministry, and other departments would enable China to reach and overtake the advanced levels of the rest of the world. The proportion of the State budget devoted to education and science would be increased.[1] Science and technology guaranteed the other three modernizations; specialized training took precedence over intellectual breadth. In addition, the forces of production were more important than its relations; Mao's egalitarian social goals would be sacrificed for pragmatic economic objectives.

The Hua-Teng coalition has sought to legitimize these policies by selective quotation from Mao Tse-tung's writings. China's decision in the early 1970's to import foreign technology may be considered her latest response to the West. Economic rapprochement with European powers was initiated in the teeth of radical opposition, which likened Chou En-lai's diplomacy to the "self-strengthener" Chang Chih-tung's "servility to things foreign" during the later years of the nineteenth century. The radicals preferred self-reliance and internal capital generation to foreign economic control. This radical view was a caricature of Mao's position, however, as he had never precluded the limited use of foreign expertise, but while Mao Tse-tung gave the main emphasis to self-reliance, Hua Kuo-feng has reversed the priorities, seeing foreign study as a guarantee of independence.

At the National Science Conference in March 1978 Hua stated:

> In order to raise our Chinese people's scientific and cultural level, it is necessary to reiterate Chairman Mao's call to study foreign countries. This means that all nations' strengths in politics, economics, military affairs, science, technology, literature, and fine arts must be investigated. We will examine foreign countries critically and on the basis of self-reliance.[2]

Hua places greater emphasis on foreign study than Mao, even if he simultaneously pays lip-service to critical self-reliance, and his call to study foreign politics is surely a tacit admission that alien institutions affect native values; import of technology from abroad may require concomitant sociopolitical change at home.

In the 1950's, Liuist pragmatism was more prepared than Maoist orthodoxy to accept the compromises dictated by the demands of a developing economy, and in doing so it subordinated politics to vocational function. Significantly, before Hua spoke Teng redefined politics: "If our scientific and technical personnel strive for socialist construction, how can they be described as divorced from politics? Socialist work also involves division of labour."[3]

Teng equated political reliability with contribution to national construction, clearly departing from the Maoist view which, like its Confucian counterpart, stressed the moral imperative of the amateur ideal. But both Teng and Mao have shared the meritocratic principle that every individual may become a ruler or educator through positive personal effort. This factor of performance has already been illustrated by reference to normative enrolment categories. The Liuists of the 1950's, however, saw that performance in academic not political terms; similarly, scientists are now considered proletarian by virtue of their specialized function. The Party now says that "feudal exploiting classes" despised all labour, but China's new leaders extol the product of mental effort, science, and honour its practitioners. Scientists and technologists are the new proletariat.[4]

This was the guiding spirit of the new education system's main architect, Chou Jung-hsin, who became Minister of Education when Teng Hsiao-p'ing was first rehabilitated in 1975 and his brief tenure ended with Teng's fall a year later. He died in April 1976, but his influence on subsequent policy has since proved considerable, as he outlined a blueprint for education's future role and the momentous changes which came in late 1977.

Shortly after his posthumous rehabilitation in August 1977, the *Jen-min jih-pao* justified the measures he had tried to introduce in the face of radical sabotage. In his *Outline Report on Educational Work,* Chou Jung-hsin claimed that lack of qualified manpower had slowed the tempo of modernization; the radicals, however, attacked him for advocating "the death of class struggle" and "marks in command." In summary, Chou had called for expert control, and to the Gang, this denied proletarian leadership. Chou's posthumous victory, however, laid the foundation for China's new education system.[5]

No doubt a personal power element was involved, but this could not disguise real disagreement about the direction Chinese society should take. The Gang espoused the Maoist integration of education and society; Chou Jung-hsin envisaged a country led by a technocratic elite. In retrospect, Chou anticipated a scientific proletariat recruited on meritocratic elitist lines, and in his report sees education as technologically oriented, training an elite encouraged by material rather than moral incentives, and increasingly able to bargain with society for the price of its services.

The premium that Chou placed on qualified manpower has thus reversed educational priorities. In a speech to the National Science Conference Vice-Premier Fang Yi called for the creation of two "red and expert contingents," a force of full-time university graduates and a body of technicians trained on the job in spare-time schools. During the 1958 educational revolution Liu Shao-ch'i saw part-time schools as a supplementary separate second-best alternative to the full-time system, imparting limited expertise and restricted social mobility. Fang Yi, in contrast, suggested that part-time institutions be levelled up to and integrated with the full-time system, giving their graduates equal opportunity and status in employment.[6]

In acknowledging that a nation's wealth lies ultimately in the wisdom and genius of its people, China's leaders have been restructuring their education system to raise academic standards and discover exceptional talent. In the long run the whole country will enjoy improved facilities, but in the short term egalitarianism is a luxury the nation cannot afford, and disparities will continue to exist between areas and institutions. In an address to the recent National Educational Work Conference, Teng Hsiao-p'ing expressed the need for balanced development, with ratios between levels and types of institutions geared to the national economic plan. China's specialized manpower sources are meagre and her development strategy requires proper co-ordination between full-time and part-time education. Teng named five priorities: (i) full-time higher education, (ii) ordinary middle schools, (iii) middle vocational institutions, (iv) primary schools, and (v) agricultural middle schools. These will be discussed in turn with special attention paid to two sub-categories, 21 July Universities and key point schools.[7]

The first priority, full-time higher institutions, promotes technological progress and guarantees standards in other sectors of the education system. Not surprisingly, the new priority being given to universities and institutes is at least partly in response to the fall in academic standards, allegedly caused by the activities of the Gang of Four during the early 1970's. In April 1978 the State Council approved an Education Ministry Report recommending that the number of institutions of higher education be increased by fifty-five, thirteen of which were old foundations abolished by the radicals during the anti-Lin Campaign in their attempt to prevent a reversal of the Cultural Revolution reforms.[8] Consequently, the Gang was accused of lowering the quality of university education and in April 1978 the *Kuang-ming jih-pao* cited the case of post-1968 graduates, later employed at a factory in Darien, who had apparently learned only basic curricula and had to be retrained on the job by advanced technicians and other workers.[9]

China's universities and institutes must train research personnel, for only by reaching foreign scientific levels can standards in the rest of the education system be guaranteed. There is thus a balance between raising standards and disseminating knowledge; increased scientific curricula content in primary and middle schools will provide more professionally motivated candidates for higher education. Hua Kuo-feng has called for free rein to individual initiative; scientific innovators and outstanding teachers are equally to be commended.

The expansion of higher education, however, is not haphazard but closely correlated with specialized needs. Specialties are to be rearranged and teaching materials imported, especially from Japan. Theory and practice are still linked, but the former is now dominant; at Chengtu Geological Institute, for example, up to 80 per cent of available time will be devoted to theoretical study and scientific experiment with the remainder allotted to practical work.[10] At last the universities have recaptured their academic base, and scientists have become China's new proletariat.

The second and third priorities are full-time middle schools; these embrace many different kinds of institutions, but for purposes of analysis, will be divided into two major categories. The first of these, the second priority, is the ordinary middle school, academically oriented and continuing to provide the main pool of applicants for the increasingly competitive university entrance examinations. The privileged position of the ordinary middle school has now been enhanced, and is at the same time indicative of the inequalities now emerging in Chinese education. At the First Session of the Fifth National People's Congress Hua Kuo-feng set the target of making ten-year education universal, by 1985 in the cities, but not in the villages, where often eight years of schooling would be in operation, including the two years of lower middle school.[11] (In the new education system primary and middle school each take five years.) The major implication here is that admission to higher education, and thus social advancement, will be infinitely easier for the urban than for the rural population. In addition, Teng's demand to raise middle school standards suggests still more rigorous selection criteria for entry to higher education and increasing social inequality.

The third priority is the vocational middle school, an umbrella term which includes specialist schools *(chuan-yeh hsüeh-hsiao),* like teacher training institutions and technical schools *(chi-kung hsüeh-hsiao).* These institutions are designed to train a professional and skilled backbone for both town and country. Their graduates' limited eligibility to apply for admission to higher education during the pre-1966 period reflected the need to maintain a precarious balance between specific manpower priorities. These schools still perform similar functions, but in 1977 recruitment to them became a part of the higher education enrolment process, their status thereby being upgraded. But, as they often admit candidates earlier rejected by universities and institutes, they are clearly considered less prestigious. No doubt, however, there will be opportunities for outstanding graduates of these schools to be promoted to higher education, as in the years before the Cultural Revolution.

The fourth priority, the primary school, stands at the base of the pyramid, but as it plays a crucial role in the discovery and development of innate ability, it must be expanded and improved. Teng called, for example, for drastic measures to speed the establishment of rural schools in Anhwei Province, lest regional neglect endanger the overall national plan.

Fifthly, Teng Hsiao-p'ing dealt with the second leg of China's education, the part-time system, focusing mainly on agricultural middle schools. These were first introduced during the Great Leap of 1958 and are still financed by commune funds. Their teaching programmes are specifically related to local needs and are formulated by provinces, municipalities, and autonomous areas. In contrast with earlier years, however, they are now more closely linked to the full-time system and have been assigned a key role in rural modernization. Essentially, they are designed to train a technical worker support force for agricultural mechanization, and recall Liu Shao-ch'i's "skeleton of leadership" in the *hsien*. But agricultural middle schools now emphasize cultural as well as technical subjects, giving outstanding graduates the chance of gaining entry to higher education. This opportunity is being justified by quotation from Mao's 1958 statement on part-time students at a Honan school[12] and Teng's 1975 suggestion that non-professionals should be enthusiastic about becoming professionals. In addition, the productive labour component in the schools' curricula is now seen as instrumental rather than a value in itself. The Agricultural Middle Schools thus combine skills with academic study.

Discussion of Teng's last priority brings up the question of part-time higher education, which has taken many forms and currently includes such variants as 21 July, 7 May Peasant, Communist Labour, and television universities. Some, like the labour university, are legacies of the 1958 revolution, while others, for example, the 21 July variety, on which attention will now be focused, came to fruition in the wake of the Cultural Revolution. In their early years the 21 July universities provided short-term training classes for workers on the job, but now concentrate on three-year courses equivalent to those in full-time higher education. On 12 January 1978 a *New China News Agency* report gave a more explicit definition of their role in China's development strategy, stating that industrial departments of the State Council, together with certain provinces, municipalities, and autonomous areas, had assigned the task of training over half the vital new technicians to 21 July universities. In early April 1978 a State Council Directive confirmed that the 21 July universities are to be considered an organizational part of higher education.[13]

Regulations governing a factory or a mining enterprise's 21 July university are formulated by its leadership according to specific conditions, but the annual plan must be approved by the relevant unit of local government. Significantly, the main enrolment targets are still the best serving workers with practical experience, but it is now stressed that they must be of higher middle graduate level, even though extra cultural tuition may be given where necessary.

Every attempt, therefore, is being made to upgrade the 21 July universities to full-time levels; curricula have been systematized, oral examinations as well as projects required, and graduates theoretically given equal treatment in employment.

This elevation policy has been accompanied by growing control from the Central Government. The Education Ministry, concerned departments of the State Council, and full-time institutions have together compiled 21 July teaching materials, the production of which is financed from the budgets of national publishing houses. Finally, regular universities have helped to train 21 July teachers; part-time institutions must now emulate the full-time schools.

If regular universities are the pacesetters for part-time institutions, full-time education has its own citadels of excellence, the key point schools. The mid-1960's brought Liuist retrenchment policies, and the key point principle epitomized the elite-mass structure condemned during the Cultural Revolution. The key point schools have now been revived and once again justified by selected quotation from Mao Tse-tung, although as late as 1976 they were being condemned as shoots of revisionism by the Gang of Four.

In the above quoted report to the National People's Congress Hua Kuo-feng called for the reintroduction of key point schools at all three levels of the education sytem. Later, a *Kuang-ming jih-pao* article provided a preliminary list of 88 key point institutions of higher education, 60 of which had been restored to their pre-1966 status and 28 newly designated. All key point universities and institutes are national bodies and centrally funded but may be divided into three categories: (i) the first and smallest group under the direct control of the Education and other relevant Ministries, (ii) two sub-groups, one geared to the needs of the whole country and the other related to the requirements of a particular district *(ti-ch'ü)*, both being led by branches of certain Ministries, with the support of provincial, city, or autonomous area authorities, and (iii) the third type directed to the demands of a province, city, or autonomous area and controlled by authorities at those levels, with assistance from branches of Ministries. As in the pre-Cultural Revolution period, key point institutions include such prestigious universities as Peking and Ch'inghua, together with other prominent technical and polytechnical institutes.[14]

These centres of excellence are not, of course, confined to higher education, and a Ministry of Education circular to provincial authorities in February 1978 laid down guidelines concerning key point middle and primary schools. Although designated by the Central Government, these schools are actually selected and run by provincial, district, and *hsien* authorities. They are clearly elitist; in Shansi, for example, they number only four hundred, accounting for 1 per cent of all schools in that province, and averaging one middle and two primary institutions per *hsien*.[15]

In conclusion, lower key point schools, like their higher counterparts, receive priority in funding, teaching staff, laboratory equipment, and library facilities. They are also specially administered by *hsien* party committees and educational departments which establish work groups to ensure adequate supervision and to convene conferences. Finally, key point schools are given exceptional treatment in the enrolment process, thereby confirming their elite status.

The key point issue is a good illustration of the way in which Mao Tse-tung has been selectively quoted to justify the discovery of individual talent and the creation of qualified manpower for China's modernization programme. Priorities in the education system have been adjusted accordingly, but whether universities and institutes succeed in their task of fostering excellence will ultimately depend on the quality of entrants. Admission criteria in turn are derived from the Party's theory of knowledge. The Liuist interpretation affirmed the Marxist-Leninist view, but simultaneously gave greater weight than its Maoist counterpart to individual aptitude and personal excellence. In the Cultural Revolution, Liu Shao-ch'i's contribution was rejected. During the middle and late 1970's, he was being accused of claiming that ability *(neng-li)* is hereditary, a view contrary to that expressed in his writings. However, his interpretation has now been taken a stage further; social practice remains the source of knowledge but even greater freedom is given to individual talent. Thus, some are born with a good ear, useful for learning music, even if that gift can only be fully developed through study and practice. In other branches of work, too, performance varies according to both objective conditions and subjective effort. In addition, collective endeavour is the comprehensive manifestation of individual activity, and differences in performance will continue to exist even in a Communist society. Individuals, such as those who contribute to scientific research, must therefore be treated according to their individual conditions, as it is only a few who make progress possible. Furthermore, youth has more potential than age and each generation will be more progressive than the last. This optimistic view sees the question of revolutionary succession almost entirely in terms of science and technology.

The premium placed on the potential of youth now sanctions the direct enrolment in higher education of an increasing number of higher middle graduates. Aptitude is of crucial importance and applicants are being given the opportunity of expressing their own subject preference for university study. They are, of course, selected through cultural examinations which are now believed appropriate for testing not only academic competence but political reliability. Mao Tse-tung had, after all, never opposed these tests per se, even if he wanted to reform them. In fact, in a directive to the Red Army University in 1936, Mao ordered the selection of those with the best examination results, providing, of course, that they were morally (read politically) suitable and physically fit. Finally, for those candidates from the so-called "black classes," academic performance is now seemingly equal to political manifestations as a criterion of eligibility for entry to higher education.[16]

University students are therefore a privileged elite and only a small minority of applicants is finally accepted. An article in the *Jen-min jih-pao* saw this implied social inequality as a fact of life; a lack of material abundance meant that only a small proportion of the population could be diverted from production to study. Only when the present unavoidable division of mental and manual labour had been eliminated through the further development of productive forces, would the Marxist millenial vision of role interchangeability of worker and intellectual be realized.[17]

These elitist sentiments were reflected in the new categories of eligible candidate for higher education announced in 1977. These enrolment targets were very similar to those of the 1950's and 1960's, but at the same time took account of Cultural Revolution reforms, for example, in relation to rusticated youth. Enrolment categories for 1977 were as follows: (i) workers, (ii) peasants, (iii) rusticated youth (but excluding those who had illegally returned to the cities), (iv) intellectual youth (those pre-1976 higher middle graduates who had refused to go to the countryside as directed were ineligible), (v) returned soldiers, (vi) cadres, (vii) the year's higher middle graduates, (viii) youth from the national minorities, (ix) compatriots from Taiwan, (x) students from Hong Kong and Macao, and (xi) Overseas Chinese. Candidates would have been about twenty, but in any case not over twenty-five years of age, and unmarried. There were, however, minor exceptions; the age limit for physical culture specialties was twenty-two. In addition, all applicants had to satisfy the three basic criteria of political reliability, a cultural level equivalent to higher middle graduation, and good health.[18]

At first glance the categories seem rigid, but when read with additional provisions, prove flexible enough to tap talent from diverse sources. For instance, students who were still in middle school but who had shown exceptional promise, could register for enrolment examinations after undergoing strict tests. Similarly, the age limit could be extended to thirty and the marital stipulation waived in the case of workers and peasants with rich practical experience who had shown special scientific aptitude. These latter concessions were also applied to the 1966 and 1967 higher middle graduating classes, who had been denied further educational opportunity by the Cultural Revolution. It must be emphasized, however, that the general condition of the higher middle cultural level was rarely waived, one instance, however, being national minority students registering for institutions in Tibet.

These regulations contrast with those issued in 1976, the last year of radical influence. The mid-1970's had seen a steady extension of coming from and returning to the communes (or factories), which apparently accounted for 27 per cent of total enrolment in 1975. There is some doubt as to whether this policy was enforced nationally, but an Anhwei broadcast stated that it would be applied to all institutions of higher education and vocational middle schools in 1976.[19] This policy has now been rejected as a general principle, but will be confined, as in the pre-1966 period, to certain institutions and applicant categories. By extension, those students already enrolled under this rubric will be ineligible to apply for other institutions. The 1977 enrolment regulations imply the re-emergence of the elite-mass structure characteristic of higher education during the mid-1960's.

Not all applicants satisfy the conditions demanded, but all must be persuaded that their social role, however minor, is a major national contribution. Moreover, if eligible candidates are selected, they study for the Revolution; if not, they join the work force in the crucial task of construction. Thus, all members of society are involved in this ideological preparation, although under Party committee leadership. Actual policy implementation, however, is in the hands of education departments and their enrolment organs.

In theory, those who meet the relevant conditions may register for examination, but the reality is often very different. In 1977, worker and peasant applicants were frequently disadvantaged, meeting opposition from work unit superiors who obstructed their applications and denied them opportunities for revision. In other cases, factory authorities had held preliminary examinations, making outstanding performance a prerequisite for enrolment registration. A Kwangtung source called this improper, as it sowed discord among applicants, their parents, and work unit leadership. These practices, however, were not confined to superiors, and even candidates had been known to abuse the revision time allotted by co-operative factory leadership.

It was concluded that suitable candidates should be encouraged to register, providing always that two basic conditions were met: (i) that production was protected and an equilibrium between existing manpower on the job and the retraining of personnel to higher levels was maintained, and (ii) that candidates selected subjects related to the specific requirements of the factory and their own personal aptitudes. Applicants were to be discouraged from registering for specialties unconnected with their qualifications and experience. Factory and enterprise authorities should permit leave of absence and arrange collective revision; qualified teachers and scientific personnel would provide specialized teaching and instruction in examination technique. Not only workers, however, but all candidates were prepared both ideologically and academically for examination registration.[20]

In October 1977 a State Council directive publicized new nation-wide student enrolment regulations. Stress was still laid on increasing the worker and peasant contingent, although proletarian status is increasingly based on scientific contribution. Student admission is, of course, primarily related to qualified manpower, and graduates are directed to employment through State allocation. An effective process of candidate assessment demands the elimination of corruption, and stringent rules were formulated to prevent the "back door" phenomenon, through which the Gang of Four had promoted its own nominees in the mid-1970's. Theoretically, at least, a centralized enrolment system would make malpractice much more difficult.

The conclusion of the campaign against the Gang, the rehabilitation of Chou Jung-hsin, and the setting of scientific priorities necessitated the postponement of the 1977 intake to February-March 1978, although admissions in future years were to revert to the traditional August-September timetable. Meanwhile, the Education Ministry convened the National Higher Education Work Conference, attended by representatives from provincial and other regional bureaux, State Council personnel, as well as university and institute delegates. The main items on the agenda were the quota system and its concomitant, a unified chain of command.

A later announcement stated that admission quotas for 1977 would no longer be distributed to basic units, but placed under the control of provinces. The Cultural Revolution reforms had assigned a key role to the masses in recommending candidates and allotted a specific number of places in higher education to individual factories and commune brigades. This system did not fundamentally change the social composition of enrolment, but it did guarantee the entry of a few outstanding youth, even if they were often Party or League members. The 1977 quota changes were doubly significant, intensifying entry competition and giving undoubted advantage to higher middle graduates. Chinese sources predicted that 1 in 30 of nearly 5,700,000 examination candidates would be successful, suggesting approximately 190,000 entrants for 1977.

Prestigious universities like Peking and Futan, with four year basic courses, proved strong magnets, each drawing 500,000 applicants. Even Inner Mongolia, a comparatively backward region with very few higher middle schools, reported that 100,000 examination candidates were competing for 4,000 places.

Higher middle graduates would have been better equipped than applicants from outside the education system to face the rigours of competition. In accordance with manpower needs, the Education Ministry directed that 75 per cent of successful candidates enter scientific and engineering faculties, and only 25 per cent the arts and humanities. City higher middle school students have greater familiarity with laboratory equipment than many of their rural counterparts, and key point institutions, increasingly dominated by science and technology, are therefore already receiving a disproportionate share of higher middle candidates, especially from urban centres. Moreover, it was stipulated that the current year's higher middle graduates would account for up to 30 per cent of the 1977 enrolment, thus seriously limiting the eligibility of other candidates.[21]

The administration of enrolment in 1977 closely resembled that of the pre-1966 period and only its major features will be outlined. National priorities and quota systems demanded a hierarchy of enrolment organs, at the apex of which stood the National Enrolment Committee. This body was guided by the statistical projections of the State Planning Commission and its membership consisted of Education Ministry and State Council officials, together with university and institute delegates. Under the direction of the National Enrolment Committee came provincial, district (or municipal), and *hsien* enrolment organs, composed of educational bureau personnel and teachers representatives, and subject to local Party committee leadership. The functions of these organs will be examined within the framework of the enrolment process.

In October 1977 a *New China News Agency* broadcast divided this process into five parts: (i) voluntary registration of applicants by late November, (ii) cultural examinations held from early to mid-December, (iii) preliminary selection in early February, (iv) provincial assessment by mid-February, and (v) admission by institutions at the end of February and the beginning of March. Each of these stages will be examined in turn.

Prospective candidates registered with their own units, and applications were then screened by relevant communes, factories, mines, government offices, or schools in accordance with the enrolment regulations. Applications were then submitted to *hsien* enrolment organs for approval and eligible candidates permitted to take the examinations.

Provincial enrolment committees were responsible for setting the papers, standardizing content, timetables, and marking standards throughout their areas. Examinations were organized and held by the *hsien,* however; in Kiangsi, for instance, one *hsien* established three examination centres and fifteen examination halls, accomodating a total of 740 candidates.

Examinations were divided into the two categories of arts and humanities, and science. Politics, Chinese language, and mathematics papers were common to both categories, but those opting for arts were additionally examined in history and geography, while science candidates were tested also in physics and chemistry. Additionally, engineering, agricultural, and medical faculties fell within the sciences; teacher training was divided between the two categories, depending on subject matter. Foreign language specialties had certain extra requirements, as did fine arts institutions.

Applicants' selection of subjects would be largely determined by aptitudes and interests already acquired in middle school. But national quotas and intense competition forced the adoption of a preference system, by which candidates could only choose two or three institutions and three subjects, all from either the arts or the sciences. Over and above these options, however, applicants could simultaneously select the names of two or three vocational middle schools, endorsing their choice with the statement ''obey the allocation.'' This last rubric was expressly designed to tap the talent of those who fell below higher education standard, but could show middle level technical competence.

These examinations were intended to test applicants' ability both to retain knowledge, and more importantly, to use it in the solution of practical problems; difficult questions were structured to discover outstanding talent. Finally, as breadth as well as depth was sought, assessment had to be based on a candidate's overall average for all the required papers.

At the third stage of the enrolment process, district (or municipal) committees reviewed the test papers marked in the *hsien.* Meanwhile, political examinations were conducted by basic level Party organizations and medical inspection carried out in designated *hsien* hospitals. It was on the basis of these academic, political, and health criteria that the district organs compiled and submitted to the province a preliminary list of candidates, the total number of whom was a little more than twice the planned enrolment.

Provincial assessment and admission by institutions were closely linked. It was the task of the provinces to correlate candidates' preferences, performance, and suitability with the national enrolment plan and the quota system. For example, the general principles of enrolment were nationally uniform, but the concentration of institutions and candidates varied considerably from region to region. In addition, key point universities and institutes enrolled on a national basis, but others' recruitment was related to local conditions. Moreover, regional imbalances even necessitated elaborate regulations to distinguish between institutions specializing in the same subject; for instance, art schools under the Ministry of Culture conducted national enrolment, while those in cities like Shanghai admitted students only from areas in which they were located. Finally, there is no doubt that the 88 key universities and institutes were greatly favoured by candidates, and the enrolment process enabled them to demand higher standards than other schools. In summary, provincial committees performed the key function of reconciling the distribution of successful applicants with national priorities.

At the last stage of the process, provincial conferences were convened to finalize the minutiae of student allocation. A Hunan source explained the order in which final assessment was conducted, and this may be taken as typical of other parts of the country. First of all, fine arts and physical culture institutions had special characteristics, and were filled as a separate category. Secondly, enrolment for the general run of institutions was completed according to the following three sets of priorities: (i) key point schools preceded the rest, (ii) outside bodies came before those in Hunan, and (iii) higher education was dealt with prior to vocational middle schools. Confirmation of selection, however, involved direct consultation with institutions. Under provincial leadership, universities and institutes made their own choice of the best applicants, according to material submitted and candidates' preferences. Their lists were then forwarded to the province for final approval, after which institutions issued admission notices to successful applicants.[22]

An analysis of available evidence concerning the social origin of successful applicants suggests the re-emergence of the elite-mass structure in higher education, and the concomitant evolution of a society, highly stratified, and very different from the one Mao Tse-tung envisaged. The first signs of this trend may be seen in the results of the 1977 enrolment process, which indicate that in the years to come Chinese society will very likely be led by a technologically oriented meritocratic elite.

Two features of admissions administration were crucial in determining the nature and direction of this intake: candidate eligibility and catchment areas.

In theory, certain enrolment targets would have fallen under the preferential acceptance rubric, which gave them priority of admission when their academic qualifications and examination performance equalled those of other candidates. These categories included workers, peasants, and applicants of similar family background, while national minority youth, compatriots of Taiwan origin, students from Hong Kong and Macao, and Overseas Chinese also received a certain measure of priority.[23] These last groups were few in number and of marginal importance, however, the privileges accorded them being designed to utilize scientific as well as technical expertise acquired abroad and to enhance the legitimacy of the Chinese Communist regime. Attention will therefore be focused on the worker and peasant categories, the first two enrolment targets listed earlier. Minimal numbers of workers and peasants would nevertheless have been represented among rusticated youth, intellectual youth, cadres, and higher middle graduates.

The eligibility of these workers and peasants would, however, have been restricted on two counts. Previous discussion focused on the special academic preparation needed by factory workers to pass the examinations, and few of them would have been of the outstanding calibre required by key point institutions. In addition, the "from the factory" rubric meant retraining in prescribed schools, and in Kweichow, for example, workers with five years service in State enterprises received wages during study. These wages were paid according to seniority, and such students would thus have been financially better endowed than students receiving scholarship aid, but their chances of social advancement were nevertheless strictly circumscribed.[24] In conclusion, qualified workers were most often directed or guided to apply for specialties and institutes closely associated with their employment, thereby acquiring enhanced technical skills as opposed to intellectual breadth. In contrast, other categories like higher middle graduates had virtually unlimited opportunity to study the subject of their choice.

Enrolment organs allocated students through catchment areas, which reflected a national-local division of labour between key point and lesser institutions. Thus the provincial assessment process involved an order of priorities, enabling prestigious national universities and institutes to select the best examinees from the large number of candidates they had attracted. Other institutions were then allotted students according to rank, with those at the end of the scale receiving the least competent higher middle graduates, in addition to the workers and peasants recruited through the factory-commune rubric.

This division of labour may be illustrated by reference to allocation patterns in minor specialist institutes. As a general rule, local medical, teacher training, and agricultural institutes enrolled those barefoot doctors, teachers in schools run by the masses, and agro-technicians who had shown exceptional promise; again, their newly acquired skills would raise professional and scientific standards in the countryside.[25] Furthermore, a number of short-term courses in major universities serve similar purposes, resulting in functional differentiation both within and between institutions of higher education.

It was this kind of policy that Liu Shao-ch'i had in mind when advocating two education systems during the mid-1960's. Part-time schools would provide expertise for communes and brigades, the celebrated "technical skeleton of the *hsien*." Now this strategy has been re-adopted to give locally-financed part-time institutions a significant, though secondary, role in the unified admissions process. Part-time schools are being re-organized in an attempt to level them up to the standards of local full-time institutes. Thus applicants who were not selected for the State-run full-time system could later apply for, or be directed to, the 21 July, Communist Labour, or television universities.[26] These part-time students, predominantly though not exclusively of worker and peasant origin, could therefore be expected to achieve a limited upward mobility, by no means incompatible with increasing social stratification.

In contrast, the key point universities and institutes have become a charmed circle, providing the best facilities, attracting the finest minds, and enhancing their own reputation. They are the pacesetters for the rest of the education system as a whole and the nature of their enrolment may well indicate the future direction of Chinese society.

Admission to three selected key point examples, Peking University, Ch'inghua University, and China's University of Science and Technology will be analyzed according to the criteria of social background, age, and examination performance. At Peking, workers, peasants, and their children were said to form the majority of entrants, while China's University repeated that pattern, but added cadres' offspring. Most significant, however, was the Ch'inghua example, which gave instances of worker and peasant entrants. One worker, aged twenty-three and a former rusticated youth, later became a commune Party committee deputy secretary and owed his great success in the examination to spare-time study. Another entrant was a 1965 higher middle graduate wireless worker from Peking who performed comparatively well through similar study. These facts suggest that social mobility is possible, but such students would, no doubt, be in a distinct minority among entrants to prestigious universities like Ch'inghua.

On the surface, then, the enrolment process followed the preferential acceptance of workers and peasants. Other details, however, suggest the need to modify this view, as Party and Youth League members represented 92 per cent of the Peking, 83 per cent of the Ch'inghua, and 94 per cent of the China University intake. These figures are important for two reasons: (i) they indicate that such nominally proletarian elements were in substantial positions of leadership, therefore occupying a very special place among workers and peasants, and (ii) Party or Youth League membership prior to university entry meant that upward mobility was taking place increasingly early in an individual's life. This second view is further confirmed by the age of entrants: over 56 per cent at Peking were under the age of twenty-one, the average age at Ch'inghua was twenty, and that for China's University about nineteen.

These age statistics, in turn, are a reflection of the new premium placed on youth by the Party's theory of knowledge. Finally, the 1977 enrolment process was designed as the most efficient method of recruiting innate ability, personal aptitude, and individual excellence, and the marks scored by entrants to these three institutions bear eloquent witness to an intensely competitive selection system. The vast majority of successful applicants at Peking scored over 70 per cent, with a quarter gaining a mark above 80 per cent as an average for all subjects; at Ch'inghua the pattern was similar with the greater proportion of candidates surpassing 80 per cent over the three disciplines of mathematics, physics, and chemistry; and the differently computed statistics for China's University suggest a roughly equivalent or slightly lower percentage. Furthermore, numbers of entrants placed competition for admission to key point institutions in even sharper relief; Peking accepted 395, Ch'inghua 818, and China's University 711, out of a projected total intake of 190,000 for all China's institutions of higher education.[27]

In summary, the foregoing analysis of the social background, age, and examination performance of entrants to these three elite institutions confirms conclusively that the apex of China's education system has become a privileged meritocracy.

This modern image of a China increasingly ruled by a technocratic elite, albeit under Party supremacy, diverges significantly from Mao Tse-tung's egalitarian social goals. He was born into a China where the servants of government were schooled by a dominant orthodoxy. His educational writings rejected the Confucian canon, but unconsciously inherited its belief in the innate goodness of man, that moral imperative and amateur ideal by which all are capable of discerning the correct ordering of human relationships, the cornerstone of good government. During the years of revolutionary struggle Mao Tse-tung formulated the Party's educational philosophy, but on the Communist accession to power, leaders like Liu Shao-ch'i (posthumously rehabilitated in 1980) had to adjust that thinking to the seemingly inexorable dynamics of a developing economy, giving greater weight to academic excellence than political criteria. They too saw education as directly related to the needs of society, but increasingly conceived of revolutionary commitment as synonymous with material contribution to national construction.

Some observers believed that the Maoist reforms of the Great Leap and the Cultural Revolution would turn back the tide of technological progress. Certainly, the excesses of the 1966-76 decade may well have cost China a generation of qualified manpower, but it would be over-simplified to see all these measures in negative terms. Indeed, Mao has been reinterpreted and selectively quoted to justify the new departures which China's leaders now feel compelled to make; such innovations as agricultural middle schools and 21 July universities have been upgraded and incorporated in China's new education system. It is tempting to say that the wheel has come full circle, yet present policies are not merely a repetition of the 1950's and 1960's; they are, rather, a refinement and extension of the Liuist interpretation.

The pragmatic figures of Chou En-lai, Hua Kuo-feng, Teng Hsiao-p'ing, and Chou Jung-hsin have been the main architects of China's present modernization programme, which requires the rapid creation of large numbers of scientists and technologists. But under their leadership, education has been given a very narrow focus, seemingly abandoning wider humanistic concerns for functionally specific goals. There are already remote signs of a backlash, but for the time being the dire imperative of economic growth may silence dissenting voices. If China's modernization aims are achieved on target by the turn of the century, Mao's more utopian social goals may be heard again.

Notes

NOTES TO CHAPTER ONE

1. Donald J. Munro, *The Concept of Man in Early China* (Stanford, CA, 1969), p. 48.
2. See, for instance, Mark Elvin, *The Pattern of the Chinese Past* (Stanford, CA, 1973), pp. 180-81.
3. Y. C. Wang, *Chinese Intellectuals and the West, 1872-1949* (Chapel Hill, NC, 1966), pp. 372-73.
4. Ibid., pp. 362-63.
5. R. F. Price, *Education in Communist China* (London, 1970), p. 97.
6. Wang, *Chinese Intellectuals and the West*, pp. 148-49.
7. "Oppose Book Worship" (May 1930), in *Selected Readings from the Works of Mao Tse-tung* (Peking: Foreign Languages Press, 1971), pp. 42-43.
8. "Recruit Large Numbers of Intellectuals" (December 1939), in *Selected Works of Mao Tse-tung*, vol. 2 (Peking: Foreign Languages Press, 1965), pp. 302-3.
9. "The May the Fourth Movement" (May 1939), in *Selected Works of Mao Tse-tung*, vol. 2 (Peking: Foreign Languages Press, 1967), p. 238.
10. "Rectify the Party's Style of Work" (February 1942), in *Selected Works of Mao Tse-tung*, vol. 3 (Peking: Foreign Languages Press, 1967), pp. 39-41.
11. "Yenan University Educational Line and Temporary Regulations (May 1944)," reproduced from Michael Lindsay, *Notes on Educational Problems in Communist China*, in Stewart Fraser, ed., *Chinese Communist Education* (New York, NY, 1965), pp. 78-82. A discussion of teaching methods also appears in my monograph *Education and University Enrolment Policies in China, 1949-1971*, (Canberra, 1973).
12. "On Coalition Government" (April 1945), in *Selected Works of Mao Tse-tung*, vol. 3, (Peking: Foreign Languages Press, 1967), p. 255.
13. "On New Democracy" (January 1940), in *Selected Works of Mao Tse-tung*, vol. 2 (Peking: Foreign Languages Press, 1965), pp. 380-81.

NOTES TO CHAPTER TWO

1. In 1950, in East China, there were said to be 85 institutions, representing 37.4 per cent of the total number, and Shanghai had 43 institutions, that is one-fifth of the total. This information was given in the closing speech at the First National Education Conference by the Minister of Education, Ma Hsu-lun, *Jen-min chiao-yü*, July 1950, p. 13.
2. The Red Rock Fighting Company *et alia*, "A Record of the Great Events in the Struggle Between the Two Lines in the Field of Higher Education," in *Pedagogical Critique* (Peking: Editorial Committee of the Peking University Cultural Revolutionary Committee), No. 2, 20 August 1967, translated in *Chinese Sociology and Anthropology*, vol. 2, No. 1-2 (Fall-Winter 1969-70): pp. 21-24.
3. Alexander G. Korol, *Soviet Education for Science and Technology* (New York, 1957), pp. vi, vii, and 143-44.
4. *An Analysis of Chinese Communist Educational and Cultural Affairs*, (Taipei: World Anti-Communist League, 1971), pp. 50-51.

5. R. F. Price, *Education in Communist China* (London, 1970), pp. 147-49.
6. Chiu-sam Tsang, *Society, Schools, and Progress in China* (London, 1968), p. 197.
7. They were as follows: The Chinese People's University, and the Universities of Chungshan, Futan, Hsiamen, Hsi Pei, Lanchow, Nank'ai, Nanking, Peking, Shantung, Szechuan, Tung Pei, Wuhan and Yunnan. This information was given in one of the enrolment handbooks, published annually by the Central Government, *1955 nien shu-ch'i kao-teng hsüeh-hsiao chao-sheng sheng-hsüeh chih-tao* [Guidance on Enrolment in Institutions of Higher Education, Summer 1955], p. 167.
8. Chiu-sam Tsang, *Society, Schools, and Progress in China*, p. 193; see also a 1953 article by Tseng Chao-lun, a leading non-Communist intellectual, "Higher Education in New China," reproduced in S. Fraser ed., *Chinese Communist Education* (New York, 1965), p. 191.
9. *Chung-kuo ch'ing-nien pao*, 6 July 1954. The qualification must be added, however, that there were cases reported of candidates for entry to higher education failing to understand the important role played by comprehensive universities. Nevertheless, there remained no doubt about the elite status of such institutions as Peking University.
10. Liu Shao-ch'i, "Speech at the Ceremonial Opening of the Chinese People's University," 3 October 1950, as translated from *Tou-pi-k'ai T'ung-hsin* [Struggle—Criticism—Transformation News], a Red Guard publication by the Preparatory Committee for the Rebels' United Com-

mittee of the Higher Education Ministry and the Education Ministry, 5 April 1967, pp. 14-16 in *Collected Works of Liu Shao-ch'i*, vol. 2, 1945-1957 (Hong Kong: Union Research Institute, 1969), pp. 235-41.
11. *1956 nien kao-teng hsüeh-hsiao chao-sheng sheng-hsüeh chih-tao* [Guidance on Enrolment in Institutions of Higher Education in 1956], p. 6. See also Tseng Chao-lun's "Higher Education in New China," in S. Fraser, ed., *Chinese Communist Education*, p. 192.
12. "Temporary Regulations for Institutions of Higher Education," Section 4, Clause 18, *Jen-min chiao-yü*, September 1950, pp. 68-69. Details concerning teaching research guidance groups are given by Tseng Chao-lun in Fraser, p. 193.
13. Price, *Education in Communist China*, p. 141 and Tsang, *Society, Schools, and Progress in China*, p. 184.
14. "In Practice Continually Open Up the True Road of Knowledge," *Kuang-ming jih-pao*, 28 June 1972.
15. Liu Shao-ch'i, *How To Be A Good Communist* (Foreign Languages Press, Peking, 1965), pp. 3-6.
16. Ibid., pp. 47-48.
17. "Directive to the Democratic Construction Association and Federation of Industry and Commerce" (1959), as quoted in *Ching-kang-shan Pao*, 8 February 1967, *Quotations from President Liu Shao-ch'i*, introduced by C. P. Fitzgerald (Melbourne, 1968) p. 62.
18. Liu Shao-ch'i, *How To Be A Good Communist* (Peking: Foreign Languages Press, 1965), pp. 63-64.
19. Ibid., p. 4.

NOTES TO CHAPTER THREE

1. The categories are listed in "The 1957 Regulations Regarding Enrolment of New Students in Institutions of Higher Education," *Jen-min jih-pao*, 25 April 1957.
2. Korol, *Soviet Education for Science and Technology*, p. 6.
3. *Chiao-shih pao*, 7 August 1956.
4. A Red Guard discussion of Mao Tse-tung's emphasis on performance, entitled "The Question of Ch'u-shen: An Analy-

sis by the Peking Social Origin Research Group," appears in *Chung-hsüeh Wen-ming pao*, 18 January 1967. The other two concepts are also outlined in detail.
5. As explained later, not all serving cadres who applied for entry to higher education were directed to do so, since some could register under the "free application" rubric.
6. *Jen-min jih-pao*, 19 June 1954.

7. *Jen-min chiao-yü*, October 1957, p. 9.
8. *Jen-min jih-pao*, 14 July 1956. However, these figures do not appear to have been all-inclusive, and were also subject to later revision. Further details regarding numbers registered are given in Chapter 4.
9. For example, *Kuang-ming jih-pao*, 6 April 1956.
10. *Jen-min jih-pao*, 27 May 1956.
11. Normal schools were generally classified under vocational schools, and primary school teachers included in the serving personnel rubric. Primary school teachers are classified here as coming from "outside the education system" because they were not currently pursuing a course of full-time study.
12. *Jen-min chiao-yü*, April 1957, p. 14.
13. *Kuang-hsi jih-pao*, 7 July 1956, and *Chiao-shih pao*, 29 May 1956.
14. *Chiao-shih pao*, 21 May 1957.
15. The promotion of teachers in workers' spare-time schools to higher education is discussed in *Kuang-ming jih-pao*, 5 July 1955.
16. Information concerning the entry of middle level specialist health cadres is given in *Kuang-ming jih-pao*, 19 May 1956.
17. *New China News Agency*, 20 May 1956. Hereafter called *NCNA* in footnotes.
18. *Wen-hui pao*, (Shanghai), 18 April 1957.
19. *Kuang-hsi jih-pao*, 7 April 1957.
20. *Jen-min jih-pao*, 9 June 1955.
21. Ibid., and see *Kuang-ming jih-pao*, 27 May 1955 for details concerning music, fine arts, and theatrical institutes.
22. *Kuang-ming jih-pao*, 7 April 1956.
23. *Chiao-shih pao*, 7 August 1956.
24. *Jen-min jih-pao*, 27 March 1957.
25. *Kuang-ming jih-pao*, 7 April 1956 and *Chung-kuo ch'ing-nien*, 1 July 1958.
26. *Jen-min chiao-yü*, May 1957, p. 50.
27. Ibid., October 1957, p. 14.
28. *Jen-min shou-ts'e* [People's Handbook], (Peking, 1959), p. 501. Significantly, this source states that there were 58 schools in 1957, in spite of the fact that such institutions had stopped enrolling in 1955.
29. *Jen-min chiao-yü*, September 1957, p. 12.
30. *Pedagogical Critique*, No. 2, 20 August 1967, translated in *Chinese Sociology and Anthropology*, vol. 2, no. 1-2 (Fall-Winter 1969/70):34.
31. "Strive to Carry Out This Year's Higher Education Plan," *Kuang-ming jih-pao*, 19 February 1953.
32. From a speech by Ma Hsü-lun in February 1953.
33. "Our Country's People's Education Serves Socialism: the Deep Transformation of New China's Higher Education," *Jen-min jih-pao*, 23 September 1954. Internal examinations and tests in institutions of higher education were assessed on the basis of the Soviet five-grade system in which "excellent" and "good" were the two highest grades.
34. See "A Decision concerning the Reform of the Education System," passed at the Government Administration Council's 97th Executive Session on 10 August 1951. *Chinese Education*, vol. 3, no. 1 (Spring 1970):57.
35. *Chung-kuo ch'ing-nien pao*, 15 July 1956.
36. Stipulations concerning serving personnel appear in "The 1956 Regulations regarding Enrolment of New Students in Institutions of Higher Education," *Kuang-ming jih-pao*, 7 April 1956.
37. Further information concerning the fifth category appears in *Chung-kuo ch'ing-nien pao*, 12 July 1956.
38. "The 1956 Regulations regarding Enrolment of New Students in Institutions of Higher Education," *Kuang-ming jih-pao*, 7 April 1956.
39. *Jen-min jih-pao*, 17 March 1956.
40. *Chung-kuo ch'ing-nien pao*, 15 July 1956.
41. Ibid.
42. *Jen-min chiao-yü*, July 1957, pp. 36-39. In addition, it must be pointed out in this context that higher education was usually residential, although day students *(tsou-tu sheng)* were often encouraged, wherever possible, presumably for economic reasons.
43. Ibid., March 1957, p. 48, and April 1957, p. 47.
44. Ibid., October 1957, p. 14. The percentages for the years 1957 and 1958 are given in *Ten Great Years* (State Statistical Bureau, Peking 1960), p. 200.
45. "Strive to Complete This Year's Higher Education Enrolment Plan," *Jen-min jih-pao*, 17 March 1956.
46. "The 1956 Regulations regarding Enrolment of New Students in Institutions of

Higher Education," *Kuang-ming jih-pao*, 7 April 1956.

47. *Kung-jen jih-pao*, 12 May 1956.
48. *Jen-min jih-pao*, 17 March 1956.
49. *Kuang-ming jih-pao*, 20 May 1956.
50. *Chung-kuo ch'ing-nien pao*, 1 June 1956.
51. *Kuang-ming jih-pao*, 20 May 1956.
52. *Jen-min jih-pao*, 14 July 1956.
53. Regulations regarding revision schools for intellectual youth were published in full in *Chung-kuo ch'ing-nien pao*, 1 February 1956.
54. *Kuang-ming jih-pao*, 18 March 1956.
55. *Jen-min jih-pao*, 13 March 1956.
56. Ibid., 17 March 1956.
57. This system of revision classes is discussed in *Chung-kuo ch'ing-nien pao*, 1 June 1956. Their division into subject categories is explained in *Jen-min jih-pao*, 13 March 1956.
58. *Jen-min jih-pao*, 17 March 1956.
59. *Kuang-ming jih-pao*, 6 April 1956.
60. For this and the following case, see *Jen-min jih-pao*, 6 April 1956.
61. The third example appears in *Kuang-ming jih-pao*, 23 April 1956.
62. *Kuang-ming jih-pao*, 19 May 1956 and 22 June 1956.
63. Ibid., 20 June 1956.
64. *Wen-hui pao* (Shanghai), 16 April 1957. For information concerning primary school teachers, see *Chiao-shih pao*, 21 May 1957.
65. It appears that the revision schools established for Overseas Chinese and students from Hong Kong and Macao were under the jurisdiction of the Overseas Chinese Affairs Organs and the Hong Kong and Macao Returned Higher Middle Graduates' Promotion Guidance Committee, situated in Canton.
66. *Ta kung-pao* (Hong Kong), 9 September 1955 and *Jen-min chiao-yü*, February 1957, p. 56.
67. *Jen-min chiao-yü*, February 1957, pp. 54-55.
68. Ibid.
69. *Ta-kung pao* (Hong Kong), 9 September

1955 and *Jen-min jih-pao*, 14 July 1956.
70. The position of the national minorities is discussed in *Jen-min chiao-yü*, October 1957, p. 6.
71. *Jen-min jih-pao*, 31 March 1957.
72. *Chung-kuo ch'ing-nien pan-yüeh k'an*, 16 April 1957, p. 6.
73. *Kuang-ming jih-pao*, 28 May 1956.
74. *Chiao-shih pao*, 29 March 1957 and *Kuang-ming jih-pao*, 25 April 1957.
75. *Kuang-ming jih-pao*, 25 April 1957.
76. *Chung-kuo ch'ing-nien pan-yüeh k'an*, 16 April 1957, p. 6.
77. Ibid.
78. *Chung-kuo ch'ing-nien pao*, 14 May 1955.
79. *Kuang-hsi jih-pao*, 7 July 1956, and *Jen-min chiao-yü*, January 1957, p. 66.
80. *Chung-kuo ch'ing-nien pan-yüeh k'an*, 16 April 1957, p. 6.
81. Ibid.
82. *Jen-min chiao-yü*, January 1957, pp. 65-66.
83. *Kuang-hsi jih-pao*, 7 July 1956.
84. *Chung-kuo ch'ing-nien pan-yueh k'an*, 16 April 1957, p. 6.
85. *Kuang-hsi jih-pao*, 7 July 1956.
86. *Kuang-ming jih-pao*, 28 May 1956.
87. *Jen-min chiao-yü*, April 1957, p. 7.
88. *Kuang-ming jih-pao*, 29 June 1955.
89. *Jen-min chiao-yü*, April 1957, p. 7.
90. *Kuang-ming jih-pao*, 16 August 1955.
91. Ibid., 29 June 1955.
92. Further details concerning the teachers' small group are given in *Kuang-ming jih-pao*, 29 June 1955.
93. A full criticism of the disparity between middle school and university level curricula, together with an assessment of revision contents, appears in *Jen-min chiao-yü*, April 1957, pp. 46-47.
94. *Chung-kuo ch'ing-nien pao*, 14 May 1955 and *Kuang-ming jih-pao*, 29 June 1955.
95. *Jen-min chiao-yü*, April 1957, p. 47.
96. *Kuang-ming jih-pao*, 13 August 1959.
97. "The Ten Great Crimes of the 1 August School," reproduced in *Chinese Sociology and Anthropology*, vol. 1, no. 4 (Summer 1969): 15-23.

NOTES TO CHAPTER FOUR

1. *Kuang-ming jih-pao*, 16 August 1955.
2. *Jen-min jih-pao*, 9 June 1955.
3. *Jen-min chiao-yü*, October 1957, p. 10.
4. *Kuang-hsi jih-pao*, 7 July 1956.
5. *Jen-min chiao-yü*, October 1957, p. 54.
6. *T'ou-k'ao ta-hsüeh shou-ts'e* [Handbook concerning Examinations for Entry to Universities] 1951, pp. 2-3.
7. *Wen-hui pao* (Shanghai), 12 May 1954.
8. Leo A. Orleans, *Professional Manpower and Education in Communist China* (Washington, 1961), pp. 131 and 136.
9. For figures relating to 1955, see *Kuang-ming jih-pao*, 29 June 1955; for 1956, *Jen-min jih-pao*, 17 March 1956; for 1957, *Ta-kung pao* (Hong Kong), 27 May 1957.
10. This table has been computed from the three sources mentioned above, with the addition of *Ch'ung-kuo ch'ing-nien pan-yüeh k'an*, 16 April 1957, p. 6. Because of the urgent need for schoolteachers, it was reported in the *Chung-kuo ch'ing-nien pao*, 20 May 1956, that teacher training could enrol 20,000 additional students if the requisite quantity of applicants were available.

    In the 1956 column only the agricultural entrants are included because forestry numbers, amounting to 2,000, were given separately. Thus, in comparison with the other two years, the real figure for 1956 should be 17,000. The same applies to 1957, where the relevant total moves from 6,000 to 7,200.
11. *Jen-min jih-pao*, 17 March 1956 and *Kung-jen jih-pao*, 12 May 1956.
12. For an analysis of actual and planned enrolment figures, see John Philip Emerson, "Manpower Training and Utilization of Specialized Cadres, 1949-68," in John Wilson Lewis ed., *The City in Communist China*, pp. 183-214.
13. This table is reproduced from *The First Five Year Plan for Development of the National Economy of the People's Republic of China in 1953-1957* (Peking: Foreign Languages Press, 1956), p. 178.
14. Two reasons for this inadequacy are sometimes overlooked: (i) not all higher middle graduates took the enrolment examinations; and (ii) middle school plans did not always make allowances for dropouts. See Emerson's "Manpower Training and Utilization of Specialized Cadres, 1949-1968," in Lewis, ed., *The City in Communist China*, pp. 199-200.
15. "Be Mankind's Spiritual Engineers," *Chung-kuo ch'ing-nien pao*, 20 May 1956.
16. *Kuang-ming jih-pao*, 24 May 1956.
17. *The First Five Year Plan*, pp. 179-80.
18. *Ta-kung pao* (Hong Kong), 27 May 1957.
19. *Kuang-ming jih-pao*, 29 June 1955.
20. *Wen-hui pao* (Shanghai), 18 March 1957.
21. These figures for the Chiaotung Technological University appear in *T'ou-k'ao ta-hsüeh shou-ts'e*, 1951, p. 42.
22. *Kuang-ming jih-pao*, 6 June 1956.
23. Wang Hsüeh-wen, "An Analysis of the Communist Bandits' Abolition of the Present Enrolment Examination Methods for Institutions of Higher Education," *Wen-t'i yü yen-chiu* [Issues and Studies], (Taipei): Institute of International Relations) vol. 6, no. 1 (October 1969): 59.
24. The 1950 Enrolment Regulations were published in *Jen-min jih-pao*, 29 May 1950.
25. A detailed outline of the educational administrative structure is to be found in Tsang Chiu-sam, *Society, Schools, and Progress in China* (Oxford, 1968), pp. 82-84.
26. The exceptions to this rule were the institutions of higher education in the five provinces and two cities of North China where, as indicated in another context, control was vested in the Education Ministries of the Central Government.
27. *Jen-min jih-pao*, 29 May 1950.
28. *Jen-min jih-pao*, 9 June 1955 and *Kuang-ming jih-pao*, 7 April 1956.
29. *Jen-min chiao-yü*, October 1957, p. 9.
30. *Jen-min jih-pao*, 9 June 1955. Similar stipulations are found in ibid., 18 September 1953.
31. *Kuang-ming jih-pao*, 16 August 1955.
32. Ibid., 7 April 1956.
33. *Jen-min jih-pao*, 22 June 1957.
34. *Kuang-ming jih-pao*, 27 May 1955.
35. *Kuang-ming jih-pao*, 7 April 1956;

Jen-min jih-pao, 25 April 1957 and 22 June 1957.

36. *Ta-kung pao* (Hong Kong), 27 May 1957 and *Kuang-ming jih-pao,* 15 July 1957.
37. *Ch'ung-ch'ing jih-pao,* 7 June 1956.
38. For a discussion of the advantages and disadvantages of unified enrolment as it operated between 1949 and 1956, see *Jen-min jih-pao,* 22 June 1957.
39. Orleans, *Professional Manpower and Education in Communist China,* pp. 38, 61 and 97.
40. *Jen-min jih-pao,* 22 June 1957.
41. Editorial in ibid., 25 April 1957.
42. For further details of this process, see *Ta-kung pao* (Hong Kong), 20 and 27 May 1957.
43. Editorial in *Jen-min jih-pao,* 25 May 1957.
44. *Ta-kung pao* (Tientsin), 8 July 1953.
45. *Jen-min jih-pao,* 20 March 1956.
46. *Wen-hui pao* (Shanghai), 18 March 1957.
47. *Kuang-ming jih-pao,* 7 April 1956.
48. *Jen-min jih-pao,* 9 June 1955, *Kuang-ming jih-pao,* 7 April 1956, ibid., 20 May 1956, and *Jen-min jih-pao,* 25 April 1957.
49. *Jen-min jih-pao,* 22 June 1957.
50. Ibid., 25 April 1957.
51. *Kuang-ming jih-pao,* 20 May 1956 and *Jen-min jih-pao,* 25 April 1957.
52. *Jen-min jih-pao,* 25 May 1954 and 25 April 1957.
53. *Jen-min jih-pao,* 9 June 1955 and 27 March 1957; and *Kuang-ming jih-pao,* 25 April 1957.
54. *Kuang-ming jih-pao,* 7 April 1956.
55. Ibid., 25 April 1957. It is worth noting here that other organizations, in addition to enrolment organs and institutions of higher education, dealt with the associated matter of candidates' welfare during the examination period. A Hong Kong source reported in 1956: "Enrolment work has been supported by government departments dealing with communications and food, and by the Youth Leagues. Such bodies as institutions of higher edu-

cation in Lanchow and Sian, and Youth League organizations in Soochow and Nanking have organized 'candidates service leagues' (*kao-sheng fu-wu t'uan*) to help candidates with food, accommodation, and medical facilities." *Ta kung-pao* (Hong Kong), 16 July 1956.
56. The dates of unified enrolment examinations are given in *Jen-min jih-pao,* 9 June 1955; examination registration dates are provided in ibid., *Kuang-ming jih-pao,* 7 April 1956, *Chung-ch'ing jih-pao,* 7 June 1956, and *Jen-min jih-pao,* 25 April 1957.
57. *Jen-min jih-pao,* 25 May 1954, *Ta-kung pao* (Hong Kong), 16 July 1956, and *Kuang-ming jih-pao,* 15 July 1957.
58. *Kuang-ming jih-pao,* 27 May 1955 and *Wen-hui pao* (Shanghai), 18 April 1957.
59. A distinction is to be made here between individual registration and individual enrolment: the former refers to candidates, the latter to institutions. Moreover, institutions conducting individual enrolment (for example, the Chinese People's University), set up their own enrolment committees. *Chou-mo pao* (Hong Kong), 4 May 1957.
60. Details of registration processes are given in *Jen-min jih-pao,* 9 June 1955, *Kuang-ming jih-pao,* 7 April 1956, and *Ch'ung-ch'ing jih-pao,* 7 June 1956.
61. *Ch'ung-ch'ing jih-pao,* 7 June 1956.
62. *Jen-min chiao-yü,* October 1957, p. 10.
63. Ibid., and *Jen-min jih-pao,* 25 April 1957.
64. *Wen-hui pao* (Shanghai), 17 April 1957 and *Chung-kuo ch'ing-nien pao,* 20 June 1957.
65. *Jen-min chiao-yü,* October 1957, p. 16.
66. Numbers registered for examination are mentioned in *Chung-kuo ch'ing-nien pao,* 5 August 1956 and *Kuang-ming jih-pao,* 15 July 1957. For entrants, see Orleans, *Professional Manpower and Education in Communist China,* p. 61.
67. These ratios and statistics are to be found in *Chiao-shih pao,* 23 August 1957 and *Kuang-ming jih-pao,* 15 July 1957.

NOTES TO CHAPTER FIVE

1. *Ta-kung pao* (Hong Kong), 17 May 1955.

2. In discussing these academic disciplines it is necessary to point out changes in termi-

nology. For example, in the 1954 categories, one term used is *wei-sheng* (health), which presumably refers to medicine and allied subjects; in 1955 the more specific *i-ke* (medical subjects) appears. It would appear, however, that as far as the examination regulations are concerned, these two terms have substantially the same meaning.

3. Fine arts, although not explicitly mentioned, would have been placed in the third category.

4. *Jen-min jih-pao,* 9 June 1955, *Kuang-ming jih-pao,* 7 April 1956, and *Jen-min jih-pao,* 25 April 1957.

5. *Jen-min chiao-yü,* April 1957, p. 11.

6. *Wen-hui pao* (Shanghai), 16 April 1957.

7. *Jen-min jih-pao,* 25 April 1957 and *Kuang-ming jih-pao,* 7 April 1956.

8. *Chou-mo pao* (Hong Kong), 27 April 1957. See also *Kuang-ming jih-pao,* 27 May 1955.

9. It is to be noted, however, that although by 1957 some teacher training institutes were conducting individual or joint enrolment, their basic subjects were the same as those for the unified system.

10. *Kuang-ming jih-pao,* 27 July 1952.

11. For example, *Jen-min jih-pao,* 13 August 1955.

12. *Jen-min jih-pao,* 9 June 1955.

13. *Kuang-ming jih-pao,* 13 August 1955 and 9 September 1955.

14. Ibid., 25 September 1953, *Jen-min jih-pao,* 13 August 1955, and *Kuang-ming jih-pao,* 7 August 1956.

15. *Jen-min jih-pao,* 13 August 1955.

16. *Chung-kuo ch'ing-nien pao,* 5 August 1956.

17. *Kuang-ming jih-pao,* 7 April 1956.

18. *Chiao-shih pao,* 7 August 1956.

19. *Kuang-ming jih-pao,* 7 August 1956.

20. *Kuang-hsi jih-pao,* 7 July 1956.

21. *Kuang-ming jih-pao,* 7 April 1956.

22. Ibid., 7 August 1956.

23. Ibid., 25 April 1957.

24. *Jen-min jih-pao,* 31 March 1957.

25. Ibid., 20 June 1957.

26. In practice, especially in engineering subjects, preferences had to be selected according to departments, which often consisted of several specialties of a similar nature. *Jen-min jih-pao,* 20 June 1957.

27. *Jen-min jih-pao,* 27 March 1957 and *Ta-kung pao* (Hong Kong), 27 May 1957.

28. *Jen-min jih-pao,* 10 August 1957.

29. *Chiao-shih pao,* 23 August 1957.

30. There was also provision in the regulations for a second session of enrolment examinations. In theory, the decision as to whether to conduct them would be taken by individual institutions which would make an announcement in the media, probably through the local enrolment work committees. As a general rule, however, new examinations do not appear to have been held. *Kuang-ming jih-pao,* 7 August 1957 and *Jen-min jih-pao,* 8 August 1957.

31. *Chiao-shih pao,* 7 August 1956.

32. *Jen-min jih-pao,* 10 August 1957.

33. It must also be pointed out that the second session of preferences was believed to confer administrative advantages over directed distribution by saving time, manpower, and facilities. This allegedly benefited both institutions and candidates. For candidates' attitudes, see *Jen-min jih-pao,* 10 August 1957.

34. *Chiao-shih pao,* 7 August 1956.

35. *Jen-min jih-pao,* 10 August 1957.

36. Ibid., 20 June 1957.

37. Ibid., and *Ta kung-pao* (Hong Kong), 27 May 1957.

38. *Jen-min jih-pao,* 20 June 1957.

39. Ibid.

40. Korol, p. 186.

41. *Kuang-ming jih-pao,* 20 May 1956 and *Jen-min jih-pao,* 27 March 1957. Outlines for such basic subjects as history, geography, and the fundamentals of Darwinism were also individually published in the press. See, for example, *Wen-hui pao* (Hong Kong) 16, 18, 19, 20, 22, 24, 25, 27, 29, 30, 31 May and 1 June 1955.

42. These details are taken from the "Outline of the National Language Examination," republished in the *Ta-kung pao* (Hong Kong), 17 May 1955.

43. This resumé of the Political General Knowledge Examination appears in *Ta-kung pao* (Hong Kong), 19 May 1955.

44. *T'ou-k'ao ta-hsüeh shou-ts'e,* 1951, p. 9.

45. *Kuang-ming jih-pao,* 6 June 1956.

46. Ibid., 7 April 1956.

47. *Ta-kung pao* (Hong Kong), 16 July 1956.

48. *Kuang-ming jih-pao,* 6 June 1955 and 25 April 1957.

49. Ibid., 6 June 1955.

50. Ibid., 18 August 1953. This average

would have covered common and basic, although not skill, subjects.

51. For the 1956 details, see *Jen-min chiao-yü*, March 1957, p. 44.

52. On the 25 September 1953 the *Kuang-ming jih-pao* stated that the number of candidates who received a total for all papers exceeding a certain mark differed

widely from area to area. In descending order of merit, the areas were listed as follows in 1953: the North-East, North China, East China, the Central-South, the North-West and the South-West.

53. *Kuang-ming jih-pao*, 9 September 1955.

54. *Jen-min chiao-yü*, October 1957, p. 6.

55. Ibid., p. 16.

NOTES TO CHAPTER SIX

1. *Jen-min chiao-yü*, October 1957, p. 7.

2. *Jen-min jih-pao*, 22 June 1957.

3. *Jen-min chiao-yü*, October 1957, p. 7.

4. *Wen-hui pao* (Shanghai), 16 March 1957. There is some discrepancy between the two overall totals for graduates and students enrolled as given in this source and those provided by Orleans in *Professional Manpower and Education in Communist China*, on the basis of *Ten Great Years* (Peking: State Statistical Bureau, 1960). But the relevance of the first source rests on the proportions of students in engineering and teacher training to the whole. See also Orleans, p. 61.

5. *Jen-min chiao-yü*, October 1957, p. 7.

6. *Jen-min shou-ts'e* [People's Handbook], *Ta-kung pao-she*, (Peking, 1957), p. 583.

7. *Jen-min chiao-yü*, October 1957, p. 54.

8. *Pedagogical Critique*, translated in *Chinese Sociology and Anthropology*, vol. 2, no. 1-2 (Fall-Winter 1969-70):30-37.

9. *Kuang-ming jih-pao*, 25 April 1957.

10. *Jen-min jih-pao*, 25 April 1957.

11. Ibid., 3 April 1957.

12. *Chung-kuo ch'ing-nien pao*, 5 August 1956.

13. *Jen-min chiao-yü*, April 1957, p. 12.

14. Ibid., p. 4.

15. *Chiao-shih pao*, 29 March 1957.

16. *Ten Great Years, Statistics of the Economic and Cultural Achievements of the People's Republic of China* (Peking: Foreign Languages Press, 1960) p. 192. The percentages for female students given in Table 10 appear in the same source on p. 201.

17. *Jen-min chiao-yü*, April 1957, p. 10.

18. Ibid., January 1957, p. 66.

19. Ibid., April 1957, p. 46.

20. *Kuang-ming jih-pao*, 3 July 1958.

21. *Ta-kung jih-pao* (Hong Kong), 31 October 1952.

22. For a rather critical assessment of this aspect of the enrolment process, see Chang Ch'ing, *Jin-jih Pei-ta* [Peking University Today] (Hong Kong, 1954).

23. The institution of special training courses was announced in the "Temporary Regulations for Institutions of Higher Education" (1950). Clause 9 stated: "The universities and institutes, in order to adapt themselves to the urgent needs of national construction, must establish, with the prior approval of the Central Education Ministry, special training courses. . . ." (*Jen-min chiao-yü*, September 1950, p. 68. See also ibid., October 1957, p. 10.)

24. *Kuang-ming jih-pao*, 11 July 1952.

25. *Jen-min jih-pao*, 11 July 1952.

26. *1955 nien shu-ch'i kao-teng hsüeh-hsiao chao-sheng sheng-hsüeh chih-tao*, [Guidance on Enrolment in Institutions of Higher Education, Summer 1955], p. 140.

27. *Wen-hui pao* (Shanghai), 6 October 1953.

28. Ibid., 13 July 1957. The scope of the "health" category is not clearly demarcated. A difficulty also arises in assessing whether or not the young workers were of cadre rank. But since the main emphasis in the article quoted is on youth, it seems more likely that the category mentioned means literally "young workers."

29. *Kuang-ming jih-pao*, 18 July 1954 and *Ch'ang-chiang jih-pao*, 24 July 1952.

30. *Ta-kung jih-pao* (Hong Kong), 31 October 1952.

31. Ibid., 18 June 1952.

32. *1955 nien shu-ch'i kao-teng hsüeh-hsiao chao-sheng sheng-hsüeh chih-tao,* pp. 198-99.

33. *Jen-min jih-pao,* 18 September 1953.

34. Ibid., 10 January 1955.

35. Ibid.

36. *Peking Review,* vol. 1, no. 12 (20 May 1958):16; *Kuang-ming jih-pao,* 3 July 1958; *Ten Great Years, Statistics of the Economic and Cultural Achievements of the People's Republic of China,* (Peking: Foreign Languages Press, 1960), p. 200.

37. *Jen-min chiao-yü,* September 1957, p. 12.

38. *Chung-kuo ch'ing-nien pan-yüeh k'an,* 1 July 1958, p. 10.

39. *Jen-min chiao-yü,* October 1957, pp. 6-10.

40. *Kung-jen jih-pao,* 4 July 1958.

41. *Wen-hui pao* (Shanghai), 3 July 1958.

42. *Chung-kuo ch'ing-nien pan-yüeh k'an,* 1 July 1958.

43. *Jen-min jih-pao,* 10 January 1955.

44. *Kuang-ming jih-pao,* 3 July 1958.

45. *Jen-min chiao-yü,* September 1957, p. 12.

46. *Jen-min jih-pao,* 30 June 1955 and *Kuang-ming jih-pao,* 16 August 1955.

47. *Chung-kuo ch'ing-nien pao,* 13 July 1958.

48. *Jen-min chiao-yü,* October 1957, p. 22.

49. Ibid., April 1957, p. 8, and *Chung-kuo ch'ing-nien pan-yüeh k'an,* 16 April 1957, p. 5.

50. *Ten Great Years,* p. 216.

51. *Jen-min jih-pao,* 7 September 1955.

52. *Ta-kung pao* (Hong Kong), 9 September 1955.

53. *Jen-min jih-pao,* 2 September 1955.

54. *Jen-min jih-pao,* 9 June 1955 and *Kuang-ming jih-pao,* 4 June 1957.

55. *Chiao-shih pao,* 4 June 1957.

56. *Nan-fang jih-pao,* 4 June 1957.

57. It is perhaps appropriate to point out at this stage that travel expenses incurred by candidates in the enrolment process, although not prohibitive, would have placed a considerable burden on those from families in reduced circumstances. Thus while it was explicitly stated that travel expenses in registering, together with medical and registration fees, were the responsibility of the individual, provision was made for candidates in need. *Chung-kuo ch'ing-nien pao,* 31 May 1957. For example, cadres and primary schoolteachers who had been examined and accepted for institutions of higher education would have their travel expenses in connection with entry registration paid by their original work unit. (See *Chiao-shih pao,* 7 August 1956 and *Nan-fang jih-pao,* 4 June 1957.) Those graduates of vocational middle schools and teacher training schools would likewise have had their travel expenses paid by the institutions from which they had originally graduated. *Chiao-shih pao,* 7 August 1956. But while in the case of the above categories payment of travel expenses by original work units and schools was automatic, those among higher middle graduates, retired and seconded soldiers, Overseas Chinese students, candidates from Hong Kong and Macao, and unemployed youth who were in financial need could request aid for travel to the institutions which had accepted them, from the enrolment organs in the area in which they had originally registered for examinations or the educational administrative departments in that area. The actual amount of assistance with travel expenses was not to exceed the price of a second class train, cabin seat or long distance coach ticket from the place where candidates congregated to begin their journey to the institution for which they had been accepted. (See *Chiao-shih pao,* 7 August 1956 and *Jen-min jih-pao,* 25 April 1957.) Travel expenses have little bearing on the question of increasing the number of students of worker and peasant origin but are mentioned here in the general context of financial aid.

58. *Chung-kuo ch'ing-nien pan-yüeh k'an,* 16 April 1957.

59. *Chung-kuo ch'ing-nien pao,* 5 August 1956.

60. *Kuang-ming jih-pao,* 7 August 1956.

61. Ibid., 17 August 1955.

62. Ibid.

63. *Jen-min jih-pao,* 21 July 1950, 11 July 1951, 7 August 1952, and 17 August 1953.

64. *Kuang-ming jih-pao,* 6 July 1955.

65. *Chung-kuo ch'ing-nien pao,* 23 April 1955 and *Jen-min jih-pao, 30 July 1955.*

66. *Kuang-ming jih-pao,* 19 May 1955.

67. *Ten Great Years,* pp. 194 and 196.
68. For projected numbers, see *First Five Year Plan for the Development of the National Economy of the People's Republic of China in 1953-1957* (Peking: Foreign Languages Press, 1956), p. 178. A useful comparison between planned and actual numbers of graduates is made by John Philip Emerson in his article "Manpower Training and Utilization of Specialized Cadres, 1949-68" in J. W. Lewis, ed., *The City in Communist China* (Stanford, CA, 1971), p. 202.

69. *Jen-min jih-pao,* 19 July 1956 and *Ta-kung pao* (Hong Kong), 21 July 1957.
70. *Kuang-ming jih-pao,* 19 July 1956.
71. Ibid., 19 July 1956 and 20 July 1956.
72. Ibid., 19 July 1956.
73. Ibid., 7 August 1957.
74. *Kuang-ming jih-pao,* 21 July 1957.
75. Ibid.
76. "Regulations Governing the Enrolment of Four-Year System Researchers in Institutions of Higher Education in 1957," reproduced in *Kuang-ming jih-pao,* 21 July 1957.

NOTES TO CHAPTER SEVEN

1. *Jen-min chiao-yü,* July 1958, p. 8.
2. Ibid., p. 9.
3. A full version of the directive appears in *Jen-min jih-pao,* 20 September 1958.
4. *Pedagogical Critique,* as translated in *Chinese Sociology and Anthropology,* vol. 2, No. 1-2 (Fall-Winter 1969-70): 44.
5. *Wen-hui pao* (Shanghai), 3 July 1958.
6. *Chung-kuo ch'ing-nien pan-yüeh k'an,* 1 July 1958, p. 15.
7. *Kuang-ming jih-pao,* 3 July 1958.
8. *Jen-min jih-pao,* 3 July 1958.
9. *Hsiang-kang shih-pao,* 18 September 1959.
10. *Kuang-ming jih-pao,* 3 July 1958.
11. For example, in *Jen-min jih-pao,* 4 June 1960 and 13 May 1961.
12. *NCNA,* 11 June 1959.
13. *Kuang-ming jih-pao,* 22 June 1962.
14. Ibid., 18 June 1962.
15. See, for example, *Jen-min jih-pao,* 11 June 1965.
16. *Chung-kuo ch'ing-nien pao,* 3 July 1958.
17. *Jen-min jih-pao,* 4 June 1960.
18. For relevant statistics concerning these years, see *Chung-kuo ch'ing-nien pao,* 3 July 1958, *Wen-hui pao* (Shanghai), 11 June 1959, and *Jen-min jih-pao,* 4 June 1960. But the *Chung-kuo ch'ing-nien pan-yüeh k'an,* 1 July 1958, gives 152,000 for 1958 and in *Professional Manpower and Education in Communist China* Orleans, on the basis of a *NCNA* source, dated 22 January 1960, mentions 270,000 for 1959. It must be remembered, however, that the statistics in the text are planned rather than actual.

19. *Chung-kuo ch'ing-nien pao,* 3 July 1958 and *Kung-jen jih-pao,* 4 July 1958.
20. *Wen-hui pao* (Hong Kong), 23 June 1959.
21. *NCNA,* 21 June 1959.
22. *Wen-hui pao* (Shanghai), 11 July 1958.
23. The allocation details for 1963 come from the *Jen-min shou-ts'e* [People's Handbook] of that year. The other sources for the tabulated figures are as follows:
    1958: *Ten Great Years,* p. 196.
    1959 and 1960: *NCNA,* 4 September 1960, in *Survey of China Mainland Press,* no. 2335, p. 13, hereafter abbreviated to *SCMP.*
    1961: *NCNA,* 2 August 1961, in *SCMP,* no. 2554, p. 16.
    1962: *NCNA,* 29 August 1962 in *SCMP,* no. 2813, p. 18.
    1964: *Chung-kuo ch'ing-nien pao,* 13 August 1964, in SCMP, no. 3288, p. 4.
    1965: *Jen-min jih-pao,* 11 August 1965.
    Slightly different totals and further estimates appear in J. P. Emerson, "Manpower Training and Utilization of Specialized Cadres, 1949-68," in J. W. Lewis ed., *The City in Communist China,* (Stanford, California, 1971), p. 204.
    It must be noted, however, that there appear to have been considerable defects in the allocation and assignment of graduates. In spite of the demands of functional specificity, graduates clearly did not always receive appointments appropriate to their previous training.
24. C.H.G. Oldham, "Science and Education

in China'' in Ruth Adams ed., *Contemporary China* (London, 1969), p. 20. Regulations concerning the enrolment of researchers appear in *Kuang-ming jih-pao*, 28 August 1959, ibid., 8 September 1959, *Jen-min jih-pao*, 19 September 1962, and through Anhwei Broadcasting Station, 26 October 1964.

25. *Kuang-ming jih-pao*, 3 July 1958.
26. Ibid.
27. *Jen-min shou-ts'e* [People's Handbook], 1962, p. 312. From 1958 to 1964 there was a single Education Ministry but in mid-1964 a separate Ministry of Higher Education was again created. Yang Hsiu-feng became Minister of Higher Education. Chiang Nan-hsiang succeeded him in this post in 1965.
28. *Jen-min jih-pao* and *Kuang-ming jih-pao*, 3 July 1958. The caveat must be added, however, that the second and third categories enumerated here for 1958 are not entirely clear. The terms "principal" *(chu-yao)* and "important" *(chung-yao)* are very vague. The first category, including the so-called key point *(chung-tien)* institutions, discussed later, was outlined with greater clarity in subsequent years.
29. *Jen-min jih-pao*, 3 July 1958.
30. Ibid.
31. *Wen-hui pao* (Shanghai), 3 July 1958.
32. *Kuang-ming jih-pao*, 3 July 1958.
33. *Wen-hui pao* (Shanghai), 3 July 1958. Needless to say, in the case of many candidates registering for institutions which came under the Central Government, such travel would not have been necessary, as some of the institutions in this category would have been situated in the province or city in which they resided.
34. *Kuang-ming jih-pao*, 11 June 1959.
35. *Wen-hui pao* (Shanghai), 11 June 1959.
36. *Jen-min jih-pao*, 4 June 1960.
37. *Kuang-ming jih-pao*, 22 June 1962.
38. *Jen-min jih-pao*, 4 June 1960.
39. *Wen-hui pao* (Shanghai), 14 June 1959.
40. *Kuang-ming jih-pao*, 16 August 1959.
41. *Jen-min jih-pao*, 3 July 1958. The two categories of cadres mentioned are not clearly defined but the "other cadre" group may have referred to cadres not of worker and peasant origin, in view of the lengthy service stipulation. The cadres would have been included in the personnel category.
42. Ibid.

43. Ibid., 4 June 1964.
44. *Chung-kuo ch'ing-nien pao*, 13 July 1958.
45. Ibid., 3 July 1958.
46. *Jen-min jih-pao*, 3 July 1958 and *Kuang-ming jih-pao*, 11 June 1959.
47. *Jen-min jih-pao*, 3 July 1959 and *Kuang-ming jih-pao*, 11 June 1959. The category "intellectual youth" does not appear in the latter source.
48. *Jen-min jih-pao*, 3 July 1958.
49. Ibid., 4 June 1960 and 13 May 1961.
50. Ibid., 23 June 1962.
51. *Chung-kuo ch'ing-nien pan-yüeh k'an*, 1 July 1958, p. 10.
52. *Wen-hui pao* (Shanghai), 11 June 1959 and *Jen-min jih-pao*, 4 June 1960.
53. *Jen-min jih-pao*, 4 June 1960.
54. Ibid., 23 June 1962.
55. Ibid. and *Kuang-ming jih-pao*, 3 July 1958.
56. *Jen-min jih-pao*, 4 June 1960.
57. Ibid., 13 June 1960.
58. *Kuang-ming jih-pao*, 3 July 1958.
59. *Wen-hui pao* (Shanghai), 3 July 1958.
60. Ibid., 3 June 1959.
61. Kiangsi Broadcasting Station, 20 June 1964.
62. *Kuang-ming jih-pao*, 22 June 1962.
63. *Wen-hui pao* (Shanghai), 3 July 1958 and *Jen-min jih-pao*, 11 June 1959.
64. *Ta-kung pao* (Hong Kong), 25 August 1960.
65. *Wen-hui pao* (Hong Kong), 4 December 1960.
66. An account of the "crimes" of the August 1st School, translated from a Peking Red Guard source, (published by Mao Tse-tung's Thought Revolutionary Rebels Joint Headquarters, August 1st School, Capital City) appears in *Chinese Sociology and Anthropology*, vol. 1, no. 4 (Summer 1969): 7-22. The history of schools for children of cadres and a denial of their elite status are to be found in *Jen-min chiao-yü*, September 1957, p. 11.
67. "Thoroughly Smash the Crimes Associated with Liu Shao-ch'i's Counterrevolutionary Educational Line," *Chiao-yü ko-ming*, 10 April 1967.
68. For a discussion of this question, see J. Gardner "Educated Youth and Urban-Rural Inequalities, 1958-66," in J. W. Lewis, ed., *The City in Communist China*, pp. 253-54.
69. *Jen-min jih-pao*, 23 June 1962.

70. *Pedagogical Critique,* 20 August 1967, translated in *Chinese Sociology and Anthropology,* vol. 2, no. 1-2 (Fall-Winter, 1969-70): 59-60.

71. Arguments concerning the alleged exclusion of those of worker and peasant origin appear in "The Question of *Ch'u-shen,*" *Chung-hsüeh wen-ko pao,* 18 January 1967.

72. *Chung-kuo ch'ing-nien pan-yüeh k'an,* 1 July 1958, p. 10. Worker and peasant origin is often used vaguely in Chinese Communist literature, but the following statistics given for this category are interpreted as referring to the "Five Red Classes" outlined earlier.

73. *Kuang-ming jih-pao,* 20 September 1958.

74. *Wen-hui pao* (Hong Kong), 4 December 1960.

75. *NCNA,* 27 September 1961.

76. Ibid., 2 May 1963.

77. Ibid., 9 November 1964.

78. *Ta-kung pao* (Hong Kong), 28 January 1960.

79. *Kuang-ming jih-pao,* 13 May 1959.

80. Ibid., 12 May 1959.

81. "Report on an Investigation of the Peasant Movement in Hunan" (March 1927), *Selected Works of Mao Tse-tung,* vol. 1, pp. 53-54.

82. Further details are given by Gardner in "Educated Youth and Urban-Rural Inequalities, 1958-66," in Lewis, ed., *The City in Communist China,* pp. 250-52.

83. *Yang-ch'eng wan-pao* (Canton), 3 September 1962.

84. Ibid., 18 August 1962.

85. The urban and rural origins of students are discussed by Emerson in "Manpower Training and Utilization of Specialized Cadres, 1949-68," in Lewis, ed., *The City in Communist China,* pp. 193-94.

86. *Pedagogical Critique,* translated in *Chinese Sociology and Anthropology,* vol. 2, no. 1-2 (Fall-Winter, 1969-70): 66.

87. *An Analysis of Chinese Communist Educational and Cultural Affairs* (Taipei 1971), p. 17.

88. *Jen-min chiao-yü,* April 1958, p. 13.

89. The part-work part-study system at Ch'inghua University is described in *Peking Review,* vol. 1, no. 25 (19 August 1958): 5. Information concerning the running of factories at Futan University is given in *Kuang-ming jih-pao,* 23 July 1970.

90. *Pedagogical Critique,* translated in *Chinese Sociology and Anthropology,* vol. 2, no. 1-2 (Fall-Winter 1969-70): 49.

91. The establishment and function of the *min-pan* schools are discussed in *Jen-min chiao-yü,* April 1958, pp. 44-45 and p. 55, ibid., May 1958, p. 21, and *Wen-hui pao,* (Shanghai) 16 August 1959.

92. The institution and objectives of agricultural middle schools appear in *Jen-min chiao-yü,* April 1958, p. 45, May 1958, p. 13, July 1958, p. 13, and in *A General Review of Chinese Communist Affairs in 1971,* Part 2, (Taipei, 1972), pp. 42-43.

93. The figures for the 1958-59 year appear in *Ten Great Years,* p. 192; those for the following four years are based on statistics given by Chu-yuan Cheng, "Scientific and Engineering Manpower in Communist China" in Joint Economic Committee of the U.S. Congress, *An Economic Profile of Mainland China* (New York/Washington/London, 1968), p. 529. These in turn have been taken from Chinese Communist sources. Details for the latter two periods are estimates drawn from Edwin F. Jones, "The Emerging Pattern of China's Economic Revolution," in *An Economic Profile of Mainland China,* p. 95.

94. *Pedagogical Critique,* translated in *Chinese Sociology and Anthropology,* vol. 2, no. 1-2 (Fall-Winter 1969-70): 55.

95. Ibid., pp. 50-56.

96. Ibid., pp. 51-52.

97. Ibid., p. 59.

98. Ibid., p. 65.

99. *Jen-min chiao-yü,* April 1958, p. 12.

100. Ibid., September 1958, p. 2.

101. Ibid., May 1958, p. 21. In 1967 Liu Shao-ch'i's supporters in the Education Ministry were accused of claiming earlier that, in future, engineers, factory directors, and Party secretaries would be promoted from among graduates of part-time institutions. These charges implied that emphasis had been placed by the Liuists on functional specificity rather than proletarian politics. *Hsin-chan pao,* 19 July 1967. During the Cultural Revolution there were instances of junior staff in industrial plants acquiring the same

political expectations through their part-time education as graduates of full-time institutions. (See J. W. Lewis, "Commerce, Education, and Political Development in Tangshan, 1956-69," in *The City in Communist China,* pp. 174-75.)

102. *Hung-ch'i,* October 1971, pp. 37-38 and "Going All Out With a Revisionist Line in Education," by the Revolutionary Al-liance General Headquarters of the Central Research Institute of Educational Science, in *Peking Review,* vol. 11, no. 2 (12 January 1968): 30-32.

103. *Hung-ch'i,* October 1971, pp. 37-38.

104. *Kuang-ming jih-pao,* 13 February 1972.

105. *Pedagogical Critique,* translated in *Chinese Sociology and Anthropology,* vol. 2, no. 1-2, (Fall-Winter 1969-70): 78.

NOTES TO CHAPTER EIGHT

1. *Kuang-ming jih-pao,* 6 January 1972.

2. Ibid., 22 July 1970.

3. The integration of education and productive labour at the University of Wuhan is analyzed at length in the *Kuang-ming jih-pao,* 12 July 1972.

4. For example, an account of concentration on "expert knowledge," after earlier reluctance, in Liaoning University's Department of Chinese Literature appears in *Kuang-ming jih-pao,* 10 January 1972.

5. *Kuang-ming jih-pao,* 13 February 1972.

6. *A General Review of Chinese Communist Affairs in 1971* Part 2 (Taipei, 1972), p. 10.

7. *Jen-min jih-pao,* 16 April 1971.

8. Ibid., 5 April 1970.

9. Ibid., 15 November 1968.

10. *Kuang-ming jih-pao,* 30 December 1971.

11. Ibid., 24 April 1972.

12. The operation of the two systems is discussed by the *Kuang-ming jih-pao,* 28 December 1971; an account of the different types of school organized in a commune in Chekiang appears in the 8 February 1972 issue of the same newspaper. The percentage for school-age children enrolled is given by the *NCNA,* 10 October 1975.

13. *Current Scene,* vol. 10, no. 7 (July 1972):1-6.

14. *Peking Review,* vol. 9, no. 26 (24 June 1966):18-19.

15. *Kuang-ming jih-pao,* 22 July 1970.

16. Information concerning 1975 enrolment policies and processes was given in broadcasts from Chinese provincial radio stations. See, for example, "Kwangsi Conference on Student Enrolment," *Summary of World Broadcasts* (hereafter *SWB*), 20 June 1975; "Fukien Conference on Student Enrolment Policies," ibid., 4 July 1975; "Student Enrolment Criteria in Anhwei," ibid., 17 July 1975.

17. These processes of recommendation and selection are discussed in *Kuang-ming jih-pao,* 16 March 1972. The role of the Party Committee Secretary is mentioned in an article entitled "Strengthen the Leadership of the Party, Seriously Work for the Successful Enrolment of Students in Universities," *Jen-min jih-pao,* 22 March 1972, translated in *Chinese Education,* vol. 6, no. 2 (Summer 1973):22-29. In addition, a 1976 source stated that mass organizations were also being consulted and presumably served an important function in propaganda work. Such organizations included educated young people's offices, trade unions, poor and lower middle peasant associations, the Youth Leagues, women's federations, and the militia. In contrast, it was claimed that enrolment administration before the Cultural Revolution had been conducted through a centralized, hierarchical chain of command and without mass participation. For the role of mass organizations in the enrolment process, see "Hunan Conference on Student Enrolment," Hunan Provincial Service, as reported in *SWB,* 24 August 1976.

18. The CCP Committee of the Huat'ung Copper Mine, "Seriously Carry Out the Work of Selecting and Sending New Students to Socialist Universities," *Jen-min jih-pao,* 12 July 1973.

19. *Kuang-ming jih-pao,* 16 March 1972.

20. The Revolutionary Committee of the Talien Engineering Institute, "Rely on the

Masses to Make a Success of Reexamination of Candidates by Institutions," *Jen-min jih-pao*, 20 June 1973.

21. "Reform of Universities," Kyodo Broadcast, 12 September 1977, as reported in *SWB*.

22. Attacks on this revisionist policy appear in "A Discussion of Chang T'ieh-sheng's Test Sheet and Answer," *Jen-min jih-pao*, 22 September 1973, as translated in *Current Background*, no. 7-12 (1974):1-5.

23. Details concerning the results of tests given to these Shanghai graduates are discussed by Pien Ku, "Cultural Examinations are Very Necessary," in *Jen-min jih-pao*, 23 October 1977.

24. For the implementation of these policies and alleged sabotage by the Gang of Four, see the Mass Criticism Group of the Peking Foreign Languages Institute, "Down With the Metaphysics of the Gang of Four, Correctly Carry Out Chairman Mao's Educational Policy," *Kuang-ming jih-pao*, 12 December 1976, as translated in *Survey of the People's Republic of China Press*, no. 6287.

25. The substance of the Gang's criticism is provided by Kao Yang, "Take the Criticism of Lin Piao and Confucius as the Driving Force in Conscientiously Carrying Out Well Student Enrolment Work for Institutions of Higher Education," *Kuang-ming jih-pao*, 15 July 1974, as translated in *SCMP*, no. 5662.

26. Ko Ming-wen, "Reforming the System of Student Enrolment is Geared to the Need to Consolidate the Dictatorship of the Proletariat—A Discussion of Chang T'ieh-sheng's Test Sheet Answer," *Jen-min jih-pao*, 22 September 1973.

27. "Colleges and Universities Enrol Students," *Wen-hui pao*, (Hong Kong), 26 November 1973.

28. Alexander Casella, "Recent Developments in China's University Recruitment System," *China Quarterly*, no. 62 (June 1975):297-301.

29. For details concerning examination subjects, see the Great Criticism Group at the Education Ministry, "The Political Deception of the Blank Sheet and the Gang of Four's Plot to Seize Power," *Kuang-ming jih-pao*, 30 November 1976. Significantly, in the Chinese Language examination, the essay topic was "A Study of 'Serve the People'," and this was clearly similar in concept to subjects set during the pre-1966 period.

30. Many sources discuss the case of the "blank sheet candidate"; four typical examples are listed below.
"Letter on the Back of a Test Sheet," *Jen-min jih-pao*, 10 August 1973; "*Jen-min jih-pao* Article Strips Gang of Four of Masks of Supporting New Born Forces," *NCNA*, 28 November 1976, in *SCMP* no. 6235; "The People's Daily Report on the Liaoning Test Paper," *NCNA*, 30 November 1976; "Gang of Four Fakes Up the 'Hero Against the Tide,'" *NCNA*, 13 December 1976.

31. Chung Chih-min, "Report Concerning An Application to Withdraw from University," *Jen-min jih-pao*, 18 January 1974.

32. "Conduct A Thorough Reform of Enrolment in Institutions of Higher Education," *Jen-min jih-pao*, 21 October 1977.

33. These examples refer to rural schools, but those for the cities followed a similar pattern. This information is drawn from material published in Taiwan. Although such sources must be subjected to the closest scrutiny, there seems little reason, in this case, to doubt their authenticity.

34. *NCNA*, 10 October 1975.

35. *Kuang-ming jih-pao*, 15 June 1972.

36. Ibid., 23 September 1970.

37. Ibid., 8 July 1972. The post-Cultural Revolution category of intellectual youth differed from its earlier counterpart. During the years 1949-65, it generally referred to those who had graduated from middle school a considerable time previously, or were of an equivalent level of scholarship, but after 1966 it embraced all those middle school graduates who were undertaking the required period of productive labour before being selected for higher education.

38. *Kuang-ming jih-pao*, 16 March 1972.

39. Rüdiger Machetzki, "China's Education Since the Cultural Revolution," *Political Quarterly*, vol. 45, no. 1 (January-March 1974):58-74.

40. *Kuang-ming jih-pao*, 16 March 1972.

41. "Shantung Meeting on Student Enrolment," as reported in *SWB*, 17 July 1975. This system of "from the commune, to

the commune" was also in operation during 1976.

42. *Peking Review,* vol. 12, no. 14 (4 April 1969):10.
43. *Kuang-ming jih-pao,* 22 July 1970 and 30 July 1971.
44. Ibid., 23 September 1970.
45. These details of enrolment during the early seventies were given by the *Shantung Broadcasting Station,* 3 April 1972 and the *Szechwan Broadcasting Station,* 3 November 1972.
46. "Hupei Conference on Enrolment for Colleges," *SWB,* 11 July 1975.
47. *Kuang-ming jih-pao,* 17 May 1972.
48. The number of entrants for 1973-74 was given by the *Wen-hui pao* (Hong Kong), 26 November 1973 and that for the following year by the *NCNA,* 16 October 1974. The 1973-74 total enrolment figure was given in P. J. Seybolt, *The Rustication of Urban Youth in China* (New York, 1975), that for 1975-76 was provided by the *NCNA* on 9 January 1976, and the 1976-77 statistics appeared in a Tanjug report of a statement by a deputy Minister of Education, Yung Wen-tao, as mentioned in *SWB,* 1 November 1977. The graduate

statistics were also taken from an *NCNA* report, issued on 15 September 1974.
49. For example, short-term training classes of this kind were held at the East China Petroleum Institute. (See *Kuang-ming jih-pao,* 13 April 1971.)
50. *Kwangtung Broadcasting Station,* 2 June 1970.
51. *Kuang-ming jih-pao,* 16 August 1971.
52. Ibid., 21 September 1970.
53. Ibid., 21 and 23 September 1970.
54. For details of Teng's policies, see "Harbin Article Condemns Teng's Outline Report," Heilungkiang Provincial Service, 24 August 1976, as reproduced in *SWB.* For radical attacks on the moderates, consult The Theoretical Group of the Chinese Academy of Sciences, "A Mighty Struggle on the Scientific and Technical Front," *Jen-min jih-pao,* 9 March 1977.
55. *Kuang-ming jih-pao,* 18 February 1971.
56. Ibid., 30 July 1971.
57. Ibid., 3 March 1971.
58. Ibid., 13 February 1972.
59. See, for example, the translation from an *NCNA* release, 27 October 1968, in *SCMP,* No. 4290, p. 12.
60. *Kuang-ming jih-pao,* 30 July 1971.

NOTES TO CHAPTER NINE

1. "Strive to Coordinate the Educational Task and the Development of the National Economy: Delegates at the National Education Work Conference Earnestly Study Vice-Chairman Teng's Speech," *Kuang-min jih-pao,* 29 April 1978.
2. "We Must Certainly Raise the Whole Chinese People's Scientific and Cultural Level: the Great Leader Chairman Hua's Call at the National Science Conference," ibid., 25 March 1978.
3. "Teng Hsiao-p'ing's Speech at the National Science Conference Opening Ceremony," ibid., 22 March 1978.
4. "Pin Red Flowers on Scientists," by Liu Tsai-fu and Chin Ch'iu-p'eng, ibid., 16 September 1977.
5. "Fabricated Accusations against Former Education Minister by the Gang of Four Exposed," *Jen-min jih-pao,* 15 September 1977, as translated in *SCMP,* no. 6431.

6. Details of Fang Yi's speech are given in other sources cited for the National Science Conference.
7. For these priorities see "Teng's Speech to the National Educational Work Conference," *Kuang-ming jih-pao,* 26 April 1978, and "Strive to Coordinate Suitably the Educational Task with the Development of the National Economy: Those Attending the National Educational Work Conference Earnestly Study Vice-Chairman Teng's Speech," ibid., 29 April 1978. The discussion of the education system follows Teng's framework, with the exception of certain specific details. Sources for the latter will be indicated in later footnotes.
8. "The State Council Approves the Education Ministry's Report: Run Fifty-Five more Institutions of Higher Education," *Kuang-ming jih-pao,* 26 April 1978.
9. "A Darien Factory Party Committee

Helps University Graduates of Previous Years to Raise Their Technical Level," ibid., 10 April 1978.

10. "Chengtu Geological Institute Formulates a Sound New Teaching Plan," ibid., 17 February 1978.

11. "Unite and Struggle to Establish a Socialist Modern Powerful Country: Hua Kuo-feng's Speech at the First Session of the Fifth National People's Congress on 26 February 1978," ibid., 7 March 1978.

12. Mao Tse-tung's statement appears in a *NCNA* report, translated in *SWB*, 25 October 1977.

13. The *NCNA* Report appears in *SWB*, 14 January 1978; the State Council Directive is discussed at length in an article entitled "Positively Develop the July 21 University to Train still more Personnel: the State Council Approves the Views of the Education Ministry in connection with Running July 21 Universities," *Kuang-ming jih-pao*, 5 April 1978.

14. The theoretical justification for key point is given in "Chairman Mao's Educational Line Must always Occupy the Leading Position: Material Relating to the Seventeen Year Struggle between the Two Educational Lines," Part 3, *Kuang-ming jih-pao*, 31 January 1978; criticism of the Gang of Four's notion of schools of revisionism appears in "Yüehyang *Hsien* Establishes Leading Groups and Teachers for Key Point Schools," ibid., 14 February 1978; the leadership of key point schools is analyzed in "The Decision to Restore and Run Well a Group of National Key Point Institutions of Higher Education," ibid., 2 March 1978.

15. The key point middle and primary sector is discussed in "Shansi Takes Measures to Run Well a Group of Key Point Middle and Primary Schools," ibid., 28 February 1978.

16. The reinterpretation of the CCP's theory of knowledge is now being given wide coverage. One example is "How Marx and Engels Investigated Natural Science," by Li Hui-kuo and Chang Nai-lieh, *Kuang-ming jih-pao*, 28 March 1978; the role of aces is discussed in "Our Cause Needs Aces," by Yang Cheng-chung, *Jen-min jih-pao*, 11 August 1977, translated in *SCMP*, no. 6420; collective endeavour and individual effort were

mentioned in Teng Hsiao-p'ing's speech at the National Educational Work Conference (already quoted); the role of youth is discussed in "Encourage Teachers to Give Their Lives for the Party's Educational Task," *Kuang-ming jih-pao*, 30 April 1978; for the direct enrolment of higher middle graduates and Mao Tse-tung's views concerning cultural examinations see "The People of Our Country Hope for the Raising of Standards in University Enrolment," *Jen-min jih-pao*, 21 October 1977; the eligibility of the so-called 'black classes' is examined in "Judge on the Basis of Political Manifestations and Technical Aptitude," *Kuang-ming jih-pao*, 26 April 1978.

17. See, for example, an article concerning this theme by Li Hung-lin, *Jen-min jih-pao*, 11 February 1978.

18. Details of enrolment categories are outlined in "Carry Out the Major Reform of Higher Education Enrolment," ibid., 21 October 1977, and "The Educational Reforms and the Prevention of Elitism," *NCNA* report, reproduced in *SWB*, 14 February 1978.

19. The 1975 percentage for "coming from the communes" appears in "The Kwangtung Conference on Student Enrolment," translated in *SWB*, 27 August 1976; the 1976 regulations are covered in "The Anhwei Meeting on Student Enrolment," reproduced in *SWB*, 4 September 1976.

20. Registration of worker candidates is discussed in "Kwangtung Enrolment Criteria," translated in *SWB*, 22 November 1977, and "Revision of Examinations versus the Needs of Production," taken from *SWB*, 10 November 1977.

21. For details concerning the 5,700,000 examination candidates, see "The Country's Higher Education Institutions' Enrolment Work Victoriously Completed," *Kuang-ming jih-pao*, 7 March 1978; the 1:30 ratio, the Inner Mongolian figures, the allocation of candidates to science faculties and the proportion of higher middle graduates appear in a *Kyodo News Agency* source, translated in *SWB*, 29 October 1977; applications to Peking and Futan Universities are discussed in a *Kyodo* report on university reform in China, reproduced in *SWB*, 17 November 1977.

22. The general principles and specific details of enrolment administration are outlined in an *NCNA* report, entitled An Education Ministry Official on College Enrolment Policies, translated in *SWB*, 28 October 1977; the reform of the quota system is discussed in "College Enrolment in Kwangtung and Sinkiang," as reported in ibid.; how examinations were organized at the local levels is explained in "Enrolment Work Must Take Exposing the Gang of Four as Its Framework," *Kuang-ming jih-pao*, 21 November 1977; examination subject requirements are outlined in "Thoroughly Reform Enrolment in Higher Education," *Jen-min jih-pao*, 21 October 1977; candidates' preferences are covered by a Kwangtung broadcast translated in *SWB*, 22 November 1977; assessment of examination scripts is analyzed in "College Enrolment in the Provinces," reproduced in *SWB*, 11 November 1977; the special arrangements for the distribution of enrolment in fine arts institutes is examined in "A Circular on Enrolment at Art Colleges and Schools," as reported by the *NCNA* and translated in *SWB*, 3 November 1977; assessment priorities in Hunan Province are analyzed in a local broadcast from Changsha, reproduced in *SWB*, 14 February 1978. No examination of the enrolment process would be complete, however, without brief reference to two other methods of broadening the avenue of talent. The first, that of day students *(tsou-tu sheng)*, was used during the pre-1966 period; the second, the exception rule *(p'o-ke)*, appears to be a new device.

    In March 1978 the Education Ministry and the State Council jointly announced that day students would be enrolled as an experiment. Later, the Education Minister, Liu Hsi-yao, stated that they would be selected from those already accepted at the preliminary stage of the enrolment process but who had not yet been given places. Improvised teaching facilities were then arranged in Peking institutions to accommodate 2,400 day students. Significantly, one half of the Peking sample were higher middle graduates from the 1966-67 academic year. Lastly, the eventual total intake for Peking University (discussed later in this chapter) may have

to be revised upwards in view of day student entry.

    But perhaps more important in the long term is the "exception rule," whereby China's University of Science and Technology enrolled twenty students below the age of sixteen, directly from middle and primary schools, without the required examination. They had initially been recommended by the masses, but then investigated by enrolment personnel, and finally given strict tests by the university. They were said to have shown outstanding aptitude for mathematics and physics. A specially qualified 'red and expert' woman teacher was assigned to teach them. The quest for talent seems interminable. For day students, see "The Decision to Increase Numbers in Higher Education by Experimentally Enrolling Day Students," *Kuang-ming jih-pao*, 3 March 1978 and "Make Great Efforts to Positively Expand Higher Education's Enrolment Numbers," ibid., 19 March 1978.

    The exception rule is discussed in "Child University Students," ibid., 5 April 1978.

    Finally, regulations for the reform of postgraduate enrolment were announced in late 1977. Once again, relevant regulations cast the net for talent as widely and as flexibly as possible. It is also noteworthy that universities are now recruiting greater numbers of postgraduates, whereas previously most research was undertaken in the research institutes of the Academy of Sciences. The qualifications required of candidates are publicized in "Thoroughly Reform Enrolment in Higher Education," *Jen-min jih-pao*, 21 November 1977.

23. For the preferential acceptance rubric, see "The Educational Reforms and the Prevention of Elitism," an *NCNA* report, reproduced in *SWB*, 14 February 1978.

24. Those who came under the "from the factory/commune" rubric were to be clearly informed of their status at the time of enrolment. A discussion of worker eligibility and wage levels appears in a Kweichow source, translated in *SWB*, 19 November 1977.

25. Details concerning enrolment in these local specialist institutes are mentioned in

"Carry Out the Major Reform of Higher Education Enrolment," *Jen-min jih-pao,* 21 October 1977.

26. This role of the part-time system is given coverage in "The Educational Reforms and the Prevention of Elitism," an *NCNA* report reproduced in *SWB,* 14 February 1978.

27. One of the sources consulted in the collation of these data refers to the first batch of 395 new students entering Peking University, suggesting that this would not be the final intake figure. Furthermore, the day students would also have to be added.

At the time of writing, the national intake figure of 190,000 would appear to include only entrants to full-time institutions.

The statistics and other information used in this survey of social background, age, and examination performance for entrants to three key point institutions are taken from: "The Country's Higher Education Enrolment Work Victoriously Completed," *Kuang-ming jih-pao,* 7 March 1978; "Ch'inghua University Performs Its Opening Ceremony," ibid., 11 March 1978; and "China's University of Science and Technology Enrols over Seven Hundred New Students," ibid., 16 March 1978.

List of Sources Consulted

I. Primary Materials

1. Newspapers and Periodicals (with translated titles, places of publication, and explanations where appropriate).

Ch'ang-chiang jih-pao [The Yangtze Daily]
Chi-lin shih ta-hsüeh pao [Kirin Teacher Training University Magazine]
Chiao-shih pao [The Teacher]
Chiao-yü chan-hsien (a Red Guard newspaper)
Chiao-yü ko-ming (a Red Guard Newspaper)
Ching-kang-shan (a Red Guard Newspaper)
Chou-mo pao (Hong Kong)
Ch'ung-ch'ing jih-pao [Chungking Daily]
Chung-hsüeh ko-ming pao (a Red Guard Newspaper)
Chung-hsüeh wen-ko pao (a Red Guard Newspaper)
Chung-hsüeh wen-ming pao (a Red Guard newspaper)
Chung-kuo ch'ing-nien pao [China Youth]
Chung-kuo ch'ing-nien pan-yüeh k'an [China Youth Fortnightly]
Hsiang-kang shih-pao (Hong Kong)
Hsin-chan pao (a Red Guard Newspaper)
Hung-ch'i [Red Flag]
Jen-min chiao-yü [People's Education]
Jen-min jih-pao [People's Daily]
Jen-min shou-ts'e [People's Handbook]
Kuang-chou jih-pao [Canton Daily]
Kuang-hsi jih-pao [Kwangsi Daily]
Kuang-ming jih-pao [Enlightenment Daily]
Kung-jen jih-pao [Worker's Daily]
Nan-fang jih-pao [Southern Daily]
Pei-ching ta-hsüeh hsüeh-pao [Peking University Magazine]
Pei-ching chou-pao [Peking Review]
Pei-ching shih-fan ta-hsüeh hsüeh-pao [Peking Teacher Training University Magazine]
Ta-kung pao (Hong Kong)

Ta-kung pao (Tientsin)
Wen-hui pao (Hong Kong)
Wen-hui pao (Shanghai)
Wu-han ta-hsüeh hsüeh-pao [Wuhan University Magazine]
Yang-ch'eng wan-pao (Canton)

Hong Kong newspapers, though not strictly classified as primary materials, are placed here for convenience in listing. In addition, *New China News Agency* sources, together with transcripts of Chinese and Japanese broadcasts, as monitored by the British Broadcasting Corporation in *Summary of World Broadcasts,* were also consulted. Finally, reference was made to such translated material as *Survey of the China Mainland Press (SCMP)* [now entitled *Survey of the People's Republic of China Press (SPRCP)*], published by the United States Consulate-General, Hong Kong.

2. Books

Liu Shao-ch'i. *On Inner Party Struggle.* Peking: Foreign Languages Press, 1951.

———— *How to Be a Good Communist.* Peking: Foreign Languages Press, 1965.

Mao Tse-tung. *Selected Works of Mao Tse-tung,* 4 vols. Peking: Foreign Languages Press, 1961-1965. (This is a translation of the Chinese version, published during the same period.)

1955 nien shu-ch'i kao-teng hsüeh-hsiao chao-sheng sheng-shüeh chih-tao [Guidance on Enrolment in Institutions of Higher Education, Summer, 1955].

1956 nien kao-teng hsüeh-hsiao chao-sheng sheng-hsüeh chih-tao [Guidance on Enrolment in Institutions of Higher Education in 1956].

1956 nien shu-ch'i kao-teng hsüeh-hsiao chao-sheng k'ao-shih ta-kang [An Outline of Enrolment Examinations for Institutions of Higher Education for Summer 1956].

National People's Congress. *First Five Year Plan for Development of the National Economy of the People's Republic of China in 1953-1957.* Peking: Foreign Languages Press, 1956.

Ten Great Years. Peking: State Statistical Bureau, 1960.

T'ou k'ao ta-hsüeh shou-tse [Handbook concerning Examinations for Entry to Universities, 1951]. The enrolment handbooks were published annually by the Education Ministries for the guidance of prospective candidates.

II. Secondary Materials

1. Books

Adams, Ruth, ed. *Contemporary China*. London, 1969.

Ayers, W. *Chang Chih-tung and Educational Reform in China*. Cambridge, Mass., 1971.

Bennett, G. A. and Montaperto, R. N. *Red Guard: The Political Biography of Dai Hsiao-ai*. London, 1971.

Biggerstaff, K. *The Earliest Modern Government Schools in China*. New York, 1961.

Chai, W., ed. *Essential Works of Chinese Communism*. rev. ed. New York, 1972.

Chang Ch'ing, *Jin-jih Pei-ta* [Peking University Today]. Hong Kong, 1954.

Chao Chung and Yang I-fan. *Students in Mainland China*. Hong Kong, 1956.

Ch'en, J., ed. *Mao Papers: Anthology and Bibliography*. London, 1970.

Ch'en, T.H.E. *The Maoist Educational Revolution*. New York, 1974.

Chiou, C. L. *Maoism in Action: The Cultural Revolution*. New York, 1974.

Chung Shih. *Higher Education in Communist China*. Hong Kong, 1953.

de Witt, N. *Soviet Professional Manpower*. Washington, 1955.

Elvin, M. *The Pattern of the Chinese Past*. Stanford, 1973.

Fraser, Stewart E., ed. *Chinese Communist Education: Records of the First Decade*. New York, 1965.

———. ed. *Education and Communism in China*. Hong Kong, 1969.

Hawkins, John H. *Mao Tse-tung and Education: His Thoughts and Teachings*. Hamden, CN, 1974.

Hinton, W. *The Hundred Day War: The Cultural Revolution at Tsinghua University*. New York, 1972.

Howe, C. *Employment and Economic Growth in Urban China, 1949-1957*. Cambridge, Mass., 1971.

Hu, C. T. *Aspects of Chinese Education*. New York, 1969.

Hudson, G. F., ed. *Reform and Revolution in Asia*. London, 1972.

Joint Economic Committee of the U.S. Congress. *An Economic Profile of Mainland China*. New York/Washington/London, 1968.

Kan, David. *The Impact of the Cultural Revolution on Chinese Higher Education*. Hong Kong, 1971.

Korol, Alexander G. *Soviet Education for Science and Technology*. New York, 1957.

Lasswell, Harold D. and Lerner, David. *World Revolutionary Elites*. Cambridge, Mass., 1965.

Lau, D. C. *Mencius*. Harmondsworth, 1970.

Lewis, J. W., ed. *The City in Communist China*. Stanford, 1971.

Munro, Donald J. *The Concept of Man in Early China*. Stanford, 1969.

Orleans, Leo A. *Every Fifth Child: The Population of China*. London, 1972.

———— *Professional Manpower and Education in Communist China*. Washington, 1961.

Price, R. F. *Education in Communist China*. London, 1970.

———— *Marx and Education in Russia and China*. London, 1977.

Raddock, David M. *Political Behavior of Adolescents in China: The Cultural Revolution in Kwangchow*. Arizona, 1977.

Rice, Edward E. *Mao's Way*. Berkeley, 1972.

Ridley, Charles P., Godwin, Paul H. B., and Doolin, Dennis J. *The Making of a Model Citizen in Communist China*. Stanford, 1971.

Robinson, Thomas W., ed. *The Cultural Revolution in China*. Berkeley, 1971.

Salisbury, Harrison E. *To Peking and Beyond: A Report on the New Asia*. New York, 1973.

Seybolt, P. J., ed. *The Rustication of Urban Youth in China*. New York, 1975.

Shih Ch'eng-chih, *The Status of Science and Education in Communist China and a Comparison with that in the USSR*. Hong Kong, 1962.

Solomon, Richard H. *Mao's Revolution and the Chinese Political Culture*. Los Angeles, 1971.

Tsang Chiu-sam. *Society, Schools, and Progress in China*. Oxford, 1968.

Wang, Y. C. *Chinese Intellectuals and the West, 1872-1949*. Chapel Hill, NC, 1966.

Whyte, M. K. *Small Groups and Political Rituals in China*. Berkeley, 1974.

World Anti-Communist League. *An Analysis of Chinese Communist Educational and Cultural Affairs*. Taipei, 1971.

———— *A General Review of Chinese Communist Affairs in 1971*, Parts 1 and 2. Taipei, 1972.

2. Periodicals

Chan-wang [Look Fortnightly] (Hong Kong)

China Quarterly (London)

Chinese Education (White Plains, New York)

Chinese Sociology and Anthropology (White Plains, New York)

Current Scene (United States Information Service, Hong Kong)

Journal of Asian Studies (Ann Arbor)

Political Quarterly (London)

Scottish Educational Studies (Edinburgh)

Wen-t'i yü yen-chiu [Issues and Studies] (Institute of International Relations, Taipei)

Index

Teachers and student relationships, 8, 39-40

Teaching methods and programmes, 8, 14-15, 47-48, 49, 59, 60, 61, 144, 173-74

Teaching-research guidance groups, 14-15, 159, 188n

Technical education, 13, 14, 41, 104. *See also* Science and Technology; Middle schools, vocational

"Ten Great Years," 46, 105, 106, 194n, 198n

Teng Hsiao-p'ing, 22, 154, 166, 168, 169, 170-71, 172, 173, 174, 185, 201n

Tientsin Polytechnic Institute, 109
    Department of Chemical Engineering, 108
    postgraduate study, 116

Tientsin Teacher Training Institute, 74

Tientsin University, 119

Ting Hua, 68

Trade unions, 27, 47, 59, 105

Transferred cadre financial aid, 111-12

Treasure pagoda system, 100-101, 102, 110

T'ungchi University, 107, 108

Twenty-First of July University, 172, 174, 183, 184, 185

Universalization and elevation, 101, 125, 137, 139-40, 147, 164

Universities. *See also* Canton; China's University; Chinese People's; Ch'inghua; Chungshan; Chiaotung; Communist Labour; Futan; Hunan; Kiangsi; Kwangtung; Nank'ai; National Scientific; Peking; Red Army; Seventh of May; Tientsin; T'ungchi; Twenty-first of July; Wuhan; Yenan
    administration of, 12-14, 20-21

comprehensive, 13-14, 40, 41, 75, 76, 99, 104, 106, 114, 116, 117, 122, 126, 134, 144, 145, 156, 161. *See also* Ch'inghua; Chungshan
    enrolment, 26-30, 61-82
    geographical distribution of, 11
    labour, 135-36, 145, 174, 183

Universities and institutes
    basic courses, 102, 103, 104, 108, 116, 164
    special training courses, 102-3, 104-5, 108, 164

Wen-hui pao (Shanghai), 76, 107, 119, 122, 125, 131, 133, 156

Western influences, 2, 3, 4, 170

Women, education of, 55, 101, 104, 150

Workers and peasants, education of, 6, 15, 17, 28, 33-41, 43-45, 58-59, 64, 105-7, 111-12, 118, 132-34, 145-47, 161-64, 178, 182. *See also* Education and productive labour; Middle schools; Seventh of May Peasant University

Workers' and Peasants' Mao Tse-tung Thought Propaganda Team, 23, 145

Wuhan Surveying Institute, 129

Wuhan Water Transport Institute, 73

Wuhan, University of, 48, 142, 143, 144, 145, 199n

Yang Hsiu-feng, 14, 76, 99

Yenan period, 5, 7, 10, 11, 12, 15, 17

Yenan, University of, 7, 8, 187n

Youth leagues, role of, 38-39, 54, 59, 60, 76, 80, 113, 129, 153n, 183
    Central committee, 48, 50